The Making
and Influence
of *I Am a Fugitive
from a Chain Gang*

The Making and Influence of *I Am a Fugitive from a Chain Gang*

SCOTT ALLEN NOLLEN

McFarland & Company, Inc., Publishers
Jefferson, North Carolina

ALSO BY SCOTT ALLEN NOLLEN AND FROM MCFARLAND
Three Bad Men: John Ford, John Wayne, Ward Bond (2013), *Robert Louis Stevenson: Life, Literature and the Silver Screen* (1994; paperback 2012), *Louis Armstrong: The Life, Music and Screen Career* (2004; paperback 2010), *Paul Robeson: Film Pioneer* (2010), *Abbott and Costello on the Home Front: A Critical Study of the Wartime Films* (2009), *Robin Hood: A Cinematic History of the English Outlaw and His Scottish Counterparts* (1999; paperback 2008), *Boris Karloff: A Critical Account of His Screen, Stage, Radio, Television and Recording Work* (1991; paperback 2008), *Warners Wiseguys: All 112 Films That Robinson, Cagney and Bogart Made for the Studio* (2008), *Sir Arthur Conan Doyle at the Cinema: A Critical Study of the Film Adaptations* (1996; paperback 2005), *Jethro Tull: A History of the Band, 1968–2001* (2002), *The Boys: The Cinematic World of Laurel and Hardy* (1989; paperback 2001)

Frontispiece: The sexual wiles of Marie Woods (Glenda Farrell) only go so far with James Allen (Paul Muni) in *I Am a Fugitive from a Chain Gang* (1932).

LIBRARY OF CONGRESS CATALOGUING-IN-PUBLICATION DATA

Names: Nollen, Scott Allen author.
Title: The making and influence of I am a fugitive from a chain gang / Scott Allen Nollen.
Description: Jefferson, N.C. : McFarland & Company, Inc., Publishers, 2016. | Includes bibliographical references and index.
Identifiers: LCCN 2016036946 | ISBN 9780786466771 (softcover : acid free paper) ∞
Subjects: LCSH: I am a fugitive from a chain gang (Motion picture) | Imprisonment in motion pictures. | Justice, Administration of, in motion pictures. | Burns, Robert Elliott. Film adaptations. | Burns, Robert Elliott. I am a fugitive from a Georgia chain gang.
Classification: LCC PN1997.I13 N55 2016 | DDC 791.43/72—dc23
LC record available at https://lccn.loc.gov/2016036946

BRITISH LIBRARY CATALOGUING DATA ARE AVAILABLE

ISBN (print) 978-0-7864-6677-1
ISBN (ebook) 978-1-4766-2678-9

© 2016 Scott Allen Nollen. All rights reserved

No part of this book may be reproduced or transmitted in any form or by any means, electronic or mechanical, including photocopying or recording, or by any information storage and retrieval system, without permission in writing from the publisher.

Front cover: Paul Muni in *I Am a Fugitive from a Chain Gang*, 1932 (Warner Bros. Pictures/Photofest)

Printed in the United States of America

McFarland & Company, Inc., Publishers
Box 611, Jefferson, North Carolina 28640
www.mcfarlandpub.com

For Lauren Porter,
my great friend from Plainfield, New Jersey

Table of Contents

Introduction	1
1. Robert Elliott Burns	5
2. *I Am a Fugitive from a Georgia Chain Gang!* The Memoir	18
3. The Making of the Film	43
4. The Reception of the Film	63
5. *Out of These Chains*: The Continuing Saga of Robert E. Burns and the Warner Bros. Film	78
6. The Historic Influence of the Film	94
Appendix A: Credits and Cast of I Am a Fugitive from a Chain Gang	143
Appendix B: Film Precursors	145
Appendix C: Film and Television Successors	147
Chapter Notes	203
Bibliography	205
Index	209

Introduction

> They refused—the state's promise didn't mean anything. It was all lies—they just wanted to get me back—to keep me here for nine more years. Their crimes are worse than mine—worse than anybody's here. They're the ones that ought to be in prison.
> —the incarcerated James Allen (Paul Muni), to his visiting brother, Reverend "Clint" Allen (Hale Hamilton), in *I Am a Fugitive from a Chain Gang* (1932)

The first of many Depression-era, so-called "social problem" films that would set the Warner Bros. studio apart from the other Hollywood "majors," where escapist fare was the main order of the day, *I Am a Fugitive from a Chain Gang* (1932), based on the bestselling book about the penal servitude of World War I veteran Robert Elliott Burns, merged the popular prison genre (MGM's *The Big House*, Fox's *Up the River*, Columbia's *The Criminal Code* [all 1930] and Paramount's *Ladies of the Big House* [1931]) with Warners' own gritty gangster genre, begun with *Little Caesar* (1931), starring Edward G. Robinson, and *The Public Enemy* (1931), featuring James Cagney.

In the *I Am a Fugitive from a Chain Gang* volume of the "Wisconsin/Warner Bros. Screenplay Series" (1981), John E. O'Connor provides the perfect description of the cultural environment into which the film was released:

> [F]ilms of social consciousness ... implied that forbidding forces were at work that were wholly unpredictable and yet capable of overtaking the hopes and ambitions of an individual. To some observers of the Depression these factors were obvious and inevitable ramifications of the American capitalist system, but to others they seemed completely capricious. Much of the literature of the 1930s depicts a people trying to come to grips with the realization that such forces were robbing them of the capacity to shape their own destinies. Business leaders had long known that the days of the

heroic entrepreneur were gone, and intellectuals had questioned for decades whether there was any room for free will in the explanations of men's actions. It was in the 1930s, however, that popular authors such as James T. Farrell, John Dos Passos, John Steinbeck and others convinced many average Americans that their way in life was more likely to be determined by giant impersonal forces in society than by any decisions they could make on their own. This message was brought home unrelentingly by *I Am a Fugitive from a Chain Gang*, the first of the Depression decade films to focus so closely on a factual story of ordinary people in such desperate distress.[1]

Though it took this historian more than three decades to write this book (as two dozen other volumes were somehow hammered out, often while bedridden like my literary hero, Robert Louis Stevenson, in the meantime), this delay "produced" a fortunate research result: Many of the film-industry trade publications (including *Variety*) and fan magazines of 1932 did not have their copyrights renewed, allowing access to much public-domain material, one of the truly beneficial primary sources for the scholar and historical detective. In a corporate society that now limits access to materials and charges exorbitant fees just to *look* at them, this public domain status, plus the availability of scanned sources on the internet, allow us *"penniless scholars"* the only way to continue our academic missions. (This historian has never chosen to write about his subjects. *They chose him.*)

Many years ago, I was very fortunate to acquire a rare first edition of *Out of These Chains*, Vincent Godrey Burns' 1942 mighty sequel to *I Am a Fugitive from a Georgia Chain Gang!*, along with some other family materials, from the Reverend's own collection. In December 1947, he inscribed and signed it for a friend, W. D. Sedgwick, also enclosing a likewise personalized poem as a Christmas gift. In this longer and more detailed version of his brother's continuing attempts to be exonerated, he admitted ghost-writing the earlier volume for his brother. *Out of These Chains* also provides an indispensable resource for reconstructing the making of the Warner Bros. film and everything that followed in its forceful wake.

The nearly incomprehensible ordeal of Robert E. Burns, channeled through his brother, Vincent's, two books, Warner Bros., Darryl F. Zanuck and Paul Muni, has haunted me for half my life. I am pleased finally to experience writing it down here. Fueled by ministerial zeal to help free his brother from a hellish existence, Vincent Burns has, not without some justification, been criticized as sometimes half-baked and a hack writer, but his cause was valid and his prose, although often florid and overblown, could at times be impressively pictorial and unforgettably powerful. He never wavered in attempting to help free his brother, who has been compared to "Jean Valjean," the long-suffering protagonist of Victor Hugo's 1862 novel *Les Misérables*.

Since I am not a "film historian," but a "historian who *often* writes about films," I have produced many past volumes covering up to 1,000 years (the films involving Robin Hood, for example)! For *your* sake, be glad I don't do that here. The *body* of this book is about Robert E. Burns (a reconstruction of the actual facts *and* a complete, detailed synopsis of the occasionally contradictory memoir *I Am a Fugitive from a Georgia Chain Gang!* both for comparative purposes, and for providing a look at what literary material actually was adapted for the screenplay); and the classic Warner Bros. film is the *heart*, with its arteries extending into the final chapter. But a very brief overview of chain-gang history is necessary to understand what transpires throughout the book.

Slavery's Son

The use of chain gangs began as a post–Civil War attempt by former Confederate states to maintain a semi-covert type of slavery, particularly involving African Americans, by "leasing out" prisoners for all manner of hard-labor projects. States using this type of legal punishment included Alabama, Arkansas, Florida, Georgia, Louisiana, Mississippi, North and South Carolina, Texas and Virginia.

Unlike a "work gang," a group of prisoners toiling outside prison walls under close supervision, the chain gangs were always shackled together and subjected to far more brutal punishment, less palatable dietary situations and a nearly nonexistent state of hygiene. The use of the chain gang, which was far more preferred than the work gang, also satisfied Southern politicians wanting to project a public image of their being "tough on crime."

Finally, by 1955, 90 years after the end of the Civil War and the date of Robert E. Burns' death, the chain-gang system had been eliminated throughout the United States. Interestingly, Georgia, the state that caused Burns so much misery for more than two decades, was the last to abandon this barbaric system.

Amazingly, the state of Alabama, in a major example of the "getting tough on crime" movement of the period, reinstituted the use of chain gangs in 1995, an extreme, archaic decision which proved a huge mistake in less than a year. Other states attempting such measures followed suit in shutting down the new camps. Only Arizona's Maricopa County has retained the institution, which can be used in cases of jail inmates offered the choice of serving on a chain gang either to avoid harsh discipline for major rule violations or earn credit toward the General Education Development (GED) certificate.

Prior to the production of narrative feature films, several early, crude documentaries were produced including footage of actual working chain gangs. As early as 1902, the Thomas A. Edison Company shot a film at a Charleston, South Carolina, penal compound in which a group of chained men, guarded by two men brandishing shotguns, was shown in a forced hard-labor situation. The entire film runs less than a minute.

Chapter 6 chronicles the post–1932 influence of the Warner Bros. film, in the social, penal and legal arenas, and the subsequent films released between 1933 and the dawn of the 21st century. The list of motion pictures is by no means exhaustive, but does include either titles directly paying "homage" to the original or containing significantly similar content, both dramatic and comic.

The three appendices include the most complete credits and cast listings ever compiled on the 1932 film, as well as similar information on its precursors and especially its successors, providing an excellent reference source on these titles, especially the Warner Bros. "social problem films" released from 1933 through 1939.

Just as *I Am a Fugitive from a Chain Gang* assisted in drawing public attention to changing penal law in the South, it also deeply affected my life. The film made me admire the early, gritty 1930s films of Warner Bros., one of the best (and least histrionic) screen performances of Paul Muni, and the indescribable brilliance and beauty of Glenda Farrell. But more importantly, as a young adult with the (unattainable) goal of doing something "significant," it *made me care...*

1

Robert Elliott Burns

> The greatest mystery of this world is what men do to one another when imbued with malice, ignorance and greed. The generations come and go, but "man's inhumanity to man," of which Robert Burns, the bard of Scotland, wrote more than one hundred and fifty years ago, still bathes the earth with human tears.
> —Vincent Godfrey Burns, "Preface," *Out of These Chains* (1942)[1]

Half of Brooklyn was still a heavily forested boy's paradise when Robert Elliott Burns was born there on May 10, 1892. His parents, James H. (born c. 1865) and Katherine W. Burns (born c. 1872), both native New Yorkers, had been married little more than a year. (They were of Irish and German-French descent, respectively.)

From the time little Vincent Godfrey Burns arrived on October 17, 1893, Robert and his younger brother were inseparable. They attended Public School No. 131 on Fort Hamilton Avenue, located just one half-mile from their home on 50th Street; and whenever they weren't closed up within these walls of learning, they were off, across the rolling hills and through the woods, hunting birds and rabbits with bean shooters and swimming in Webster's Pond, from which Robert once saved a drowning boy by quickly grabbing up a sapling and holding it out to him.

The Burns brothers remained close until Robert was about 14, when he quit high school and became much more isolated, running his own paper route and often shutting himself off, alone and racked by periods of depression. He would alternate brooding with fits of temper, starting arguments with little or no provocation, sometimes to the point of violence, which would cause him to leave the house and not return for long periods of time. At age 15, he took a bookkeeping job with Italian fruit importer Ferdenand Gatto, who lived with the family for a time, and gave his salary check to Katherine each week. This practice greatly augmented James' salary as shipping clerk for a New York clothing store.

A sister, Dorothy, had arrived in 1898; and further on, in 1906, twins—James, Jr., and Jennetta—joined the ever more crowded family. In 1912, when Vincent began college, Robert, who always had romanticized the tales told by his Union Civil War veteran grandfather, simply disappeared. For 18 months, he remained incommunicado, until just as surprisingly, returned home one day with enough money to pay off all his father's debts. He also entertained the whole family with adventurous tales of working in Western wheat fields and learning a sailor's trade toiling on several Great Lakes steamboats.

Now 25, Robert decided to settle down by returning to the business of accounting, but this attempt again could not dissuade him from being the rambling rover, this time under strict discipline and in far more dangerous places, with names like Flanders, Château-Thierry and the Argonne. After beginning training on April 18, 1917, with the U.S. Army at Fort Slocum, New York, he shipped out with the Medical Detachment of the 14th Railway Engineers; and from September 1917 until November 1918, he continually was hip deep in mortally wounded soldiers, many of whom he helped bury himself.

On May 28, 1917, Vincent, while a student at Harvard University, registered for the draft. He was inducted into the U.S. Army in Brooklyn on January 5, 1918, and attended Officers' Training School at Camp Dix, New Jersey, until April 24, when he was assigned to Battery B of the 307th Field Artillery at Camp Jackson, South Carolina. On May 3, he was transferred to Battery A of the 4th Regimental Field Artillery and, at the end of that month, accepted a commission as Second Lieutenant. On August 21, 1919, he was honorably discharged, having avoided the overseas horrors experienced by his brother.

By the time Robert returned Stateside in May 1919, he was a physical wreck, and his tendency to become depressed and violent had increased manifold. His behavior had become extremely erratic during those 14 months among the mud and blood, the dying and the dead.

The job he had been promised "to be waiting for him when he returned" had long ago been filled by someone else. And his sweetheart had fallen into the arms of another man. After pounding the pavements all day, looking for jobs that no longer existed, he paced the floor of his room into the wee hours, loudly cursing the fact that he had been suckered into the Great War touted as the bringer of Freedom and Democracy to the common man everywhere.

1. Robert Elliott Burns

It was nothing but a racket. It was the war-mongers, greedy capitalist profiteers who didn't give a damn about anyone else—that was why he, and so many of his dead, maimed and shell-shocked brothers, had gone off to "serve their country." The former war hero now was known around the neighborhood as "that radical Burns." His nocturnal hell raising (which now would be diagnosed as a symptom of post-traumatic stress disorder [PTSD]) often would wake the neighbors, but Vincent would explain that his brother was not mentally nor morally responsible for what he said and did.

One day Robert garbed himself with a painted-up sandwich board reading, "I FOUGHT FOR YOU IN FRANCE, AND NOW YOU HAVE NO PLACE FOR ME, NOT EVEN A JOB!" and trudged six city miles from Bay Ridge, Brooklyn, to the South Ferry at Atlantic Avenue. Passersby laughed, jeered and threw stones, until he boarded the ferry and then jumped off at the battery, where he began a little perambulation up lower Broadway. A large crowd gathered around him to exercise some instinctual mob mentality, until enough motor traffic backed up to require police intervention.

Robert was arrested and tossed into the local slammer, just long enough for him to cool his heels and the precinct to return to a semblance of normality. He was released after the sun went down. As expected, the following morning's papers featured Robert's photo, with bylines such as "Doughboy in Jail!" and "The Soldier Who Couldn't Get a Job." Following this ordeal, Vincent rented a room for Robert at the Brooklyn YMCA, where he could study for night classes; and their father was hopeful that a new job with a local magazine would help him gain stability and even discover some purpose in his life.

In January 1922, Vincent now was a student at the Union Theological Seminary located at Broadway and 20th Streets. A severe thunderstorm, marked by a torrential downpour and frightening flashes of lightning, raged outside, as Vincent heard a knock at his dormitory door. In the hall stood a stranger *and* Robert, drenched to the skin, his face gaunt with deep bags under both eyes. Obviously the night classes and the magazine work had not accomplished what had been hoped.

Robert told Vincent that he again was leaving New York, that very night. Asked *where* he would be heading and *what* he would be doing, he could offer no answers. He only knew that he had to remove himself from the world of commercialism, of "wolf eat wolf," as he called it. Vincent later wrote that it had been difficult even to recognize his own brother, that it seemed more like he was looking into the tear-filled eyes of a madman.

Inside the room, Vincent scraped together $50, telling Robert that a bed could be provided for him at the seminary that night, but his agitation proved he was in a terrible hurry.

"No, Vince, I must be on my way," he told his brother. "Thanks—and someday I hope to be able to pay you back for all that you've done for me. You've been a true brother in my time of need. Goodbye."

"Goodbye, Ell," said Vincent, customarily calling Robert by his boyhood name, adding, "And good luck," watching his brother's slim, soaked and exhausted figure disappear into the unending sheets of rain under clashes of thunder.[2]

South of Mason-Dixon

True to form, Vincent heard nothing from Robert for several weeks. When word finally arrived, it came in the form of a letter from John Echols, an Atlanta attorney, reporting that Robert Elliott Burns, arrested for conspiring in a holdup, was being held without bail in the Fulton County Jail. Prior to his trial date, Echols expected some form of remuneration. Since the letter contained no details of the seriousness of the crime, Vincent asked his father to send Echols $100 while he remained tending over his flock at the City Park Chapel, the settlement house extension of the Brooklyn First Presbyterian Church. Vincent deeply regretted not immediately traveling to Fulton County after hearing the outcome of the incident: At his arraignment, Robert had plead guilty to highway robbery, for which Judge Thomas had sentenced him from six to ten years hard labor on a Georgia chain gang.

When Robert had reached Atlanta, having hopped freight cars most of the way, his clothes were in tatters and his shoes had worn off his feet. While seeking refuge in a Salvation Army Rest Camp, he met two fellow vagrants, Flagg, an Australian sailor, and Moore, just another "nobody." Flagg mentioned that he knew where they could obtain work, and suggested they all meet the next morning.

Desperate for any kind of employment, Robert was ready at the appointed time. Outside a small grocery store on Atlanta's south side, Flagg described his harebrained plan on how they were going to rob Samuel Bernstein, the "Jew" owner, by throwing shredded cabbage in the man's face before relieving him of the $1,000 he was holding. Robert refused immediately, but Flagg called him "yellow," pulled a gat and forced him to frisk the owner as Moore went through the cash register.

The owner had nothing on his person, but grabbed for a gun, which Robert, the experienced war veteran, wrestled away from him. While he and Moore were anxious to flee the scene, Flagg simply ripped the telephone out of the wall and walked out after them, hoping at least to have gained something from the register drawer. Following a two-mile jog along the railroad tracks, they stopped to count the haul from the caper: a whopping $5.80.

Charged with only the sole count, Robert was advised to plead guilty by Echols, who explained that his sentence would prove far more severe after a trial. Though Robert was allowed to speak to the judge about the circumstances of his postwar health problems, inability to find work, and coercion in joining the other two men in robbing the grocery store of $5.80, he nonetheless was shipped off to the Fulton County chain-gang camp.

Robert had no knowledge of the South, even after he had ridden the rails deep into it. The Fulton County camp, in particular, was quite a shock to a man who thought of a prison as a huge concrete fortress filled with blocks containing six-by-six-foot cells. Other than a few toppling down shacks, the camp included a blacksmith shop, for the sole purpose of harnessing a man in iron ankle rings held together by a 13-link chain to which another "upright" chain and heavy ring was fastened. At night, all the convicts in a shack would be bound together by a heavier chain slid through all the large rings on their upright chains. The whole concept was a holdover from centuries of slavery which only had "ended" about 60 years earlier.

The convicts were roused from their filthy racks at 3:00 each morning. If a man was slow in excitedly getting ready to swing his sledgehammer until dusk, he was beaten with a club. In the mess area, they all sat down to a breakfast of fatback, corncake and a cup of liquid called "coffee," complete with a host of floating flies. After working on the crude county roads all day, they returned to their shacks, and a half dozen men, charged with "laziness," were whipped with a wide leather lash. Supper consisted of the obligatory fatback, corn pone, sorghum and more "coffee." Nothing resembling hygiene was practiced.

Combined with his already unstable condition, this brutal regimen took a further toll on Robert, who realized that six years in the camp was out of the question. Possessing no death wish, he made up his mind to break out of the wretched hell hole. Allowed to apply for a transfer, he eventually was sent to the Campbell County camp, which was no better; and, rather than having to sleep in a stinking shack, his slumber time took place in an even more foul "pie wagon," a conveyance resembling a mobile carnival enclosure, only built with iron struts rather than wooden walls.

One day in June 1922, while the Campbell County convicts were repairing the tracks for a small railroad outfit, Robert was particularly impressed by the accuracy with which a large, powerful black man swung his sledge. Whispering to him as the guards, rendered apathetic by the high humidity, lazed about, Robert asked the man if he could hit the iron rings on his ankles with sufficient force to bend them into an oval shape, enough to allow him to slide them off when he got a chance. Realizing that anything less than a direct hit on the ring would result in a shattered ankle, "Sam" hammered away, perfectly connecting with both rings three times.

On Monday, June 21, 1922, Robert, again noticing that the guards were being laid low by the heat, painfully slipped off the iron rings and headed for a thicket beside the road, then ran as fast as he could into the woods. He could hear the guards shouting and blasting away with their shotguns as he kept his pace. Not even with bloodhounds on his trail could the sadistic Campbell County guards apprehend Robert, who managed to catch a ride to Atlanta, from whence he rode the rails and hitchhiked all the way to Chicago.

Windy City

For the next seven years, Robert worked as a laborer, real-estate manager and publisher of *The Greater Chicago Magazine*. His move up the ladder was instigated by a divorced landlady, Emilia Del Pino Pacheo, who, having fallen in love with him, used her family's connections to set them up as proprietors of an apartment house. Though he didn't share her feelings, Robert married Emily, who eventually discovered his true identity by reading a letter from his family. When Robert fell in love with another woman, Lillian Salo, the highly emotional and conniving Emily turned him over to the local authorities.

Robert's harrowing story soon made national headlines, and he was heavily supported by Chicago businessmen and the chief of police, who actually proposed a get-away plan. Vincent, having rushed to the Windy City, and supported by letters from the poet Carl Sandburg and social-work pioneer Jane Addams, founder of Chicago's famed Hull House, gained an audience in Springfield with Republican governor Louis L. Emmerson, who apparently planned to deny the Georgia extradition warrant.

From a late edition of a Chicago newspaper, the brothers were shocked by a front-page story declaring that the mayor of Atlanta, bearing the incredible name of Isaac Newton Ragsdale, had recommended a pardon for Robert, an initiative supported by several members of the Georgia legislature. Robert's attorney, Cameron Latter, immediately planned a Southern trip to see if these claims were true.

The catch: Robert would have to waive extradition (which had been approved by Governor Emmerson but stalled by a writ of *habeas corpus*) and voluntarily return to Georgia, assured that he would not be reassigned to a chain gang. Instead he would pay $350 for the cost of his return, a fine of $2,500 (half in advance; the remainder following the pardon) and be given an office job in Atlanta for 60 to 90 days while the Prison Commission arranged for his release. The details of this deal were arranged by attorney and former Georgia congressman William Schley Howard.

The aptly named Georgia governor Lamartine G. Hardman, a Democrat but, according to Robert, also "a Baptist fundamentalist of the old school," pledged to remain neutral in the matter of clemency, while letting the three members of the commission (all of which he personally appointed) decide the case. (By this time, Robert understood that the $2,500 was graft money to be split among the three commissioners.)

Finishing his letter to Vincent, dated June 21, 1929, Robert, still in Chicago awaiting word from Atlanta, wrote:

> I want to take this opportunity to again express my deepest thanks for your unflinching loyalty, love, and devotion, but I do not think it is fair to have you spend your time and money in my cause. The whole thing is my cross and I will have to bear it myself as best I can, and I believe I am strong enough physically and mentally to bear the burden.[3]

Newspapers across the nation published editorials supporting the pardon of "the World War veteran" and "a prominent Chicago citizen of seven years." In its supportive piece, the *New York Herald-Tribune* concluded,

> Southerners may argue that the experiences on the chain gang are no worse, and are certainly more public, than the things done to convicts in the secrecy of Northern prisons. The fact remains that the chain gang lives in the popular imagination outside the South as an institution shrouded in the dark taint of slavery and Southern sheriffs find it almost as difficult to recover fugitives as it once was to recover fugitive slaves. It is no help to the modern South. In the present case, with all the other elements in his favor, it seems fairly safe to bet, not on the State of Georgia, but on Mr. Burns.[4]

However, by this time, Robert's words to Vincent about having enough strength to bear his cross may have begun haunting him. He upheld his part of the bargain, but after stepping back onto Georgia soil, he soon was shipped to the Campbell County camp, from whence he had escaped, and hammered into leg irons and chains. He not only had to complete his original six-year sentence, but an additional six years tacked on for his escape. He had paid the money supposedly used to bribe the Southern officials, but now was broke and back on the chain gang.

Terror of Troup County

Since he already had escaped from the Campbell County site, Robert soon was transferred to the camp at La Grange, in Troup County, located in southwestern Georgia. His pledge to Vincent that he could "physically and emotionally bear the burden" was quickly shattered, as proved by one of his distressing letters:

> I am treated the same as a low, uneducated criminal—my business is completely ruined and destroyed—my faith in God and man is failing fast—and my health—body and mind are cracking under the strain! If this is justice, Vince, then I won't live through it![5]

In July, Vincent and his mother traveled to Atlanta, to speak before a session of the Georgia Prison Commission at the State Capitol. Prior to the session, they visited La Grange, located amidst cotton fields and pine woods, at the end of a three-mile dirt road paralleled by crude shacks on stilts inhabited by poverty-stricken, exhausted and ill African American families who stared at the taxi as it kicked up enough dust to cloud their vision and fill their lungs. As the sunbaked men, women and children choked on the cloud of sandy clay soil, the Burns contingent finally reached the camp.

They were instantly appalled by what they saw and heard. A dog was howling, and even a mule was coughing, as a brutish armed guard approached the taxi. Following a brief interrogation, a trusty accompanied them inside a large building with a low ceiling. Chicken wire was strewn across iron bars through which the convicts could speak to visitors: blacks on the right side; whites on the left.

Vincent and Katherine observed a ring of guards, playing cards and smoking cigarettes. One of them loudly yelled, "Burns!" and out shambled a withered, darkly tanned, grime-caked creature with bloodshot eyes that spoke of endless days of hopeless brutality and anguish. Behind the chicken wire, Katherine, unable even to touch her pitiful son, had tears streaming down her cheeks. Neither she nor Robert could utter a word. Finally Robert turned to Vincent and yelled, "For God's sake, why didn't you come sooner?"[6]

The hearing in mid–July 1929 appeared to offer high hopes, at least to Vincent, particularly since Flagg, the career criminal who had forced Robert into the robbery at gunpoint, already had been pardoned. Though

Vincent and two attorneys made eloquent appeals for Robert's release, the three members of the Prison Commission were steely-eyed and hard as the rocks beaten by the blows of the chain-gang sledgehammers. The farce ended with the assistant solicitor of Fulton County, a full-blown bigot named Stephens, personally summoned by the implacable Judge Rainey, referring to Robert as a "habitual criminal," "menace to society" and "ow[ing] the State of Georgia a term of servitude." Concluding his lambaste, he then tore into Vincent, growling, "And whether Yankee parsons come down here or not we'll keep him on the chain gang until it is collected!"[7]

Two months later, while Vincent was visiting Katherine in Pittsfield, Massachusetts, she learned from a *newspaper article* that Robert's pardon had been denied. Frantically rushing back to Georgia, they approached the governor's Atlanta office on Labor Day 1929, only to find that he was enjoying a holiday at his summer residence. A week later, accompanied by William Schley Howard and a trio of Atlanta ministers, they asked Governor Hardman if he could override the Prison Commission's decision with his own right of pardon.

After assuring Mrs. Burns that he personally would inquire about Robert's physical condition and perhaps move toward a pardon, Hardman neither took any further steps nor had any other communications with the family. Robert had been duped into a seemingly unending web of lies, deceit and political corruption, the shadow of which has haunted some Southern halls of "justice" ever since.[8] Further appeals, both in Georgia, and by Vincent in Washington, D.C., proved fruitless.

Mrs. Burns remained in Atlanta for several more weeks, but finally returned to Massachusetts after learning that the Prison Commission could not even consider a pardon until the convict had served at least a year on the chain gang. The original Chicago promise of Robert being released after voluntarily returning for a period of 60 to 90 days had been bunk from the outset.

Robert survived the brutal 12 months at La Grange and, in July 1930, another hearing was held in Atlanta. This time, Vincent arrived, armed with five bound volumes, each holding 86 affidavits from some of Chicago's finest residents. Aided by Metro-Goldwyn-Mayer's Nicholas Schenck and a local film executive, Colonel Schiller, many of Atlanta's business barons also joined the Burns cause. However, this second hearing was nearly identical to the first, but with the judges nodding off before the infamous Assistant Solicitor Stephens again paraded about, spewing vitriol in every direction, making sure that, on this occasion, some of it soaked Robert, his attorneys, Vincent *and* Katherine Burns.

In August, when Vince and Mother were allowed to visit Robert at La Grange, this time outside on a bench, Robert, knowing that he would be expected to serve *11 more years* on the chain gang, told them of another bold escape plan he had brewing in his head. Katherine was dead-set against it, but Vincent, who had been contacting officials in the hope of getting Robert transferred to a trusty position, advised him to wait until the chains had been removed from his legs.

The pardon again was denied, but Vincent's efforts did push through approval to make Robert a trusty. During the afternoon of Tuesday, September 2, 1930, the famous fugitive, having received his New Jersey veteran's bonus of $150 hidden in a pack of smokes sent by his brother, was recognized and given encouragement by a darkly tanned, straw-hatted, poverty-stricken farmer at a small store beside the road on which the gang was working near Mountville, Georgia. Shortly after, while the guards' attention was focused on the chained prisoners, the farmer came walking down the road to speak with Robert.

Deftly flashing the corner of a $50 bill at the destitute man, Robert asked him if he could possibly park his car at a specific spot in the woods along the road between 7:30 and 8:00 a.m. the following day. The farmer was game, and also agreed to hide in a nearby thicket, where he could imitate the whistle of a mocking bird when the coast was clear. Finally, Robert would join his new comrade on a circuitous route to Atlanta and freedom.

On September 3, 8:00 a.m. came and went. Later that afternoon, Robert again saw the dark man in the straw hat walking toward him down the road. He couldn't make it, the farmer told the trusty, who promised him an additional fin if he'd try it the next day, alongside a different stretch of the red Georgia clay.

The same thing happened on September 4. For the *third* time, Robert went over the plan with this strange "Georgia cracker,"[9] raising the bribe to $60, plus an additional $100 if he reached New Jersey safely. Again nodding affirmation, the farmer added one stipulation: that he only drive Robert as far as College Park, a suburb about ten miles from Atlanta, from which a trolley could be caught.

September Morning Breakout

On the morning of September 5, the Troup County chain gang was typically stretched out some 300 feet, overseen by a guard at each end, with a third patrolling the distance between. To even make it to the spot where the farmer agreed to conceal his automobile, Robert had to run about 40 feet, through the ditch, a ragged hedgerow about two-feet high and into the forest, expectedly with lead shotgun pellets flying all around him.

Instinctively using his body as a sundial, Robert, having begun work at 5:00 a.m., knew it had to be about 7:30 when he finally heard the mocking bird's whistle. First making sure all the guards were sufficiently occupied, he ran like hell toward the silhouette of a man among the trees, and then the pair took a narrow cart path about 300 yards toward a running auto and *another man*, armed with a horse pistol!

Robert thought he'd really been given the business on this *fourth* occasion, but the guy with the gun jumped into the passenger side, as Robert, hearing shotgun blasts ripping through the foliage behind, climbed into the rumble seat, where he crouched down as far as he could. Following a brief, bumpy jog out of the woods, he could feel the smooth pavement of a highway beneath him. He handed a fiver through the shredded curtain behind the front seat, asking the farmer to stop farther down the road, at a store where he could purchase a blue shirt and a pair of overalls. It was time to ditch the chain-gang stripes.

But Robert had to white-knuckle it for another hour as the farmer made several stops in an attempt to find the properly sized clothes. The companion did the best he could, buying duds in which Robert could take a swim, and he had to improvise after they pulled off into a wooded area where the $60 was paid, the wardrobe change was made, and the trio all piled into the front seat for the final miles into College Park.

Refusing to drive any farther, the farmer stopped as soon as they reached the suburb and shook hands with Robert as he exited the car. *Right across the road* stood the Campbell County chain gang, from which he had been transferred five months earlier. To avoid being recognized, he quickly ducked into a nearby barber shop, where he could buy a haircut and shave while waiting for the trolley.

As he moved toward the barber chair, he instantly realized that the man with the razor in his hand was a church deacon whom he had known from services held at the Campbell County camp! Dropping into the chair, Robert blurted out what he needed. Luckily, the "Deacon Barber" of College Park failed to recognize him on this nail-biting occasion.

The man proceeded so slowly and prattled on at such length that Robert missed the trolley. The barber shop was attracting a steady flow of customers as his close shave finally came to an end. He quickly paid and walked out. The convicts still were straight across the street. Rather than risk detection while pacing around until the arrival of the next trolley, he began walking toward Atlanta.

The heat and dust of the day had not abated as he continued his grueling pace toward the city, but now Robert could hear the sound of the trolley behind him on the road. In Atlanta, he entered a Decatur Street clothing store where he bought a $10 suit, shorts, white shirt, tie and a pair of socks. Also picking up a single-buck suitcase, he stuffed his "farmer" clothes into it and handed the clerk a $50 bill, a move that cost him another seemingly endless wait, 15 minutes, as the greenback had to be cleared at the nearest bank.

His first decent meal in more than a year was a special treat. A bus trip to Chattanooga seemed safer than taking the train to Washington, D.C., but as he walked toward the entry door, a large man was informing the driver about someone who had escaped from the La Grange chain gang. He now looked like just "anyone else," he thought to himself, so his boarding raised no suspicions and he settled back to await his speedy exit from the state that had caused him so much misery. A 20-minute stop at Rome, Georgia, included a sweat-soaked brush with two local sheriffs at a soda counter, but the bus soon entered Tennessee, arriving at Chattanooga at 7:30 p.m.

A six-hour wait for the bus to Louisville brought another nerve-wracking experience, and Robert did his best not to loiter in any one spot too long, renting a locker for his suitcase, eating at a restaurant, then returning to the station to overhear another mention of the La Grange fugitive, this time by an attendant on the telephone.

Jersey at Last

On Saturday, September 6, Robert, sleep deprived to the point of hallucination, finally passed out as the Greyhound bus cruised along the Lincoln Highway through a light morning fog toward Newark, New Jersey. Having pulled into his destination, the bus driver walked toward the back as the passengers scrambled out—all except one.

Roused from a chain-gang nightmare, Robert started up, pulled up the brim of his fedora, and blearily look around, through the windows on either side. Half stumbling toward the front exit door, he picked up his grip and walked toward a diner. Coffee, a lot of it, was what he needed; and as he began to gorge himself on some crullers to boot, he noticed a man perusing a familiar article in the most recent local newspaper. There was his photo, taken from enough distance so his unshaven face couldn't be recognized, standing in his chain-gang stripes, beside a horse-drawn cart, with some African American convicts behind him. The nightmare had been bad enough; now the newspaper was inducing a wide-awake flashback.

While Robert, with $1.80 left in his pocket, was heading toward the subway which would transport him to the town of Palisade, Vincent, his wife and daughter were staying with Katherine in Pittsfield, Massachusetts, 150 miles distant. Never having received word about the outcome of the last Georgia hearing two months earlier, they were uplifted by a morning edition of *The Berkshire Eagle* including a rather erroneous feature about Robert's bold second escape. Naturally Mrs. Burns voiced her usual concern that her tortured, weakened son would be killed during the extensive, relentless manhunt.

Vincent's house in Palisade was pitch dark and the mailbox was overflowing. Robert continued walking, checking back, but no light ever shown within. He found a phone booth, luckily having enough change to make a long-distance call to Pittsfield. The receiver rang and then he heard the voice of his sister on the line. Not revealing his identity, he asked for Vince, but he was away and wouldn't return until around 11:00 p.m. Robert gave his sis the number on the pay phone and anxiously awaited by the booth for a return ring.

Ever so promptly, Vincent called back at exactly 11:00, suspecting that it would be Robert who'd be lightly rapping his fingers on the inner walls of the phone booth. Picking up the receiver, Robert told Vince of his plan to reach Hackensack, asking his brother to send some money to "John Pashley"—a somewhat elegant alias—care of General Delivery. As always with Vincent Burns: *done*.

On the morning of Monday, September 8, Vincent, his family and Mrs. Katherine Burns motored to Palisade and awaited Robert's return. Frightened by a tense, hirsute face peering in the kitchen window, Vincent's wife announced the appearance of a stranger as the bell at the back door began to ring. Mother scuttled toward the door as quickly as she could, throwing her arms around her disheveled and unkempt son, immediately wanting to know the details of his against-all-odds flight from that Southern hell. Just as Vincent told him that he immediately would drive him to Jersey City, the front doorbell rang. It was a cop.

2

I Am a Fugitive from a Georgia Chain Gang! The Memoir

> *What was it that had gained the upper hand over humanity? Was it greed? Yes, that was it. "The love of money is the root of all evil." That was what the good Book said, and it was all too true. So greed spawned hate, and hate became jealousy and revenge, and these four Horsemen overrode the finer impulses of humanity—unselfishness, understanding, forgiveness, love, and they brought with them war and poverty and ruin and death....*
>
> *A fatalistic, pessimistic philosophy may drive a man to drink, to failure, to suicide. In those days we feared for my brother's life. When things were at their worst, however, a lucky break came to him to change his outlook.*
>
> —Vincent Godfrey Burns, *Out of These Chains* (1942)[1]

The police officer entered the Burns home. Vincent attempted to convince him that the stranger the neighbors had seen loitering outside and now was standing within eyeshot of the cop was "Mr. John Pashley," but he recognized "Elliott" instantly from the "Fugitive Wanted" cards that had been issued by the Georgia authorities.

The tension in the room was tangible but the officer was quite kind, offering the best wishes of Palisade Police Chief McDermott and advising Robert to leave town and find a hideout in a much less conspicuous location. But anywhere, the fugitive now would face a new problem, the rampant unemployment and long lines of men seeking any kind of work to make a few bucks to feed themselves and their families. The Great Depression

"No Men Wanted" placards far outnumbered the "Help Wanted" signs, which instantly drew an enormous procession of job-seekers. And then there were the equally lengthy bread lines....

In October 1930, Robert was 35 years old, but naturally appeared far older due to his chain-gang experiences, including a monumental load of stress, and baking to a chestnut hue in the hot Georgia sun every day. Carrying bogus identification indicating that he was John Pashley, a first-class sailor in the Seamen's Union (the card had been given to him by a fellow inmate on the La Grange chain gang), he applied for an advertising position with the *Newark Ledger* newspaper. Hired for a 10-percent commission on all the space he could sell, he was overjoyed. Within the first two days, he earned a $45 check from selling $450 worth of advertisements, and greatly impressed the very imposing-looking department manager.

Attempting to avoid Mr. McCullough, the classified advertising manager, with whom he coincidentally had worked on a competitive basis in Chicago, Robert opened a savings account and purchased some new clothes. The next thing on his mind was some female companionship, regardless of the fact that he was still legally married to the backstabbing Emily in the Windy City. After meeting a local woman, they enjoyed going to the movies, one of which was MGM's *The Big House* (1930), starring Wallace Beery, Chester Morris and Robert Montgomery. Robert didn't have any trouble watching the picture but wasn't particularly impressed with his date's mentioning the fact that he resembled a picture of an escaped chain-gang convict she'd seen in some newspapers not that long ago.

Not wishing to repeat this close-call experience, Robert began a lengthy correspondence with Lillian Salo, the Chicago woman he really loved. Amongst other things, he planned to save up enough money to bring her to Newark to share a nice apartment. Attempting on two occasions to pay her travel expenses to New Jersey, he met with a rude awakening during the second attempt, when the devious McCullough could hold his tongue no longer. Robert lost not only his job but also what had become a certain level of freedom and comfort he enjoyed in Newark.

Lillian was supposed to arrive on the train early in the evening, so he withdrew all his greenbacks from the bank, packed his small collection of belongings in a suitcase and rented a furnished apartment on the outskirts of the city. But his excited waiting at the train station mirrored his first attempt a short time before: Though he refused to leave the platform, observing every woman who disembarked from every car and not seeing Lillian, train after train left him bitter and nearly heartbroken.

Wandering aimlessly, and angrily, through the fog, Robert had no idea what to do at that point. Someone brushed against him on a mist-drenched sidewalk, and the fugitive could hear his heavy shoes pivoting on the pavement behind him. He increased his pace, but the sound of the steps kept coming closer. The bright neon lights of a bar flashed amiably ahead, and he headed straight for it, although the steps were still immediately behind.

Robert turned, expecting a beat cop or maybe even a detective but, of all people, it was Moore, one of his "companions" in the notorious Atlanta grocery store heist of 1922. He also had escaped from the chain gang and had lambed it to Newark. Over Ballantine's beer, they toasted every cracker son of a bitch who had brutalized them, but then Robert, his brain ever formulating his next move, his subsequent plan, said,

> Moore ... it's about time someone had the guts to come right out and tell the truth about the barbarities they practice down there. When I think of those lads who are still there, taking the beatings they do, sweating in those chains, driven worse than slaves, a chill goes up my spine. Someday, Moore, the Federal Government is going to do something to clean up the chain gangs of the South.[2]

Bertha Wagner

Moore, mentioning that someone needed to write a book about the chain-gang abomination, continued to castigate the peckerwood regime, but Robert noticed an attractive woman, her tear-stained face half hidden by long brown hair, across the room, leaning on a table near the front window. He slowly approached her, sat down and leaned in, calmly asking about her troubles.

The loss of a job and a sweetheart in the same day. Well, Robert sure as hell knew all about that. This was his introduction to Miss Bertha Wagner, whom he assured would look just like Myrna Loy if she'd just stop weeping her makeup all over her pan.

An intelligent dame, she had been a junior-high teacher active in political causes that led to her dismissal by the school *and* her boyfriend. Robert convinced her that there were far worse things handed out by Fate, and called a taxi to take his new female find to her hotel. By the time Thanksgiving loomed on the horizon, the two were fulltime sweethearts.

But the realities of the Great Depression affected them as they did most U.S. citizens. On the day before the holiday, as they relaxed on a bench in Newark's Military Park, Robert asked a hungry, shoe-shining ragamuffin to join them for a nice lunch at a nearby diner, just before returning to hear a very cogent speech made by an articulate socialist who naturally attracted a crowd of passersby. When a heckler attempted to prevent the man from continuing, Robert couldn't help but stand up for the Constitution, receiving in return a savage blow to the face with a walking stick. Considered an agitator, Robert was nearly placed under arrest by two local flatfeet, but was saved by none other than Bertha. Vincent later wrote,

> A well-spoken word from a determined woman may often become the strongest force on earth and may turn any tide. It proved so in this instance. The cop released my brother.
> "Don't get excited, lady," said the policeman. "We don't want any trouble about this. We'll let your boyfriend go. But we're not letting him go because we think he's entirely innocent. We're letting him go because we think you're a sensible woman."[3]

The police then ordered the cane-swinging heckler to beat the retreat or face being tossed into the local slammer.

Soon after, Robert learned that the family of the shoeshine boy truly were in dire straits: The mother was dead, the continually coughing father had been gassed in the war, the youngest daughter had a serious cold, and the other two children, the boy and another girl, were supporting the whole outfit entirely with funds earned after school hours. Paying a doctor to treat the little girl, Robert, who promised to look into the man's veteran's bonus status, rented their empty, unheated attic, where he contracted a terrible strain of influenza. Vincent, who hadn't seen him in weeks, was shocked to see him so ill; and Bertha had checked out of her hotel, leaving no forwarding address.

Robert had fallen into a deep depression, mired in an endless litany of expressions of self-pity. At the other end of the psychological spectrum, Vincent bounded toward his bed, where he had propped himself up on some old pillows. Every bad situation has a positive aspect, Vincent advised his brother, and each of these can be documented, he continued, revealing that he had been keeping detailed notes of his brother's ordeal. Now, he ordered Robert to describe his whole adult life, from the time he was discharged from the U.S. Army to sneaking back home after the tension-wracked escape from the camp at La Grange. They were going to write a *book*!

Eyewitness Account

Vincent had been writing down notes and collecting press material since July 1929, when an article about Robert had appeared in the Chicago-based *True Detective Mysteries* magazine. He had sought out the editor,

John Shuttleworth, advising him of errors and hatching a plan for a much longer and accurate account of Robert's sensational adventures. Shuttleworth agreed to the idea, especially since Vincent was expecting his brother to break free a second time. Such a courageous, bold move could help increase circulation manifold.

Over the course of ten days, Robert's memories flooded out and through Vincent's penciled handwriting, resulting in an enormous stack of papers that would be given to a secretary to be typed into manuscript form. Following his brother's literary-induced catharsis, Vincent didn't see him for months. During Spring 1931, he had moved out of the drafty attic and opened an ill-fated advertising business in Newark, before hitchhiking 20 miles to Carteret, where he applied for a job as a slag dynamiter with the United States Metals Refining Company.

Mr. "Richard N. Crane" landed the job (the most difficult in the entire operation, exposing him to extreme heat, toxic fumes and dust), a $5 advance on his salary, and moved into the owner's house, renting a nice three-buck per week room. One Saturday, he worked an extra day, earning $150 to blow up an old brick smokestack at a vacant factory recently bought by an oil company. When 2,000 picnicking spectators arrived to see the highly touted "Dynamite Dick," he became leery of the police detail dispatched to the scene. His three-charge procedure eventually brought down the tower, the crowd went wild and, rather than draw undue attention to himself, he agreed to pose for a newsreel photographer. The following week, "Dynamite Dick" Crane was seen, much larger than life, in theaters across the nation, with the actual fugitive from a Georgia chain gang making his silver-screen debut.

Very fortunately, no one recognized the intrepid blaster as Robert Elliott Burns, and "Crane" was promoted to assistant foreman of the slag crew. Simultaneously, he received a letter from his "undying love" in Chicago, Lillian Salo, who revealed that she had been reading his life story in *True Detective Mysteries* and wondered if he was still unmarried. She also explained why she had missed her previous planned visits to New Jersey, adding that she hoped to hear back from him. During a lengthy correspondence with her, Robert stashed away as much dynamite dough as possible.

The serialized version of "I Am a Fugitive from a Georgia Chain Gang!" edited from the original manuscript Vincent had prepared, was published in six issues of *True Detective Mysteries* from January through June 1931. By the end of its run, the tale had reached an estimated ten million readers. Georgia Democratic governor L. G. Hardman, urged by the outraged Prison Commission, responded by multiplying the price on Robert's head by 10, from $50 to $500.

Literary Revelation

The foreword to the memoir begins:

> I AM a fugitive!
> I am a fugitive from the law—but NOT FROM JUSTICE!
> Discharged from the army, after the World War, a broken man, I committed a petty crime in Georgia, was caught, convicted, sentenced to ten years on the Georgia Chain Gang.

(Interestingly, the brief opening does not include mention that Robert was *forced* into committing the petty crime.)

An "Introduction by the Rev. Vincent G. Burns" follows, after which Robert's recollections begin on "a beautiful day in May 1919" at Camp Devens, Massachusetts, where the U.S. Army's 14th Engineers are being mustered out of service following their return from the hell of the Somme and Meuse-Argonne. Robert drew the $300 he was owed and greatly looked forward to freedom and returning to his job and sweetheart, both promised to be waiting for him upon his surviving the war and passing the Statue of Liberty as he landed back in New York.

Losing his lady was bad enough, but being an ex-soldier was "a drug on the market." When his $300 was gone, he became a depressed, bitter, aimless drifter.

Like a film, the memoir quickly segues from New York to Atlanta. The mood is set as sleet falls on a 50-cent flophouse barely heated by wood burning in a tin stove. Flat broke, Robert accepts a dollar from an Australian stranger named Flagg, accompanied by Moore, a "young, dumb one." Incredibly, Flagg promises the pay of $100 for his assistance on the following day.

No sleet falls on the following morning, which dawns "fine and clear and warm." During breakfast, Flagg, also a veteran of the late war, keeps their discussion confined to their mutual military experiences, never mentioning the job he has in mind. Moore does not speak.

In Atlanta, on Pryor Street East, at 9:00 a.m., Flagg, the criminal mastermind, reveals his robbery plan involving a pistol and a handful of cabbage, to be tossed into the face of the "Jew" owner of the grocery store. Robert wants nothing to do with such a cockeyed scheme, but Flagg's taunting, combined with the persuader in his pocket, convinces him that he has to go through with it. Besides, he "hadn't much to live for, anyway—and now, either decision I made would not clear me. I might as well be shot for a goose or a gander."

Robert's participation in the caper netting $5.80 involves frisking the owner and finding only a gun. Twenty minutes later, he and his two accomplices are lounging in the slammer of the local police station. Several victims of recent robberies file by, recognizing Flagg, but neither Moore nor Burns. Flagg is indicted on 21 counts; Moore and Burns, though no one can positively identify either of them, are each indicted on one count. Moore, pleading guilty, receives a sentence of eight to 12 years; Burns, declaring the same but allowed to speak in his own defense, lands a stretch of six to 10, at hard labor.

Robert had no idea that Georgia had no penitentiary, absolutely no prison of any kind. All convicted lawbreakers were sent to outdoor camps and "prison farms." At Bellwood, in Fulton County, stood a few old wooden shacks. Here he was outfitted with new attire: a two-piece ensemble of "stripes," four sizes too big, and without benefit of underwear or socks.

At a blacksmith's shop, a heavy iron ring was riveted to each of his ankles, and a "strad" chain consisting of 13 links (like the 13 winds in a hangman's noose) was attached to these, preventing him from taking a stride. Smack in the middle of the strad was linked another chain, the "upright," three feet long and ending with a ring about two inches in diameter. He had to carry the upright chain in order to walk at all. The iron rings ground the skin into raw meat, making infection a constant hazard, and could only be removed with a hammer and chisel. The whole rig, partially held in place by strips of leather, weighed about 20 pounds.

Trucked a short distance to Sandy Springs camp, Robert was introduced to his new digs, a long wooden structure of rough boards and iron-barred windows, with filthy cots along each side and stinking open toilets in the middle, bookended by a mess hall and a so-called wash room. Segregation was absolute law, and 100 white men were confined to this side of the camp, with blacks on the other.

Prior to enjoying his evening slumber, each prisoner had to hold his upright ring so a guard could pass through "the building chain" which linked together all the prisoners, making escape impossible. Removal of the pants was quite a difficult task, since they had to be pulled cleverly through one of the ankle rings, and not many of the convicts wanted to sleep bare-assed, anyway.

If using a toilet became necessary, a prisoner had to yell, "Getting up!" and wait for a guard to reply, "Get up!" waking all his fellow convicts and rattling all the linked chains while barely being able to reach the disgusting throne.

Robert's morning "alarm," occurring at 3:30 a.m., was the building chain being quickly dragged through all the prisoners' upright rings. If the convict didn't quickly rise to the occasion, he could find himself dragged hard to the floor or onto a neighboring cot. Such an act of rebellion could result in the extreme displeasure of one of the guards.

Dim lamp light barely allowed sight of what passed as "breakfast": hoe cake (white floor fried in animal fat), three small chunks of fatback, sorghum and a cup of "bad coffee." Unfortunately, this was the day's best meal, and usually was furiously pounded down by the camp's more recent arrivals.

Out in the yard, overseen by the warden under eerie torchlight, the convicts were arranged side by side in two lines of 10, with two guards assigned to each group. Each man held his upright ring so a "squad chain" could be run through, binding them all together. One truck was assigned to each group, and those who couldn't sit down painfully stood during the bumpy ride to the work site. The guards, each armed with a pistol and automatic shotgun, sat on the front seat with the driver. Upon reaching the roadside or quarry location, work would begin as soon as the sun rose.

Robert and his cohorts worked with sledgehammers and dynamite, but being closely chained together and overseen by willingly brutal guards made rebellion or escape quite unlikely. Blinded by sweat, a convict was forbidden to stop working until he shouted, "Wiping it off!" and waited to hear a guard's reply of "Wipe it off!" before doing so. A drink of water was carried around by a trusty about every hour, and at 11:30 a.m. a lunch of soil-caked corn pone and "cow peas," infested with filth and worms, was dragged about in an iron bucket, from which the men dipped with a tin plate. They actually were allowed to rest, wherever they dropped, dragging the others with them, until 1:00 p.m.

Five hours later, as dusk descended, the guards called out, "Lay 'em down!" and the incessant back-breaking toil temporarily ended. Back at the camp in darkness, each convict was searched, his chains examined and, finally, threatened with having "his ass knocked off" by the warden should he even consider committing the slightest infraction of the interminable litany of rules. All powerful within the confines of the camp bordered by *two* fences of razor-sharp barbed wire, the warden was a superior man whose word could have been chiseled in stone.

Hygiene was nearly nonexistent. One hundred men were forced to share three tin wash basins, and as for drying after "washing," that could be forgotten altogether. A scrap of garment, a filthy old bag, perhaps, if any such cloth could be dredged up from the floor, but never an actual towel would be provided. Five minutes after the first truck rolled in, "Get your feed!" was shouted out, and those convicts who could stomach another serving of the same disgusting slop bellied up to the long, picnic-like wooden tables before dragging each other to their iron cots, to flop down upon the grimy, thin poor excuses for mattresses and pillows.

Prior to the guard's placement of the building chain, the warden would make a personal inspection, intent on selecting a few convicts who obviously slacked off on the job that day. Robert recalled that six such unfortunates were chosen on his first night at the Sandy Springs camp. Dragged into the mess hall, where they barely could be seen by their fellow inmates, these men certainly could be *heard* during what ensued.

"So, you son of a bitch, you won't work, eh?" echoed the voice of the warden. "Get your pants down."

Held down by guards, the convict, his pants yanked to his chains, laid helpless, bare-assed on a picnic bench while a three-inch wide, six-feet long leather strap flogged him as he tortuously screamed until the point of unconsciousness, his warm blood running down between his legs and soaking into the wood floor beneath him. After he was jolted back to his feet and his bloody stripes pulled back up over his ass, the exact same treatment was applied to the other five men.

As with the iron rings that ground into their ankles, these whippings were not at all soothed by the application of medicine of any kind. Worse yet, the pants would adhere to the coagulating blood and prove excruciating when ripped forth from the wounds. The memoir states,

> So many prisoners died from the beatings they received that Governor Walker of Georgia was obliged to abolish the leather in 1923 to still the national agitation against this medieval brutality.
>
> The chain gang is simply a vicious, medieval custom, inherited from the blackbirders and slave traders of the 17th and 18th centuries, and is so archaic and barbarous as to be a national disgrace.
>
> There was a saying on the chain gang, and it ran as follows:
>
> "Work out"—meaning make your time.
> "Pay out"—meaning purchase a pardon or parole.
> "Die out"—meaning to die—or
> "Run out"—meaning to escape.

Following Robert's first night of hearing the hideous screams of these tortured men, he thought to himself, "Was it the hell I once read of in *Revelations*, or was I going insane?" The memoir continues,

2. I Am a Fugitive from a Georgia Chain Gang! *The Memoir*   27

> Any kind of reformation, and idea of trying to inoculate of decency, manners, or good and right thinking in the convict, is prohibited. All the convicts get is abuse, curses, punishment, and filth. In a few weeks all are reduced to the same level, just animals, and treated worse than animals.

Robert waited until each Saturday, when every man was given a "clean" pair of stripes and a small piece of Borax soap to wash his hands and face. A combing of the hair was also allowed. Though the brushing of teeth was nearly impossible, tobacco was rationed out: square plugs of chew on Wednesdays and cigarettes on Saturdays. Robert had the good sense to trade his chewing tobacco for the chance to grab a quick shave.

Sundays included a rest period, so the guards kept the building locked until 8:00 a.m. This interval allowed Robert time to read *if* he find any relevant material, since the illiteracy rate among the convicts was about 80 percent. Having much of this extra time to *think*, he continued to ponder the four possible means of leaving the living hell of the chain gang, and this was his conclusion:

> Not that I wanted to cheat justice. I leave that to the reader. If I had been sentenced to one year—which under the conditions of the chain gang and the extenuating circumstances of my crime, would have been plenty—I would have tried to make it. But six years—that was plain vengeance and also complete destruction.
> "Well," thought I—"Die out."
> I'll "Die out" trying to "run out." That was the definite conclusion I finally came to after two weeks at Fulton County.

On the Sunday following his drastic decision, Robert wrote a letter to the three members of the Georgia Prison Commission, the state's equivalent of a parole board, asking to be transferred to a different camp. While talking to several other convicts, he learned that some smaller counties ran facilities with fewer inmates and guards. Two weeks passed, and then 12 white inmates, including Robert, were moved to the Campbell County gang, which previously housed only blacks. Unfortunately, the living conditions were even worse than those at Fulton, with the convicts confined to sleeping in the reeking, lice and maggot-infested, iron-barred "pie wagons," stacked on four structures of three bunks each, with no room to move around. Meager washing was done outside from a bucket, and the "mess hall" was a small stockade surrounded by barbed wire. Nightly whippings also occurred in the open, with each poor bastard sprawled out on a piece of rough iron as he was flogged with the heavy leather strap.

However, no squad chains were used in Fulton County, with the whites and blacks integrated, working together on road projects. Two guards were assigned to each 12 prisoners, and just in case some brave or reckless soul decided to make a run for it, attempting to carry 20 pounds of iron chain along with him, well-trained bloodhounds were ready for a swift pursuit.

Following six weeks of considered observation, including witnessing one convict being flogged severely for trying to saw into his ankle rings with a modified razor blade, Robert developed a far wiser plan, concluding that the only reasonable time to attempt an escape would be a Monday morning, the period during the week when a man could be well rested. And the only possible way to remove a round ankle ring was if it were altered into an elliptical shape. But how?

Integration of the Campbell County camp provided Robert with his answer, if only he could manage to speak to one particularly powerful black man now unnoticed by the guards. This man, who had been on the gang so long that he handled a 12-pound sledgehammer with unerring ease and accuracy, just might be able to bend his ankle rings into ovals while Robert placed them against one of the rails they were tearing up from a line no longer in use. If the man missed the exact mark by only a fraction, however, the result could be multiple fractures of the tibia and fibula, and the loss of a foot.

On a day in June 1922, as the guards were becoming overheated by the blazing sun, Robert asked the black man for help. Admitting that he didn't deliberately court trouble, "Sam" still was willing to do his best, providing that the recipient of his hammer didn't accidentally turn the ring before the blow struck.

Pulling the 13-link chain as taut as possible, Robert set the right-ankle ring against the rail, allowing his new friend three blows to render the iron into what appeared to be an elliptical shape. They then repeated the exercise on the left leg. All said and done, Robert emerged with nothing broken, vowing to repeat the procedure another day should the change in the rings not be enough to allow the proper slippage to begin his run toward freedom. With supper over, and on his way to the pie wagon, Robert's turn at inspection came and went. The guard somehow hadn't noticed any change in the ankle rings.

Lying on his bunk in the darkness, Burns spit on his hand, lubricated his feet and was able, using a little force, to slip the rings over them. He had saved up some of the "allowance" mailed by Vincent, and now had four days to make a plan for his escape on the next Monday morning, taking into account the bloodhounds, finding new clothes, his problematic Northern "accent" and the undoubted dangers of repeating shotgun blasts.

On the morning of Monday, June 21, 1922, while ripping up an old bridge with his fellow convicts, Robert yelled, "Getting out here!" indicating a need to relieve himself.

"All right," a guard answered, pointing to a particular spot in the shrubbery, "get out here and don't be long." The second guard, 50 feet away, was focusing on other convicts.

In the bushes, Robert removed his shoes, slipped off the rings and, relying on his military training, began to crawl away. The requisite two-minute period elapsed and the guard shouted, "Come on, get back to work!"

Robert leapt to his feet and ran like hell as the dumbfounded guard blasted away. With buckshot around his ears, he poured on more speed until he reached a wooded area. Eventually he stopped to play with the dogs chasing him, which ended much of their barking and baying. Deep in the woods, always using the sun as his compass, he kept moving swiftly to the north.

Occasionally he would stop for a drink of water, to cool off a bit, before starting again, until realizing it must be reaching about 5:00 p.m. Now it was time, he thought, to change out of his convict stripes. Near a shanty occupied by a black family, he carefully absconded with a shirt and pair of overalls hanging on a wash line. At a very welcome river, he jumped in and swam, long enough to lose the dogs along the bank, before crawling out on the opposite side.

Now Robert felt comfortable just walking at a brisk pace; and, following another hour's progress, he reached a paved highway along which traffic was flowing in both directions. He thumbed a ride in a Ford coupe driven by a friendly man, who had a basket of peaches on the seat beside him. Told to help himself, he was astonished to learn that his driver was headed to Atlanta, just nine miles away, and that he had run about 27 during his flight from the chain gang.

In Atlanta, at 8:00 p.m., Robert bought some better-fitting clothes, got a shave at a local barber shop, ate at a diner and then found a 75-cent hotel, where the clerk, who had been on the Sandy Springs chain gang, recognized him. Not only didn't he blow Robert's cover, but the man gave him six dollars, and offered him whiskey, heroin and prostitutes, none of which he accepted. Instead, Robert quietly asked his generous and obviously debauched friend not to broadcast his spectacular escape to any other good-time folks who might accidentally blather on about his achievement. One of the hookers remained, however, and during her conversation with Robert, ducked out to bring back railroad timetables from which he could plan his trip, by way of Chattanooga, for the following day.

In the morning, while waiting for the train, Robert saw a large police contingent gathering at the station. His nerves on edge but determined to leave Georgia as soon as possible, he walked steadily toward a passenger car as the cops began running toward him—and then right *past*, chasing a tramp who had suddenly appeared on the scene.

Following a four-hour trip by train, Robert, fearing that the crew were suspicious, jumped out at the first station in Tennessee and began walking along the highway toward Chattanooga and, ultimately, Chicago, where he planned to settle down to an honest life's work. In the Windy City, he arrived with 60 cents left in his pocket.

At the famous Chicago Stock Yards, Robert landed a day job paying $3.20 every evening. A year passed and he still was free, walking along Ingleside Avenue, where he chose to rent a room at number 6444. Here he met the landlady's daughter, Emilia Del Pino Pacheo, a somewhat older divorcee who soon fell in love with him, catering and helping like a wife and accepting him into her family. Robert, however, not reciprocating her feelings, explained exactly how he *did* view the situation, but this only dissuaded her for a few days.

The situation changed when Emilia opened a letter to Robert written by his father, thus discovering his "secret" and beginning a lengthy period of emotional blackmail bound by his desire to run a big-city business. The "couple" actually operated two professional operations: an apartment house, which appealed to "Emily," who initially split the income with him; and *The Greater Chicago Magazine*, an endeavor challenging Robert's more artistic and intellectual nature, and which he funded entirely on his own.

As to their legal relationship status, the memoir states, "She lived with me as though she were my wife. This you will please understand was not objectionable to me, but was absolutely voluntary on her part."

Serving as both publisher and editor of his magazine, Robert worked into the wee hours nearly every night. He also became a popular speaker at various functions netting him extra money with which he could pay off debts incurred while running the operation. Finally, in August 1926, as Robert attempted to distance himself further from Emily, she demanded that either he marry her or face the consequences of escaping from the chains of Georgia.

Robert accepted the hard medicine. He also developed excellent credit, expanded the circulation of his magazine, made wide circles of friends, and joined the Chicago Association of Commerce and Real Estate Board. He often lectured to large audiences for free, supporting every type of worthwhile cause, including the movement to hold the Second World's Fair in the city.

Here, the memoir states:

2. I Am a Fugitive from a Georgia Chain Gang! *The Memoir*   31

> The record I made in Chicago, the friends I acquired—and remember, I started as an unknown and every step up was self-made—are overwhelming and convincing proof that I did live a clean, honest, wholesome and creative life, and as such was both an honor and an asset to Chicago.
>
> And yet, and were those, so saturated with prejudice, jealousy and hatred, as to deliberately lie and slander me by saying I was and still am a menace to society!

Robert tolerated and pitied Emily, but morally could not become her husband, even if legally he was so on paper. His lectures and presence at social events brought him into contact with hundreds of women and he, deprived of actual shared affection, naturally became interested. However, when Emily became seriously ill in November 1928, he saw to it that she received the best care, going so far as to have every medical aspect upgraded, until she was discharged on Christmas Eve, when she became enraged: He didn't love her.

This was the last straw for Robert. He ignored her as much as possible, always staying out until well past midnight, and considered initiating divorce proceedings. In February 1929, he met Lillian Salo, a music student from Minneapolis working as a Chicago dime-a-dance girl.

Now Robert was really in love. Planning to set up house with Lillian in late March, he explained it all to Emily, whom he promised more than an equitable divorce; in fact, she would receive not only alimony but also stock in the magazine company. She would be set for the rest of her life, so she made a promise, on her rosary beads, to grant the divorce. True to form, however, she reneged, causing a violent scene in his office, where she threatened either to "destroy" him or "kill" him!

Aided by employees, Robert calmed her down, and she again agreed to a divorce. However, on March 28, 1929, from the Jackson Park Post Office, she mailed a quite informative letter to prison authorities in Georgia. Thus began the downfall of the self-made, successful, philanthropic Chicago version of Robert E. Burns, and his reduction back to a *Fugitive from a Georgia Chain Gang!* Real love, planning a happy household in the northern suburb of Des Plaines, perhaps a family—all this led to the disaster of returning to Hell on Earth. The memoir reads:

> Does honesty pay? Why of course it does! Had I not acquired all of this by honesty, adherence to ideals; by courage and real worth of character? Surely organized society could not overlook this hard-won and deserved victory over so many obstacles and not see that the man behind it all was now a man, tested by life's bitter experiences and found to be of pure metal.
>
> Some twenty-four hundred years ago Confucius said, "It is better to fall, and rise again, than never to have fallen."

For two months, Robert enjoyed a nearly ideal life with Lillian, listening to her sing and play her violin, and treasuring her company when he delivered his evening lectures and attended other events. Divorce proceedings with Emily and her attorney did not pan out as well, with his refusal of their exorbitant terms resulting in, not a divorce, but being served with a writ of separation. When this case was dismissed by a judge from the Domestic Relations Branch, Emily filed two civil suits against Robert.

He utterly ignored this frivolous litigation; but, on May 22, 1929, two men, without an appointment, arrived at the magazine building. Following a meeting with his editor, Merle McBain, Robert allowed them into his office. One of them pulled a gat while the other brandished a shield. Both were detectives, bounty hunters on a mission for Georgia prison officials.

Holding a piece of paper, one of them inquired, "Are you the man referred to in this letter?"

Robert had no choice but to be honest. "Yes," he replied. Turning his business affairs over to McBain, he was locked up at the State Street Police Headquarters "with the riff-raff of the underworld." Visited by an extensive parade of reporters, attorneys, friends and other supporters, Robert was called in to meet with a high-ranking police officer who described a plan that could keep him in Chicago for years, preventing the Georgia officials from taking him back to the chain gang.

The next morning, at a hearing addressing his petition for a writ of *habeas corpus*, Judge David said,

> Georgia—the Great State of Georgia—the home and birthplace of that vicious organization, the Ku Klux Klan. Where they sell the water of the Chattahoochie River at five dollars per gallon to baptize the ignorant and illiterate, that they may be initiated into the wonders of the Klan, and so continue their holy and Christian persecution of the Jew, the Catholic, and the Negro; and become acquainted with the fine art of lynching and midnight beatings and terrorism.
>
> The purpose of the law is for protection of society and *not* for vengeance. It seems to me that Georgia in this case does not want justice but vengeance. Personally, I cannot see anything in this most peculiar situation but vengeance. Society has nothing to gain by returning this man to a brutal prison, neither has it anything to fear if he continues to remain free.

Bail was not granted to Robert, but he was released into the custody of the sheriff who, rather than locking him in the county jail, assigned a deputy to accompany him wherever he went. The following morning, he returned to court, where the judge agreed to release him on a $5,000 bond, which was paid by the vice-president of H. O. Stone and Company, the oldest Chicago business firm, having operated successfully for 93 years in the city.

Back at his office, Robert and all manner of prominent supporters, realizing that Georgia governor Hardman would not even consider the case until he was returned to the chain gang, focused their efforts on appealing

2. I Am a Fugitive from a Georgia Chain Gang! *The Memoir* 33

to Governor Emmerson of Illinois to deny the extradition warrant after it actually arrived. A businessmen's support group, "The Burns Citizens Committee," was established on West Washington Street.

After Emmerson scheduled a hearing in Springfield, Illinois, for June 1929, Emily gave a series of scurrilous interviews to several newspapers, blatantly lying that Robert had committed bigamy and embezzlement. She even made the ludicrous assertion that he was *not* in the AEF during the Great War. Soon, Vincent arrived in Chicago to accompany his brother to the hearing. At this point, the memoir speculates on Robert's ensuing legal difficulties:

> In the light of subsequent events, especially at my two hearings before the Prison Board in Georgia, and other happenings which I will relate, there was always a vague, indistinct and elusive power that seemed to work against me continually. What or who this power was I do not know. But this I do know, that the only known enemy I had was my wife and she could never, single-handed and alone, have created and put into action the force that was used to obstruct my parole.
> Some other force was there. In searching my mind for an explanation, I was at a complete loss to account for it.
> Thus it became apparent that besides having a host of friends who were straining every effort to save me from going back to prison, it is possible that I had powerful forces lined up against me.

On the day the hearing continued, Assistant State's Attorney Chatt reported that a full investigation of Emily's charges was not sufficient to bring any criminal action against Robert. In Springfield a few days afterward, an official of Governor Emmerson's legislative committee reported that a decision on the extradition matter would be completed in a day or two. Regrettably—and astonishingly—the governor's decision was to sign the warrant sending him back to Georgia.

After considering five different possibilities of defeating an actual fulfillment of his chain-gang sentence, Robert voluntarily chose to return to Georgia for a period of 45 to 90 days, during which he would be made a trusty, and to pay all the expenses the state had incurred in its efforts at extradition. Advised through several reputable channels that it was the proper choice, Robert had to raise about $3,200, much of which was contributed or loaned by friends and business associates.

The hearing with Judge David, Assistant State's Attorney Chatt and the representative from Georgia assured them that, upon his return, Robert would not be chained and forced into road work, but be assigned a clerical job. He then deliberated the situation with Lillian Salo, who promised to wait for him: whether he went to Georgia and, keeping their word, the state allowed him to return to Chicago in 45 to 90 days; or, instead, decided to flee the country, with her in tow, to begin a new life in some faraway land like Australia, a possibility they previously had discussed. The memoir quotes Robert as thinking to himself, "Walking a few blocks to my attorney's office, where I was to meet Mr. Stanley, I had a violent premonition that that was the last time I would ever see Lillian."

Back in Georgia, he returned to the Campbell County camp, from which he had escaped seven years and five days earlier. He recognized no one, prisoner nor guard, and was introduced to the warden, Paul Phillips. Though he was assigned to the same pie-wagon bunk, he was made a trusty, with yard duties tending to clothing, rations and reading his fellow convicts' mail. These light duties continued for five weeks, during which Lillian moved to Atlanta and was allowed to visit him, accompanied by his attorney, John Echols.

However, on July 29, 1929, Echols arrived to inform Robert that the Prison Commission required $500, to be paid *that day*, in order to recommend his parole. Robert replied that it would take a few days for him to have that amount of money wired from Chicago, and Echols returned to Atlanta. A mere *two hours* later, two thugs, armed with .45 automatics, drove up in a Buick. One of them was Warden Hardy of the Troup County chain gang, who had an official document transferring Robert to this camp, located at La Grange, Georgia, where they arrived at 9:00 p.m. that evening. He was locked up, alone for a time, in a concrete enclosure with a steel-barred door called "the bull pen." The memoir states:

> Among its inmates were the desperate, fearless, hardened men from other camps; prisoners who had escaped and were recaptured, and those who were without friends or political aid. They were sent here for safe keeping: to prevent by every known human ingenuity their escape. It was a place shunned by everyone of Georgia's 5,000-odd felons.

For the next 14 months, Robert joined the other convicts in being rudely awakened at 3:00 a.m., to sleepily shuffle toward two filthy, rusted wash tubs before entering the mess hall for a serving of customary cold "middlings," hoe cake, sorghum and "coffee." Though he had been away from the camp horrors for more than seven years, the rituals in the yard, Ford trucks and on the roads came back to him as if he'd never escaped. After dark, chained in the bull pen, he was endlessly questioned by his new "companions": auto and cattle thieves, heist men, safecrackers, rapists, murderers and cop killers. During his incarceration, he witnessed insubordinate convicts subjected to the sweatbox and "the jack," a medieval-like torture device, stocks that leave a man hanging in midair by his wrists and ankles, looking like a piece of meat hooked up in a butcher's smoke house. Surrounded by many men plotting their various means of escape, Robert still maintained his faith that the Prison Commission would grant him a parole or pardon.

The initial hearing for clemency was held in Atlanta on August 10, 1929, lasting 30 minutes with Robert absent, shoveling soil with a group of blacks on a road in Troup County. More than two weeks later, he finally learned from another convict that his petition had been denied. On August 17, Governor Hardman, a staunch Christian, wrote a letter to Vincent, indicating that he would personally review the case. However, when Vincent and Katherine traveled to Atlanta to meet with him, they were received with callous indifference, and informed that Robert might be eligible for parole after serving a term of one year back on the chain gang. All of the positive support continuing to flood in from across the nation was glaringly negated by the web of lies perpetrated by Emily, exactly the kind of slander that was ripe for yellow-journalism-type newspaper headlines. Her campaign included attacks on the magazine company; and when the stock market crashed in October 1929, Robert's account at the City State Bank of Chicago was completely annihilated.

"Recreation" at the camp consisted of a weekly sermon by a fire-and-brimstone, evangelical preacher. Of course, the convicts were segregated, with whites sitting on splinter-ridden wooden benches on one side, and blacks on the other. The memoir explains:

> He always would finish in the same vein and with the same thought. These were almost his exact words: "If you suffer and are in pain and misery, it is God's will. It matters not what your lot may be, the only thing of earthly importance is to save your soul. If the only way a man's soul might be saved was by hanging him by the neck until dead, or electrocuting him, if these things were the only ways his soul could be saved, it would be better to kill him and save his soul than to let him live and lose his soul."
>
> I don't profess to be a deep student of theology, but somehow I can never accept such a belief. I feel that if a man has a soul he has a responsibility to cultivate it. God or truth can be of help to him. But morally and spiritually a man must learn to stand on his own feet and follow the divine voice that speaks in his own heart.

Katherine and Vincent continued to travel to Atlanta, Washington, D.C., and Chicago, where they collected over 80 affidavits from prominent individuals attesting to Robert's positive qualities, achievements and charitable efforts. The memoir notes, "Surely so large and influential a group of men and women would not commit perjury to free a menace to society, as I had been labeled by Assistant State's Solicitor Stephens."

Robert again was eligible for a hearing in July 1930. During the previous month, five Georgia chain-gang convicts actually had been *worked to death*. One of them, an African American at the La Grange camp, had reported he was so sick that he could not work. In return for this comment, the man was forced to labor in a soil pit, the toughest job on the crew. He attempted to maintain the brutal pace demanded by the guards while repeating that he was ill, but was given no chance to rest. Finally, he collapsed and died from sunstroke. The guards tossed his corpse into a truck and another convict took his place. That evening, a medical examiner arrived to fill out a bogus death certificate and make the situation appear as if proper protocol had been followed.

By the time Robert's second hearing was held on July 9, even a considerable percentage of Georgians, informed both by the press and word of mouth, were calling for his release. Among the affidavits and letters presented by Vincent were those signed by New York governor Franklin Delano Roosevelt, former president Calvin Coolidge, former secretary of the navy Josephus Daniels, New York attorney George Gordon Battle, and Commander of the American Legion John Fromm. Robert leafed through these documents when Vincent and Katherine were allowed to visit him on the Fourth of July holiday, and he was most impressed by those submitted by the people of Georgia, including businessmen, attorneys, a congressman, and even the world-famous golfer Bobby Jones, who hailed from Atlanta. When July 9 dawned, even people in Troup County, including many of the La Grange camp guards, believed that he would be set free.

Lasting a mere *five minutes*, this hearing was quite different than the first, with Judge G. A. Jones, a close friend of Warden Hardy's, filling in for Mr. Stanley as second member of the Prison Commission. Chairman Rainey, Robert's attorney, Schley Howard, and Vincent were the only others present. Damaging "testimony" against Robert had arrived in the form of a letter to the Prison Commission from Solicitor General John A. Boykin, who reiterated that the convict had escaped, hadn't paid his time to the state of Georgia and was a continual "menace to society."

At this point, the memoir, attempting to explain the continual refusal of the state to parole or pardon Robert, includes a brief, but thorough, history of the "prison contract system" that led to the institution of chain gangs. It begins:

> Georgia suffered heavily in the Civil War. After the War, she was faced with the problem of reconstruction on a new social foundation. The people were poor, their wealth had been destroyed, there was nothing to tax and nothing to pay taxes with. Many difficult problems demanded instant solution.
>
> One of these problems was the disposition of convicted lawbreakers. There were no penitentiaries or workhouses. In the face of a rising tide of lawlessness the problem demanded an immediate solution. It worked about as follows:
>
> A man was convicted of a crime and sentenced, say, to three to five years. A prison

contractor would appear at the county jail, look the man over, estimate his worth in terms of labor, and bid for his services at the rate, say, of twenty-five dollars a year. The State accepts the bid.

The memoir continues to describe this process, whose administration eventually shifted from the state to the counties, but continued as a racket involving government employees and politicians at all levels. This history concludes:

> When the Georgia officials read this they may deny my allegations vigorously, admitting, perhaps, that this may have once been the case, but is not true today. My answer to that is stated in unequivocal terms: If they deny these allegations, I say they lie.

This chapter continues with the statement that "Georgia has always been prejudiced against Catholics, Jews, Yankees and Negroes." Mentioning the "unprintable nature" of the continuous bigotry heard by Robert, it concludes with a warning:

> If you were to visit Georgia and were arrested, accused of some violation of the law, the first question the Judge would ask you would be: "Where do you come from?" and the next, "What church do you go to?" If the answers to these questions brought out the fact that you were a Northern Catholic or a Jew, you would be in need of help.

Robert made the difficult decision that, if the result of the second hearing mirrored the first, his only choice would be to attempt escaping again, preferring the chance of death to spending six to ten years more in the horrors of the chain gang. Katherine was positive that he would be released, but Robert knew better, and told his mother about his plan to take it on the lam from any more outrageous politically corrupt injustice the state could dish out. Once again, his parole was denied, but he was made a trusty, which meant that the chains were removed from his ankles.

Working on the road in the vicinity of Mountville, Georgia, Robert met a harshly sunbaked, prematurely aged farmer with whom an escape plan was struck: paying him a carefully stashed $50 to hide his automobile in the woods between 7:30 and 8:00 a.m. the following day. But on the morrow, when Robert's shadow indicated the scheduled time had arrived, no hide nor hair of the man could be found. The farmer was unable to pull it off, so a slightly altered attempt was arranged for the following day, using a tall pine tree as a mark for the auto's hiding place.

The next morning: Again, no farmer; but when the suntanned man in the overalls appeared on the road hours later, Robert propositioned him a third time, promising to send him an additional $100 should he make it to freedom. This time, now devised for an initial $60, resulted in the Georgian's telltale "mockingbird" signal from the woods beside the road, and

Robert took off, hell bent for bracken. He sped through the brush in the ditch into the woods, with buckshot flying around his head, and toward the man's car, where the rumble seat had been prepared for his escape. Another man brandishing an imposing horse pistol briefly stopped him in his tracks, but he proved to be the farmer's enforcer.

Robert paid the men $5 to purchase some new clothes, which required several stops before they could pull off the road for his wardrobe change and to collect their money—hence the presence of the farmer's armed friend. Driving as far as Atlanta was out of the question, however, so Robert was dropped off in College Park, where, coincidentally, the Troup County chain gang currently was working.

Resorting to one of his previous dodges—the barber's chair—he dropped in for a shave in order to have his visage partially disguised, as he waited for the College Park Trolley to deliver him to Atlanta. On Decatur Street, he bought a $10 suit, which he had altered at a shop around the corner. Completing his new appearance by having his shoes shined, he headed for the train station; but, realizing this choice involved several pitfalls, he opted for taking the Greyhound to Chattanooga. Following a 4:00 a.m. layover in Rome, Georgia, where he underwent a perceived close call with two sheriffs, the bus resumed its course, reaching Chattanooga at 7:30 p.m. He checked his suitcase and waited for the bus to Louisville, which would arrive there at 1:30 a.m.

However, after overhearing several Greyhound employees discussing the La Grange escapee with a clerk on the telephone, he decided to travel by the Royal Palm train to Cincinnati. On the train, he befriended a lovely, intelligent young woman traveling to Chicago, and she was not only weighted down by bags and hat boxes, but also in need of rest and a bath after being on board for more than a day. To provide cover for himself in Cincinnati, he convinced her to lay over there for a day to take care of personal needs. This plan worked perfectly; and, after bidding her goodbye, he slept and bathed himself before boarding the bus for Columbus, Ohio. Destination: Pittsburgh, where he planned to begin using the alias "John Pashley," the name of an old buddy from the chain gang who had passed on a Merchant Marine card featuring a photo that closely resembled his own reflection in the mirror.

At 4:30 a.m. on a Sunday morning, sitting at a table at Silver's all-night café, Robert was back in his beloved city of Newark, New Jersey. At the Hackensack train station, he telephoned his mother's home in Pennsylvania, reversing the charges. She was out but, not knowing the person to whom he was speaking, merely left a message that, at 11:00 p.m., "R. E. B." would be awaiting her return call.

Spot on, at 11:00 p.m., the phone jangled and Robert quickly snatched up the receiver. He first heard the voice of his beloved mother, then his brother, who agreed to mail $25.00, addressed to "John Smith," care of general delivery, to Hackensack. For months on end, Robert went from job to job, having to bolt for one reason or another, often—by mere coincidence—facing the chance of being recognized. In the midst of the Great Depression, even the prospect of *getting* a position, especially with having honestly to fill out a job application, was very unlikely. As the memoir draws to an end, it describes this dismal scene:

> I am sitting in my plainly furnished cheap room, alone, writing this record of events with hands horny from heavy toil. I am now John Pashley—an itinerant laborer—friendless—weary of body and mind—only my heart after years of tragic events beats bravely on—hoping against hope that someday its sturdy beats will eventually hammer out a place for me somewhere—somehow—some time.

The third paragraph from the end reads, "'Mr. Burns will certainly get first-hand information about sleeping in chains if he is ever my guest again,' said Warden Hardy in the *Atlanta Journal*."

When this memoir was published in *True Detective Mysteries* from January through June 1931, the [co]-author declared brazenly:

I AM A FUGITIVE FROM A GEORGIA CHAIN GANG!

Hardman's Hard Line

After Georgia's Governor Hardman read the memoir and raised the bounty on Robert's head, Vincent then made a sly move by writing a letter (signed by his brother) to the politician, reviewing the case and asking for a pardon, which he then mailed from Long Island City to John Shuttleworth at Macfadden Publications' New York office. But after reading the detailed and persuasive missive, Hardman retained his hard line, refusing to answer personally, instead spouting a curt single line to the press that Burns would have to return to Georgia before they would even reconsider his case. Vincent then sent a second letter, which he signed, but the governor and his commission still wanted more for one-third of the $5.80 which Robert supposedly heisted from that unharmed grocer nearly a decade before.

When Vincent received a request from a New York newspaper reporter for an interview with Robert, he checked out the man's reputation. All appeared kosher, so Robert agreed to meet with the journalist in an old roadhouse on the edge of Newark. During his talk, he reportedly included some astute socioeconomic conclusions based on his many life experiences:

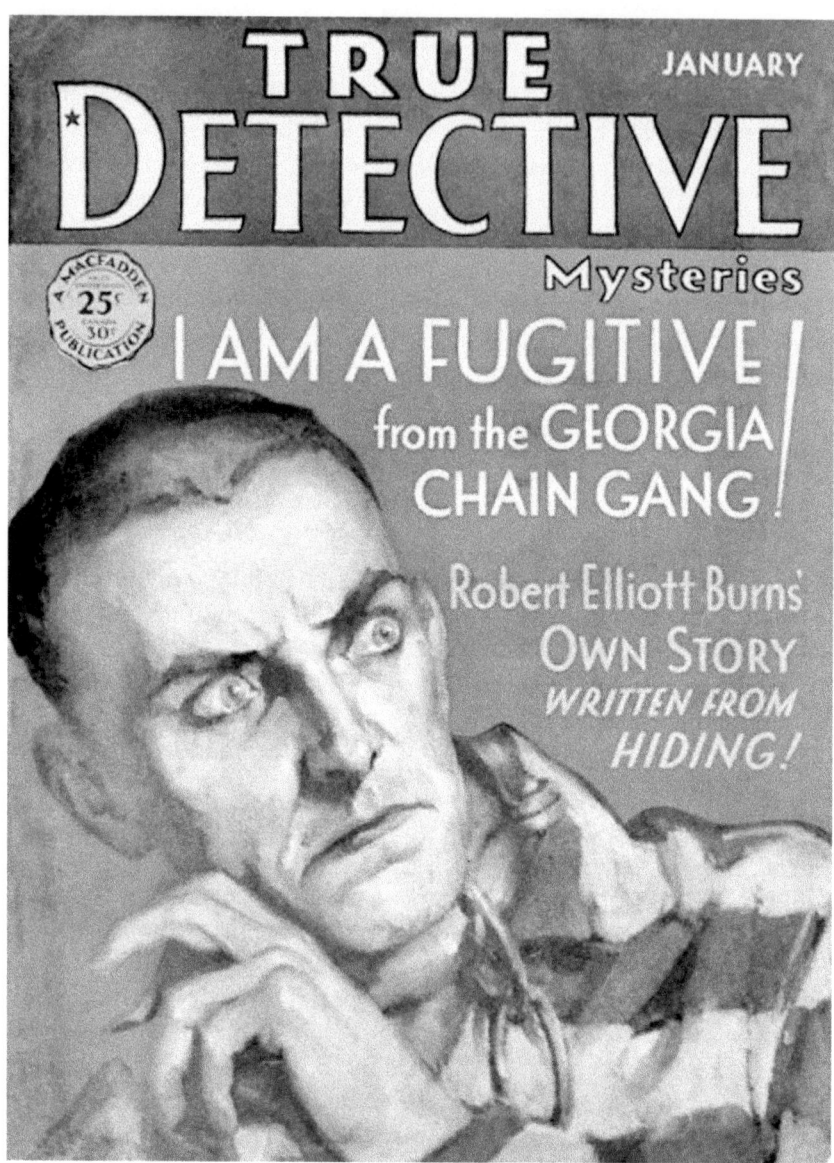

The memoir of Robert E. Burns' travails on the chain gang was first serialized in six installments published in *True Detectives Mysteries* magazine from January to June 1931.

> The man who is most respected is the man with the biggest club.... All the saints of all the ages have tried to change it, but today we are only one step removed from savagery. And the time is coming when we'll find this out to our sorrow in the larger scene of international politics...
> Music, drama, literature and art ... are the things that bring unity and meaning to life.... The desire for brotherhood and the love of beauty may yet lift mankind out of

its quicksands of hate, its bogs of greed and its swamps of war. These things alone relieve the deadly monotony of the devilishly wicked economic slaughterhouse. Unless we do something to really change it, it will change us by blood and fire and our world will never be the same again!⁴

(Written at the dawn of U.S. involvement in World War II, this account, published in Vincent Burns' *Out of These Chains* [1942], undeniably shows his ministerial pen embellishing with religious fervor and literary metaphor the socialist political beliefs he and his brother shared.)

Soon after Robert accepted a new job as night watchman with the metals refinery, a drunken coworker came stumbling in, babbling he knew the true identity of "Richard Crane" and offering to forget all about it if he could just grab some bars of gold. When another watchman joined them and then assaulted the inebriate, he yelled out the name "Burns" with a threat of exposure, but Robert anxiously waited for weeks without being summoned by anyone.

Tipped off that everyone at the refinery and the local police now knew his true identity, Vincent told him to meet him in Elizabeth, New Jersey, halfway between Carteret and Newark. One month later, the brothers began adding new material to the six *True Detective Mysteries* installments, and with three brand new chapters containing far more details about the chain-gang operation, Vince worked with a secretary to create a new, book-length manuscript.

From Pulp Nonfiction to Bestselling Book

Following a plethora of rejections from major New York publishing firms, Vanguard Press published *I Am a Fugitive from a Georgia Chain Gang!* in January 1932. A majority of reviewers were enthusiastically positive about the book, and sales were tremendous. A half-century later, it would be reevaluated as an "unsteady compound of hearsay, myth and stereotype," an embellished memoir that "struck a resonant chord with the men and women of [Burns'] generation, especially after the start of the Great Depression."⁵

In his introduction to the 1977 University of Georgia Press edition of the book, Matthew Mancini astutely notes:

> However understandable the anger and embarrassment of Georgians might have been over Burns' book, the fact is that throughout its history the South's development has been inextricably connected with forced labor of all kinds. That Burns presented his story in a way that reinforced stereotypes, rather than advanced a serious analysis of the problem, should not come as a surprise. He was unjustly sentenced to a shocking hell and

wanted to tell about it. The instruments he had at his disposal for explaining the system were stock images—stereotypes. Therefore he could not help but use metaphors and similes, as well as direct descriptions, that in turn could not help but cause many Georgians to feel embarrassment, loss of face, and, consequently, furious anger.[6]

More simply, the perspective of the book, dictated by the tortured fugitive and written by his brother, a minister and aspiring poet, is *not* that of an academic—a historian nor a sociologist—therefore the characterizations of the Southerners are simplistic stereotypes. But they certainly all have a conspicuous basis in fact.

3

The Making of the Film

> [I]t will probably make a good picture for [Paul] Muni and he will probably be great in it but I doubt if it will ever meet with such a hearty approval from an audience, especially now that everyone has a problem of their own to solve.
> I personally do not care for a story of this kind and would not like to make it.
> —Warner Bros. director Roy Del Ruth, after reading the temporary script for *I Am a Fugitive from a Chain Gang*[1]

Before the memoir was published in book form, Vincent Burns realized that the six serialized installments of the memoir were ripe for transformation into a motion picture script. He took the published segments, bound them into a manuscript, and sent the bundle to MGM's New York office, where it didn't make it past the first script reader. It was quickly returned with the remark, "This is not screen material!" scrawled in pencil. Such hard-hitting misery didn't fit the Hollywood hokum churned out by the *ars gratia artis* studio where anything resembling real life rarely invaded the feel-good world view of the sociopolitically arch-conservative Louis B. Mayer, a friend and staunch supporter of President Herbert Hoover.

The success of the book version generated significant interest in the film capitol, however. Though an MGM executive, having no knowledge of the earlier New York snub, made Vincent an offer, Robert wisely preferred Warner Bros., the only studio in Hollywood run by Democrats. Three decades later, when writing his autobiography, Jack Warner would claim the project became "the first sermon I had ever put on film."[2]

Jack's brothers in New York always were concerned with the box-office appeal of any project, and Harry Warner convinced Abe, ever more willing to placate their stock investors, that Darryl Zanuck could hold down expenditures and spark audience interest, even while adapting a potentially controversial subject for the screen. By 1932, Harry, intending to compete with such competitors as RKO and Universal, who produced films with slightly higher budgets, was looking for a property with some prestige.

After selling the film rights to Jack Warner, who was aware that Zanuck had been advised by story-department assistants about potential censorship problems, for $12,500, Robert again established his own business, a small gift shop in East Orange, New Jersey. On Easter Sunday, March 27, 1932, he suddenly shocked Katherine and Vincent by admitting that he would be traveling from Newark to Hollywood via Chicago by train the next day. Zanuck had offered him an opportunity to act as advisor on the chain-gang scenes and to work with the screenwriters on making the character of "James Allen" as authentic as possible.

Mrs. Burns was mortified, insisting that New Jersey was the only state in the Union where he would have any chance to remain safe from extradition back to Georgia. But Robert assured her and Vincent that Warner Bros. had promised him a safe haven on the studio lot. "They will stand by me," he insisted.[3]

Just hours after Vincent dropped Robert at the train station, he picked up a copy of *Variety* featuring a byline revealing that the author of *I Am a Fugitive from a Georgia Chain Gang!* was on his way to Hollywood. A few days later, his fear that Georgia authorities would soon be in Tinsel Town increased when every major newspaper in New York and New Jersey ran this story:

> The hunt for Robert Elliott Burns, famous escaped convict and writer of the bestseller, "I Am a Fugitive from a Georgia Chain Gang," who was sentenced to ten years' imprisonment for stealing a handful of change, will be shifted to the West Coast this week on a report that he is in Hollywood helping to film a movie of his Georgia chain gang experiences…. Judge G. A. Johns, vice-chairman of the Georgia Prison Commission, said last night a film trade publication had carried items about Burns being in Hollywood to assist with the proposed picture, and that the Commission would begin an immediate investigation, and if the facts were verified would send a Georgia police officer to Hollywood to arrest him…. Word from Los Angeles today said unverified reports had stated Burns was supposed to be there under an assumed name…[4]

Warner Bros. Before the Burns Brothers

The Warner Bros., like other pioneering studio moguls (Carl Laemmle, Samuel Goldwyn and Jesse L. Lasky) officially began Southern California-based filmmaking operations during 1912–13. Abe Warner served as company treasurer in New York, while Harry, Sam and Jack began film production in Culver City, California. In 1918, they had saved enough capital to invest $25,000 in some real estate at 5482 Sunset Boulevard, where "Warner Bros. Pictures" was officially inaugurated.

Harry settled in New York, where he became president of the company, with the financially astute Abe retaining his position as treasurer. In "Hollywood," a neighborhood which had merged with Los Angeles in 1910, Jack and Sam shared production duties after opening the new studio on April 4, 1923. Their first major star was not a human being, but a dog, "Rin Tin Tin," a multitalented German Shepherd, who, like the Burns brothers, was a veteran of World War I. Having made his film debut in *The Man from Hell's River* (1922), the dog played his first starring role in *Where the North Begins* (1923), on which future director Lewis Milestone served as editor. "Rinty" was a notable worldwide box-office hero, appearing in a total of 27 films, until his death at the age of 13 in 1932. The dog is credited not only with popularizing the use of dogs as film characters in general, but specifically advancing Darryl Zanuck's career and helping to save the Warner Bros. from a potential bankruptcy.

As early as 1925, Warners' head of publicity, Hal B. Wallis, announced that the studio would begin producing "talking pictures." Harry Warner was anxious to compete with the other Hollywood majors by making films allowing audiences nationwide to see and hear the greatest stage and musical stars of the age. At the Warner Theatre in New York, the studio publicly demonstrated "the second turning point in the history of entertainment," the Vitaphone sound system, in August 1926.

Vitaphone, a division of the Western Electric Company, had offered its revolutionary system to several producers, but Sam Warner was the only one with the insight and fortitude to buy a license for the invention, which played a film's soundtrack on phonograph records, to be synchronized with the projected film. Convincing his three brothers to accept this "sound idea," Warners produced the epic *Don Juan* (1926), starring the great matinee idol John Barrymore, Mary Astor, future Charlie Chan Warner Oland, and a very young, exotic Myrna Loy. The film's sound consisted of a complete synchronized score recorded for Vitaphone by the Philharmonic Orchestra. Vitaphone's George Groves, who developed a multi-microphone setup to record the 107-member orchestra, became the first music mixer ever to work on a film soundtrack.

Other soundtrack efforts for feature releases followed, with Harry and Jack finally deciding that music *and* dialogue needed to be featured in a true "prestige" production, in this case an adaptation of Samson Saphaelson's play *The Jazz Singer* (1927), to star "show-business" phenomenon Al Jolson, who had been recording popular songs since the World War I era. The finished film includes only a few musical numbers and dialogue sequences with Jolson, but this groundbreaking film was a smash hit, ranking Warner Bros. at the forefront of cinema's "sound revolution." Audiences who never had a chance to see "the foremost personality in the entertainment world" perform live on Broadway now had a chance to witness him sing his distinctive interpretations in *any* town that had a movie theater.

Half of *The Jazz Singer*'s $500,000 budget went to Jolson, making the project Warner Bros.' most expensive film to date, but a profit of $250,000 allowed them further to convert and expend their studio soundstages for producing sound pictures. Tragically, Sam Warner didn't live to see the success of the film, whose milestone achievement was due to his initial belief in the efficacy of using the Vitaphone system to make sound films. Only one day before *The Jazz Singer* premiered, he died from the quick onset of a cerebral hemorrhage on October 5, 1927.

Fulfilling their late brother's foresight, the remaining three produced the first truly "all-talking" feature, *Lights of New York* (1928), a project, featuring Helene Costello and Cullen Landis, that also established Warner Bros. as *the* studio that produced gritty, hard-edged, streetwise films involving currently raging crimes such as bootlegging, racketeering and murder. Made on a B-film budget of $23,000, this first Warner Bros. sound gangster epic grossed $1 million. This, combined with Al Jolson's continued smash successes, especially in *The Jazz Singer* follow-up, the even better received *The Singing Fool* (1928), in which he gave a performance earning him accolades as "a truly great artist," gained Warner Bros. the exalted position of creating "The New Era in Motion Pictures."[5]

Jack Warner did double duty, dealing with company executives in New York while managing the Sunset Boulevard studio, handling contract negotiations and making casting decisions. The youngest but dominant brother, he oversaw the most important productions, often claimed others' ideas and innovations as his own, and faked a heavy Yiddish accent for visitors. Lesser projects—the bread-and-butter melodramas, action pictures and lower-budget crime thrillers—were entrusted to Zanuck, who also handled most of the day-to-day operations, including screenplay development.

By autumn 1928, Warner Bros. was fully equipped for sound production, and far ahead of the competition in releasing talkies to its theaters. The brothers had bought a controlling interest in First National, a Burbank studio with large, newer production facilities and an extensive distribution system. During the days, the Sunset studio was hooked to the Burbank studio equipment via a telephone wire. In the evening, the First National crews would take over and shoot through the night. By the year's end, Harry Warner had paid all the debts and still marked up a $2 million profit. Following the stock market crash of October 1929, he increased the company's power even further by buying the remaining First National stock from the financially strapped William Fox.

During 1930, Warner Bros. signed Edward G. Robinson and James Cagney, both of whom had begun their careers on the New York stage. Following a colorful gangster part in *The Widow from Chicago* (1930), directed by Edward Cline, Robinson scored the far more important titular role in Mervyn LeRoy's *Little Caesar* (1931). Preceding the release of *The Widow from Chicago*, Cagney appeared in two minor Warner Bros. gangster melodramas, *Sinner's Holiday* (1930), based on the Broadway play *Penny Arcade*, in which he had costarred with Joan Blondell (whom the studio also signed for the film version), and *The Doorway to Hell* (1930), playing the right-hand man of mob boss Louis Ricarno (played by, of all actors, Lew Ayres, hot from his heartbreaking performance in Universal's *All Quiet in the Western Front*, directed by Lewis Milestone). Then Cagney instinctively unleashed one of the developing gangster genre's most powerful and timeless characterizations, playing his final shocking scene as a hideous, trussed-up corpse, in William Wellman's *The Public Enemy* (1931).

Fictional Gangsters to Real Chain-Gang Fugitive

When people on both Coasts were questioning his whereabouts, Robert already had arrived at Warner Bros., causing considerable consternation among the employees until Darryl Zanuck arrived at a secretary's desk to whisk him off to a private area. The *I Am a Fugitive from a Chain Gang* screenplay had been assigned to young writers Brown Holmes (born in Toledo, Ohio; age 24) and Sheridan Gibney (born in New York City; age 28), who set out to adapt the book into a coherent narrative, while avoiding the more specifically controversial elements. "Georgia" was dropped from the title by Zanuck, who didn't want to add extra fuel to the fire already raging among state authorities who considered that, now, California as well as New Jersey was harboring a dangerous felon. (No specific Southern state is mentioned in the film.)

Holmes and Gibney had been ordered to complete a treatment by the end of April, before Zanuck left on a European trip. Due to the episodic nature of the book, 15 solid weeks would be required, with the help of the more experienced, 38-year old San Franciscan Howard J. Green, to fashion a final draft of the screenplay. The James Allen character was to be written specifically for Paul Muni, who had signed a four-picture contract with the studio on March 15.

A Star for Robert E. Burns

Born Meshilem Meier ("Muni") Weisenfreund in Lemberg, Galicia, Austria-Hungary (now part of the Ukraine) on September 22, 1895, Paul Muni (his legally changed name) always insisted in being called *Muni*. The entire Weisenfreund family had been itinerant performers in the ghettos of Eastern Europe, a reality that always gave "Muni" a fear of living in poverty. After performing in London for a time, he and his folks emigrated to New York, where they became involved in the Yiddish theatre.

Muni played his first stage role at age 12 after the family relocated to Cleveland. From 1907 on, he played a great range of roles and became quite adept at applying a variety of heavy makeup styles. Moving again, this time to Chicago, the family all contributed to the small theater opened by Nathan, Muni's father. His older brother, Joseph, recalled that, around 1912, as he watched his younger sibling on the stage, "a 'tingle' went down my spine. I always knew Muni was good, but, at that moment, I realized that he had that 'spark of greatness.'"[6]

When Hollywood producers began searching for "actors who could speak" after the coming of sound, Muni was screen-tested by Fox Films, who signed him to a three-year contract. Unfortunately, the films *The Valiant* (1929), a box-office bomb (that nevertheless earned Muni an Academy Award nomination), and *Seven Faces* (1929), in he played seven different characters, and prompted comparisons to Lon Chaney (which he did *not* appreciate), soured him on the film industry, and he returned to New York to appear in *This One Wins* (1930) at Broadway's Morosco Theatre. Referring to Fox, he said, "They'll have to sue me if they want to pick up my option."[7]

Uneasy Alliance of Fugitive and Filmmakers

After Darryl Zanuck introduced himself to the frail-looking fugitive, he was joined in his office by Sheridan Gibney, who was quite surprised by Robert's appearance. According to Vincent Burns, Gibney admitted,

Burns, I didn't expect to see a man like you. I thought you'd be a big, husky guy. In fact, I didn't expect to see you at all. I didn't think you'd have the nerve to come out here. I guess you must realize your own danger. If I were in your shoes, I think I'd be scared to death even to show myself out here—to anybody! I guess you can get by with it, though. There's nothing of the ex-convict about you. You might be a toothpaste salesman or a drummer for a line of women's wear.[8]

Robert merely smiled and thanked him for the "compliment," explaining that, the minute things began to get "warm," he'd immediately be on his way again. His presence at the studio, however, was absolutely necessary. The book had been intended as a testament to his mistreatment by a corrupt penal system, and he wanted to make certain that its message remained intact in the film.

There was nothing "Hollywood" about this fugitive who was risking his freedom to serve as the film's advisor. Gibney and his cowriter certainly couldn't depict his physical appearance or personality on the screen, but his crusade would remain as powerful as possible. "We're going to make your story into one of the biggest and best pictures this studio has ever turned out," Zanuck promised, "and we've got one of the country's greatest actors, Paul Muni, to play the leading role." (Both the prediction and the boast proved true.)

The choice of Muni pleased his real-life counterpart, who was openly enthusiastic about a better-looking and—speaking version of "himself" being portrayed on the screen. Recently, Muni (encouraged by his wife, Bella, to give Hollywood a second chance) had caused a sensation as the Al Capone–like Tony Camonte in Howard Hawks' gangster epic *Scarface* (1932), and now had to take a six-week leave from the hit Broadway play *Counsellor-at-Law* to act in the new film.

Warner Bros. checked Robert, who had been assigned a bodyguard, into a room at the Hotel Roosevelt, where he immediately wrote a letter to his brother. As part of their "security plan," Robert sent all his missives to a friend in San Antonio, Texas, who then mailed them on to Vincent.

The following day, Robert was set up in his own office on the Warner Bros. lot. He also was given the pseudonym "Frank Bates," the job title of "chief electrician" and assigned a "fixer" who would handle any legal problems that might arise. This "fine gentleman of the old school," as Robert referred to him, already was in the process of working out deals with the local sheriff, chief of police and district attorney, and would soon meet with California governor James "Sunny Jim" Rolph, who currently was on a two-week trip to Washington, D.C. (In November 1933, Rolph, a Republican, would become criticized severely for his public approval of the lynching of the murderers of San Jose department-store heir Brooke Hart, thereafter becoming known as "Governor Lynch." Stricken by a series of heart attacks, Rolph died about six months later.)

In a subsequent letter to Vincent, Robert wrote of his feeling that Rolph would not grant extradition if Georgia authorities ever arrived in Hollywood. He also expressed how impressed he was with personnel at the studio, specifically Jack Warner, executive producer Hal B. Wallis and John G. Adolphi, who originally had planned to serve as assistant director on the film. (Adolphi eventually was replaced by Al Alleborn.)

Adolphi worked closely with Robert in developing ideas on shooting the chain-gang sequences, including a scene involving the Georgia Prison Commission. Adolphi also had seen a screen test in which Vincent auditioned to play his cinematic counterpart, Reverend Robert Allen (though his Christian name is depicted as "Clint" in a letter shown during the completed film). Robert wrote to Vincent that Adolphi approved of the screen test but that the final decision on casting would be made by Zanuck, who soon would be stopping over in New York with Adolphi on their way to Europe. Robert strongly emphasized that his brother meet with them in order to discuss this unique opportunity to appear in the film.

"Fugitive from the Director's Chair"

Warner Bros.' highest paid director, Roy Del Ruth, who considered the subject "heavy" and "morbid," eventually passed on the temporary script, believing that filmgoers already would be so depressed by the current economic situation that spending a few precious coins to experience even more despair would be unthinkable. (In a studio memorandum to Hal Wallis, Del Ruth actually refers to the public as "the mob."[9])

The director's chair instead was filled by Mervyn LeRoy, whose rise in the film industry, first (as an actor) at Paramount and then Warner Bros., was generated by a deft combination of nepotism, talent, efficiency and a shared societal view with Zanuck. His previous successes with *Little Caesar* and *Five Star Final* (both propelled by the electric performances of Edward G. Robinson in 1931) made him the perfect choice for the new unflinching material. Although he had been planning to make the musical *42nd Street*, he shifted to *I Am a Fugitive from a Chain Gang*, and the other project was assigned to veteran Warners contract director Lloyd Bacon (whom James Cagney later would call his favorite collaborative filmmaker).

Muni, however, was *not* happy with the choice of LeRoy, whom he considered too young (31) and inexperienced for such powerful material. He had been hoping for a major, established director; and the meticulous actor, though giving one of his most focused and best film performances, would prove occasionally difficult to work with on the set.

I Am a Fugitive from a Chain Gang actually marked LeRoy's 25th film as director, so Muni's objection was unwarranted on this count. One of LeRoy's earlier films, *Numbered Men* (1930), adapted from the play *Jail Break* and starring Conrad Nagel, involves the imprisonment of an innocent man, and provided excellent background for this new assignment. By the time the *I Am a Fugitive from a Chain Gang* shoot was completed, Muni and LeRoy were good friends, and would work together again.

Robert literally threw himself into his new job, arriving at the studio early each morning, eating a Spartan lunch of milk and crackers, and often working late into the evening. Gibney and Holmes took copious notes, describing his movements, mannerisms and facial expressions as he acted out the painful, brutal events of his life on the chain gang, as well as his two carefully planned, intense and dangerous escapes for LeRoy.

Robert cared little about financial gain, nor any of the kind of extravagant publicity needed to sell the film. The obsessiveness of his behavior, including his tendency to launch into lengthy dissertations about various aspects of filmmaking, began to bother some of the crew members. He instantly became very nervous upon hearing gunfire and police sirens used in films being shot on other sets. Vincent, revealing that his brother had finely developed aesthetic sensibilities, but also an uncompromising, cocksure nature, later claimed:

> He was coldblooded in his demands.... He wanted only that his story should be exactly as he'd lived it, the details right, the facts exact.
> "You movie people are pretty sloppy," he would say. "You mean well, but you slip up in the execution. *Understatement* is the secret of power on the screen. Most of the time you are suffering from a disease called '*overemphasis*.' You must let the horror of the chain gangs speak for themselves. Don't overdo it. Make it mild. Remember, the public won't believe it if you show them the complete truth. Therefore, only hint at it. Their imagination will do the rest. Now, if I were directing this picture, this is what I would do..."[10]

This inflexible (but very understandable and defensible) attitude continued for five weeks. Whenever Robert ran into Zanuck, asking him about the film's development, the head of production would answer, "Burns, your story's coming along great!"

One of the biggest challenges involved transforming the rambling first-person viewpoint used in the book. Holmes, though only 24, had worked on four previous major Warner Bros. projects (including the racy

The Maltese Falcon [1931] and the even more daring *The Strange Love of Molly Louvain* [1932]) and capably wrote the original 86-page treatment, dated April 25, 1932, which was expanded by the slightly more "mature" Gibney, an operatic librettist and would-be playwright who had completed the screenplays for two previous studio films, *Week-End Marriage* and *Two Against the World* (both 1932). The two then collaborated on a temporary script and handed it over to Zanuck, who added his own personal annotations and brought in the seasoned Howard Green, a former newspaper man (with experience on both Coasts and the Midwest) who wrote in a direct, realistic style, to integrate the changes and suggestions into a final shooting script, completed on July 23.

This writing team accomplished a major feat in transforming the memoir, with its constant shifting back and forth between Robert's actual experiences and Vincent's obvious commentary about the constant flow of wrongs committed by the State of Georgia and other specific institutions. Holmes and Gibney deserve praise for navigating their way through this literary maze to adapt the important dramatic material, indeed following Robert's apparent emphasis on understatement while avoiding any of his brother's proselytization that would have made for an insufferably moralizing film. Even before Green, prompted by Zanuck, began working on the final screenplay, much already had been achieved by Holmes and Gibney.

Green tightened the overall pace, and added several effective visual touches, including a montage incorporating crosscutting to compare the shackling of the chain-gang prisoners with the harnessing of the mules who pull their wagon to the rock pile. He also added exciting and moving action to Allen's second escape by having "Bomber" Wells (the unforgettable Edward Ellis) sacrifice himself to save his friend by tossing sticks of dynamite at the pursuing guards' cars until he is gunned down and falls off the dump truck into the ditch. (The truck escape sequence originally depicted the escape of, not Allen and Wells, but two African American convicts.)

Holmes and Gibney's "explicit critique of capitalism" (including the use of a pot-bellied war profiteer and a soapbox socialist)—which arguably would have been just fine with the Burns brothers—was toned down. Transitional sequences and character introductions were added to smooth the flow of the narrative, which had been somewhat confusing.[11]

One of Holmes and Gibney's most powerful scenes, the ending showing the pathetic, nerve-wracked Allen still on the run, was retained. Initially, Green didn't want to ease off the sociopolitical commentary. He later admitted, "If I had my way, I am afraid that the script would have been a blasting tirade against the whole system. Mr. Zanuck sensed this and upbraided me for it."[12]

Several earlier endings had been quickly jettisoned. These included one depicting Allen shaking hands with another chain-gang fugitive he suddenly encounters on a street corner, a rather unbelievable incident, though based on an event in the memoir. Others involved Allen simply creeping across a state border under cover of night, or escaping to another country.

The film's depiction of unemployment did reflect the hard times experienced by many returning World War I veterans in 1919, but not the general economic situation during the 1920s. The fiscal setting of *I Am a Fugitive from a Chain Gang* is solidly indicative of the Great Depression in 1932. Often referred to with such simplistic terms as "The Roaring '20s" and a "period of prosperity," the earlier decade *was* far different than the one that followed in the wake of the stock-market crash of October 1929. Robert's inability to hold a job and his tendency to live in "gypsy"-like fashion was, not solely due to the economy of the United States in 1922, but more an individual circumstance, one created in part by his own (perhaps bipolar) personality and the afflictions of his having been "shell-shocked" during the war.

Holmes and Gibney were shrewd in their decision to suggest much of the chain-gang horror, rather than depicting it outright. During a scene in which Allen is flogged with a wide leather strap, reaction shots of his resolute face and those of the other convicts, who show various levels of concern, powerfully intimate far more agony than an actual on-camera enactment.

Zanuck's Streetwise Savvy

Zanuck personally beefed up the suspense and sexual elements, including the scene, based closely on the memoir, featuring a prostitute, Linda (Noel Francis), at a hotel run by a former chain-gang inmate, Barney Sykes (Allen Jenkins). Though Linda sits on the bed and beckoningly places her right hand on James' left knee (as a jaunty instrumental version of W. C. Handy's "St. Louis Blues" plays on the Victrola), he wants nothing to do with her in a sexual way.

"If there's anything I can do to help you," she informs him with a very sincere expression, "just say the word."

He takes her hand in both of his, but with a subtle expression of regret, replies, "Thanks, there's nothing you can do."

She looks over at the door through which Barney had left just moments ago, then offers James a drink, but he also turns that down. He is too absorbed by his razor-sharp focus on leaving the state as soon as possible.

But Linda pours herself a shot of bootleg hooch, walks back over to James and tantalizingly sits down on the right arm of his chair, assuring him that he is "among friends" as the scene fades out. The suggestiveness of her actions, combined with a close-up, tilt-down shot that carefully shows Linda's sleek body from head to toe, gives the viewer plenty to stir the imagination. (Though brief, the performance of Noel Francis, who often played small supporting parts as smoldering strumpets in early 1930s Warner Bros. films, is noteworthy.)

Zanuck didn't have to invent anything for this sequence, since the Burns original, set in a "75-cent Atlanta hotel," states:

> I didn't want any women, and I wanted to conserve my strength. I wanted to get out of Dixie…
>
> "Girls, you got me sized up wrong. I am no goodie-goodie, but I am no professional criminal either, and I don't intend to go on breaking the law, or following any racket. All I want is to get out of Atlanta and Dixie, get some job and be on the square."
>
> With this, one of the girls went out, wishing me luck; but the other came over and sat down on the bed beside me.
>
> "Gee," she said, "you're what I call a real guy. I wish I could hook up with a real man with guts like you, get out of this damn racket, and go straight once more. If I help you to get out of Atlanta will you take me with you?"
>
> I felt sorry for her; such a pity, I thought, for she was fairly good looking, and about twenty-five years old. But—"He travels fastest who travels alone," so I politely explained to her that such a course was impossible. However, I compromised by telling her that if she would help me and I got through o.k., I would send for her and help her go straight.
>
> She eagerly accepted the proposition and asked me how she could help. She was all excited and thrilled. I must have touched something in her when I declared myself for "the straight and narrow" instead of "the free and easy" path.

Holmes and Gibney gave James Allen, not Robert's Chicago occupation as a magazine publisher aided by his in-laws, but that of a construction worker who craftily and steadily studies and works his way up to engineer, the very example of the "American Dream" as he becomes one of the city's leading citizens. His accomplishment as a builder of bridges is ironically deconstructed later in the film when, during his second chain-gang escape, he dynamites his way to freedom by blowing up just such a structure, thus blocking off his rifle-blasting pursuers. Much of the footage depicting Allen's engineering work eventually would be cut from the finished film (although still photographs of one major scene featuring Muni and Helen Vinson have survived).

3. The Making of the Film

Based on Robert's real sellout by his selfish wife, Emilia Del Pino Pacheo, Holmes and Gibney, greatly augmented by the additions of Green (who gave the character more screen time), also developed the tough and ultimately stone evil Marie Woods, the attractive 26-year-old landlady whom Allen marries. Marie, another of the film's strong erotic elements, is played by 31-year-old Glenda Farrell, who very obviously left behind the Burns brothers' accurate "stout, dark-haired ... about forty years of age" description of Pacheo. In the 1981 Warner Bros. *I Am a Fugitive from a Chain Gang* "Screenplay Series" book, John O'Connor notes,

> In 1932 ... Hollywood's characters still tended to be simple and un-confusing, designed to make unmistakable sense to a mass audience that had become accustomed to the broadly acted and simplified characters of the silent screen. There was no trouble identifying villains in the work of Holmes and Gibney—the big businessman, the warden and his guards, the prison commissioners, and Allen's wife, Marie, all qualified. Still, there were some confusing contradictions and ambiguities. The wife's character was cast as 26 years old and sexy ... and her lines made her motives clear. A vicious and vindictive woman, she sought to dominate her husband as well as grow rich off him. She enjoyed reminding him that she knew his secret and would not hesitate to turn him in if he displeased her. Yet somehow the script suggested that she deserved sympathy too. After all, she loved Allen even if she was taking advantage of him. It was he who was unfaithful.[13]

O'Connor oversimplifies the nature of cinematic characters developed during the silent period, plus the "sympathy" generated by Marie is due as much to the believable, naturalistic performance of Glenda Farrell, an exceptional, Oklahoma-born actress who had benefited from many years of both stock company and Broadway experience before making her Hollywood film debut as the female lead in *Little Caesar*, as to anything actually included in the screenplay. (And the boozing Marie *also* is unfaithful, an aspect added by Green during his rewrite.)

Allen's truthful behavior in the scenes involving Marie, however—and the way Muni plays him—closely follows the memoir at times. For example, Holmes and Gibney faithfully and economically paraphrased this paragraph of dialogue in the book:

> Emily, I hate to tell you this, but I must. I like you, admire you, and appreciate your great interest in me, but I don't love you. Love is something that one must feel. I *know* I don't love you. I don't love you or anyone right now—perhaps never will. I cannot will myself to love you, any more than I can change the color of my eyes. Someday I may fall in love with another woman. Then I would be compelled to love you. If you want to continue under these conditions, all right, but I shall never feel any different toward you. Perhaps I may never fall in love; in that case life with you will be as it is now, comfortable, pleasant, serene. But I am speaking plainly, bluntly, frankly. If romance blows the bugle, I will have to say goodbye and fall in love.

"Bates" Escapes from Warner Bros.

After working for a total of five weeks with Wallis, Zanuck, LeRoy, Holmes and Gibney, Robert suddenly disappeared from the Warner Bros. lot, never to return. One day during the second week of May 1932, when Muni went to Burns' office, he found, not "Frank Bates," but only a note, reading, "Getting hot here. Moving on." Muni immediately took the note to Zanuck, who realized that Burns again was on the lam.

A short time earlier, Robert had received an envelope with a Los Angeles postmark addressed in pencil to Frank Bates. Inside was a single sheet of stationery from a local fleabag hotel, on which was scribbled,

> I am a friend of yours. I happen to know that there is a detective here who will try to apprehend you sometime during the next few days. My advice to you is—SCRAM!

Aside from his colleagues at the studio who knew his true identity, "Frank Bates" had no friends in Los Angeles. Therefore, this hastily written, unsigned note gave Robert E. Burns quite a chill. His only confidant outside the Warner Bros. lot was his bodyguard, who considered the letter nonsense but nonetheless told Robert that he would be sure to be more on his toes than ever.

That promise was tested soon after, during a meeting with Gibney about the content of the shooting script, when a woman who worked in the front office noticed a strange man who was attempting to gain entrance to the lot. Receiving an affirmative comment from his bodyguard, Robert quickly headed to his office, where he stuffed his few belongings into a briefcase.

The last person to see Robert Elliott Burns at Warner Bros. was Sheridan Gibney. After leaving though a side exit of the building, Robert retrieved the rest of his meager possessions from the hotel room, tossed them into the car he'd bought in L.A., and headed toward San Bernardino on Route 66.

Back at the studio, the Georgia detective stormed into one of the executive offices, fuming about the harboring of a fugitive, whom they had aided and abetted, in violation of federal law. Responding that Warner Bros. was only in business to make the best motion pictures possible, the executive concluded, "I know as little of his escape as you do" while handing over the brief note that Paul Muni had found in his dressing room.[14]

Hell's Highway (1932) and Other Chain-Gang Precursors

While the writing team worked for 15 weeks to complete the *I Am a Fugitive from a Chain Gang* screenplay, RKO Radio studios was gearing up for its own chain-gang film, *Hell's Highway*, starring Richard Dix and Tom Brown, hoping to hit theater screens before Warner Bros. was able to release its much-touted spectacular, which began shooting on July 28, 1932. The *Hell's Highway* screenplay was a collaboration between Samuel Ornitz, Robert Tasker and Rowland Brown, who also directed the film.

During the silent period, two short chain-gang documentaries were produced, one by the nascent Edison Company in 1902, and the other a 1917 effort by the educational Bruce Scenics company, but these received limited distribution. Significant precursors to *Hell's Highway* and *I Am a Fugitive from a Chain Gang* include *Master of the Range* (1928), a silent Western starring Cliff Lyons (a longtime member of the John Ford "stock company" who performed stunts and small roles in over 400 films), MGM's musical feature *Hallelujah* (1929) and a Walt Disney cartoon, "Chain Gang" (1930), which stars Mickey Mouse (featuring the voice of Disney himself) escaping from the slammer with Pluto (in his film debut) hot on the criminal rodent's heels.

Little is known about the B programmer *Master of the Range*, in which Lyons plays a cowboy sentenced to toil on a California road gang, but *Hallelujah* is a major milestone in African American cinema. Though faced with the expected stereotypes of the period, director King Vidor was one of the few contemporary Hollywood directors who ambitiously made a concerted effort to work progressive themes into his films. One of the first mainstream studio films featuring an all African American cast, and shot primarily on location in Tennessee and Arkansas, it is an innovative combination of admirable footage and early sound techniques that introduced the striking actress Nina Mae McKinney to audiences and earned Vidor an Academy Award nomination. Unable to convince MGM chairman of the board Nicholas Schenck to finance the financially risky film, Vidor pulled the cash from his own bank account (unfortunately resulting in his having to drop two truly great artists, Ethel Waters and Paul Robeson, from the intended players).

Vidor sought "authenticity" for the struggles of Zeke (Daniel L. Haynes) with religion and temptation, from the accidental killing of his brother, to his redemption as a preacher and subsequent fall from grace, to his responsibility for the deaths of "Chick" (McKinney) and her hustler boyfriend, "Hot Shot" (William Fountaine), and the salvation provided by his family after he returns from prison, where he has suffered the hell of the chain gang. *Hallelujah* was embraced by popular white journalists, but the reaction of the black press was mixed. Vidor's portrayals of African Americans were based on stereotypes, resulting in characters either idealistic or animalistic, but his sincere intentions provided a step forward, creating an archetype for subsequent all-black musicals. Banned by the Southern Theatre Foundation, the film was booked into only a few scattered venues below the Mason-Dixon Line.

In the July 30 issue of *Motion Picture Herald*, Warners announced that "I Am a Fugitive" would be released on December 17. Curiously, on August 6, the same publication reported that the film would star "Glenda Farrell and James Bell."[15] In his first film appearance, the Virginia-born, 40-year-old Bell does perform in the film, but in the small, uncredited role of "Red," a sickly convict who collapses on the rock pile and dies after being brutalized by a guard.

Glenda Farrell, however, is essential as Marie (who possesses some of the "gold digger" qualities she would exhibit in many later Warner Bros. films, but in far more likeable and comical ways). She is viscerally sexy in her introductory scene, and builds Marie's selfish, vindictive nature like a musical crescendo (which is particularly impressive, since her screen time is limited). She captures exactly the description of this scene in the original screenplay:

> INT. BOARDINGHOUSE ROOM
> It is a rather nice room. Marie and Allen have just come in. She is twenty-six, dark and sexy looking. She is the kind of girl that must have her man. Allen is inspecting the room as she talks. He is paying but little attention to her, but she is eyeing him critically, and she likes him.

The subtle nonverbal touches Farrell integrated into her performance, as in the way Marie slowly withdraws Reverend "Clint" Allen's "chain-gang" letter from between her breasts before she hands it to James, are striking.

Picture Play's Nobert Lusk wrote:

> Mr. Muni handles his meaty role with the reserve of a master craftsman.... Miss Farrell is so attractive one wonders why Allen ever took a room at her house, unless he really wanted to get entangled.[16]

In August, *Motion Picture Herald* published a feature article by Charles Aaronson, in which he included quotes from an interview with Broadway impresario Lee Shubert, who presented his arguments for the superiority of stage productions to those of the film industry. In general, Shubert pointed out that, while motion-picture producers focused on "types" and "cycles," closely aping the successful releases of their competitors, those who created for the stage had no such proclivities. (Here, Shubert's use of the words "type" and "cycle" refers to what French film critics later identified as thematic *genres* in the context of the Hollywood studio system.)

3. The Making of the Film

Shubert said, "Often the best material is passed up while a cycle is in the process of development. The motion picture producers, by so doing, are killing their own business."[17]

With *I Am a Fugitive from a Chain Gang* targeted for a November 19 release, Warner Bros. and Darryl Zanuck faced resistance on several fronts *because* the material was so unusual. No other film historian has described the genesis of this thematic and fiscally problematic film better than Thomas Schatz:

> [This] picture ... marked a high point in Zanuck's regime and the coming of age of Warners' Depression-era style. It didn't come easily. Zanuck and the Warners faced resistance to the project on both coasts, but they pulled together and quite literally muscled the film through the institutional machinery.[18]

Mervyn LeRoy's Shooting of the Film

The production of *I Am a Fugitive from a Chain Gang* began on July 28, 1932, with the stipulation that LeRoy was to complete the shoot, primarily on five studio soundstages and on the backlot, in one month. The first two days of shooting were perhaps the easiest: all interiors, involving the flophouse, the diner hold-up and the courtroom sentencing scene. This scheduling allowed LeRoy to dispense with actors Preston Foster and Berton Churchill, who then moved on to other Warners projects. The next three days involved interiors of the chain-gang camp, filmed on Stage 8.

The exterior chain-gang camp set had been built at the Warner Ranch in Calabasas, California, and a major scene involving the inmates swinging sledgehammers on a rock pile was shot in a working quarry at Chatsworth. This part of the shoot was truly grueling for all concerned, particularly the chain-gang actors. Another major location involved filming the "coming home" from World War I scene at an old train station in Pasadena. The one other outdoor sequence, involving Allen's showing Helen (Helen Vinson), his new (and real) love, the bridge he has helped to build, was ultimately cut by Zanuck. Much of the exciting truck escape scene was shot in miniature.

Overall, the production went very smoothly, with LeRoy usually working his cast and crew 10- to 14-hour days, six days per week, though the shoot ultimately stretched to six weeks, with the delay attributed generally to his decision to shoot a lot of coverage, (thus providing more camera-angle choices during the editing phase), and specifically to the difficulty of shooting the underwater shots of Muni used during Allen's first escape.

Hell's Highway (1932), RKO Radio's powerful chain-gang drama starring Richard Dix, hit theaters two months prior to *I Am a Fugitive from a Chain Gang* (1932).

On August 20, *Motion Picture Herald* reviewed *Hell's Highway* for exhibitors. Though the subject matter was considered humorless and "unromantic," "McCarthy" predicted good business for the picture:

> It is a realistic story of men condemned to the chain gang in a convict labor camp, of the terrible conditions under which they exist, the cruelties, the hates and fears engendered

in the hearts of men condemned to such punishment.... It's bitter drama of bitter men, but despite its harshness it should prove to be a sensational picture. During the past few months a number of newspapers have been devoting much space to conditions in chain-gang prison camps, stories can be expected to have whetted the public appetite to see in picture form what those conditions are supposed to be. In addition, there is the public interest in almost any news story about a big jail break.[19]

Production on *I Am a Fugitive from a Chain Gang* was wrapped on September 7 at a total cost of $195,845 ($16,750 of which went to Muni). Meanwhile, RKO Radio began its publicity campaign for *Hell's Highway*, which was released nationwide on September 23. Warner Bros. countered with two-page trade ads, headed, "Millions will demand the genuine screen versions of these famous best-sellers. They want no substitutes!" Along with the *I Am a Fugitive from a Georgia Chain Gang!* book, the studio included images of Warden Lewis E. Lawes' *20,000 Years in Sing Sing* (the film version of which stars Spencer Tracy), David Karson's *Silver Dollar* (Edward G. Robinson), Einar Thorvaldson's *The Match King* (Warren William), Harrison Kroll's *The Cabin in the Cotton* (Richard Barthelmess) and Bradford Ropes' *42nd Street* (Warner Baxter).

In October, *Modern Screen* published a brief review of *Hell's Highway*:

> Realism ... with a capital R. RKO studio brings the first of the chain gang stories to the screen, omitting none of the brutality of such a theme. As the star, Richard Dix probably has never offered a finer piece of acting. Young Tom Brown, as Dix' younger brother, and every member of the supporting cast deserve highest praise.
> Essentially this isn't entertainment. It's a piece of life.[20]

Ultimately, LeRoy's work, including the large amount of coverage, was turned over to Zanuck, who (as he would throughout his career at Warner Bros., 20th Century [his own production company] and 20th Century–Fox) oversaw the editing of the finished film, including the addition of dramatic touches, such as sound effects, to heighten the suspense, and an overall tightening of the pace (though Holmes and Gibney already had done an admirable job with the latter aspect).

In early October, the studio ran trade ads thanking *The Film Daily* for recognizing

> the tremendous influence Warner Bros. have had on the upturn of picture business! Thank you for pointing out that Warner Bros. pointed the way to *news-value pictures* with "Public Enemy," "Star Witness," "The Mouthpiece," "Dark Horse." You've put your *finger* on one big reason why "Blessed Event," Chatterton's "The Crash," Barthelmess' "Cabin in the Cotton" are standout successes of today.... And tomorrow you'll give us an even bigger *hand* for these coming giant productions, every one backed by the tidal power of flaming Public Interest...
>
> "I AM A FUGITIVE FROM A CHAIN GANG" with Paul ("Scarface") Muni
> This very minute headlines are screaming the sensational facts bared in the national

best-seller which made its author front-page news. Every newspaper in the country has helped to sell this show!

Following an October 1932 preview (a rare luxury for a Warner Bros. film), Zanuck claimed that he made one of the most significant changes to the overall impact of the story. Rather than merely end the film with the titular character still on the lam, he took credit for the more direct indictment of the "system" of Depression-era U.S. society by putting the dramatic punch of the words "I steal" into Muni's mouth. Of course, this line already had been part of the temporary script developed by Holmes and Gibney. (In his 1974 autobiography, Mervyn LeRoy also takes credit for the scene.)[21] (These differing accounts demonstrate how careful a historian must be when dealing with "evidence" provided by Hollywood and other public figures about their own lives and careers.)

I Am a Fugitive from a Chain Gang (1932). When asked by his sweetheart, Helen, "How do you live?" James Allen (Paul Muni) responds, "I steal" before mysteriously disappearing into the dark.

The film was press previewed for Charles Aaronson, who hit all the right points in his "Showmen's Review" for *Motion Picture Herald*. Calling it "stark and unrelenting," he praised Paul Muni for "standing head and shoulders above everything else" and advised exhibitors to emphasize "in hammering terms" the realism, brutal accuracy and real-life horror of a brilliantly made film based on the true memoir of an *innocent* man still on the lam from the law. Referring to the experience as "strong medicine," Aaronson suggested that *I Am a Fugitive from a Chain Gang* should be sold as "extraordinary" in every way.[22]

4

The Reception of the Film

"I think it's going to set the country on fire."—Bertha Wagner

I hope so—not so much for myself as for those poor devils who are still down there. If it arouses the country enough, there will be some kind of a clean-up in the chain gangs. The wardens and guards will have to be more human and those poor unfortunates will find life a little more livable. *They'll never get me back there, I know that—not in anything else but a coffin.*
—Robert E. Burns (Their discussion after first seeing *I Am a Fugitive from a Chain Gang*, outside the Branford Theatre, Newark, New Jersey, November 15, 1932[1])

Warner Bros.' trade-paper advertisements for *I Am a Fugitive from a Chain Gang* trumpeted,

MAKE ROOM AMONG THE SCREEN IMMORTALS FOR THE PICTURE THAT PUT A PRICE ON ITS AUTHOR'S HEAD ... WARNER BROS.' DEFIANT MASTERPIECE THAT WILL HAVE CONSCIENCE-STRICKEN AMERICA TALKING IN ITS SLEEP!

"I AM A FUGITIVE FROM A CHAIN GANG" with PAUL MUNI. HIS FIRST PICTURE SINCE "SCARFACE"—AN ENTIRELY DIFFERENT ROLE.

Cast of 40 including Glenda Farrell, Helen Vinson, Preston Foster. Directed by Mervyn LeRoy. Already awarded 4 stars by *Liberty*.

Meanwhile, *Hell's Highway* still was gaining space in various periodicals. The November issue of *Motion Picture* reviewed the film, suggesting that ex-cons might comprise the best audiences, but also praised the lead actors:

Alumni of the rock piles may admire the fidelity with which the sordid details of prison life are portrayed. Other observers will get whatever pleasure this sad and brutal story affords in the exciting episodes of the fire and the escape of the convicts, and in the touching portrayal of the two brothers by Richard Dix and Tom Brown.... The final scene is a masterpiece of irony, as the self-satisfied citizens pass along the highway built at the cost of so much brutality and sweat and sin, and blandly admire the view. For those who like vicarious suffering.[2]

Richard Dix also received a "Best Performance of the Month" honor from *Photoplay* magazine.[3] Dix's award was well deserved for his earnest performance in this hard-hitting and realistic portrayal of chain-gang brutality, but the screenplay, by Samuel Ornitz, Robert Tasker and director Rowland Brown, bears no similarity to any of the actual events involving Burns. Instead, the writers based their "expose" in part on the recent sweatbox hanging death of a convict on a Florida chain gang.

After Warner Bros. dropped an elaborate plan to present a roadshow version of *I Am a Fugitive from a Chain Gang*, the New York premiere was held at the Strand, the company's largest first-run theater, on Thursday, November 11, 1932. No one was more excited about its reception than Darryl Zanuck, who received news that the 2,758-seat venue had generated the studio's best opening-day business since *Little Caesar* had thrilled audiences in the Big Apple nearly two years earlier. The box-office had to turn away an overflow of patrons, and made plans to remain open from 9 a.m. on Friday to 3 a.m. on Saturday. The second day's sales proved even better, when the Strand hit a new high in a single day's admissions for any feature ever exhibited at the theater.

On November 12, Warner Bros. also began 230 first-run engagements, for which they had ordered a record-breaking number of prints, throughout the U.S. and Canada. Interestingly, the solidly Democrat studio used President-elect Franklin D. Roosevelt in the full-page trade advertisements.

One of the largest engagements, promoted by a "big exploitation campaign," opened at the Georgia Theater in Atlanta, contradicting reports that the film would not be shown in the South.[4] Across the U.S., newspapers began to run a six-chapter serialization of the story, illustrated with photographs from the film.

One week after the premiere, Warner Bros. ran advertisements reporting,

> "I AM A FUGITIVE FROM A CHAIN GANG" with PAUL MUNI RUINING RECORDS EVERYWHERE! ALREADY 2nd WEEK ON BROADWAY AFTER TOPPING "LITTLE CAESAR" FIGURES AT STRAND! *VARIETY* REPORTS—"RECORD OPENING IN NEW HAVEN"—"LEADING EASILY IN NEW ORLEANS"—"HIT OF YEAR IN COLUMBUS!"

The Strand continued to run the film from 9 a.m. to 3 a.m. daily, expecting to continue this 18-hour schedule for up to five weeks. Warner Bros.' Strand

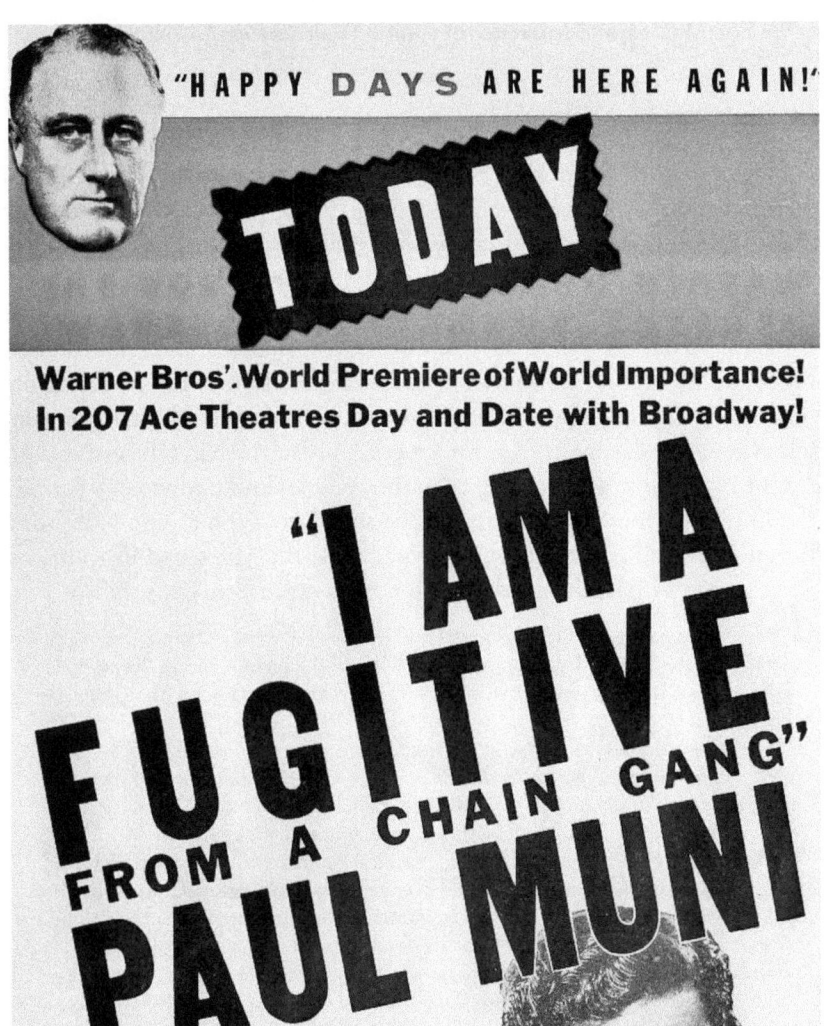

A Warner Bros. trade-paper advertisement for the opening of *I Am a Fugitive from a Chain Gang* (November 1932).

in Brooklyn, whose opening had begun during the first week of December, also announced a record hold-over. The studio also mentioned the film in their major advertisements for other new releases, including *Silver Dollar* (1932), starring Edward G. Robinson, and *The Match King* (1932), with Warren William.

Burns Back in New Jersey

Having made it back to New Jersey in just five days, Robert Burns remained close to the safety of his little gift shop, which he expanded by selling all sorts of valuable merchandise that he bought for ridiculously low prices at "Depression sales" all over the area. Much to his delight, Bertha Wagner, a woman he'd met during his time in Los Angeles, walked into the shop one day while the radio was playing a performance of Richard Wagner's *Lohengrin*, her favorite opera, and she viewed it as romantically symbolic of their becoming reacquainted. Both of them had tried to find each other after dating in L.A. for a week, but Bertha had left to stay with an aunt in Florida, to escape the clutches of a jealous and violent fiancée.

Though Robert couldn't attend the showing of the film in New York, Warner Bros. had provided a mezzanine box at the Strand, so Vincent and a large group of friends could see the film in style. Vincent recalled:

> Something happened that night which I have never witnessed before or since in any movie theatre. At the conclusion of the showing of the picture, the audience stood spontaneously in a body and wave after wave of applause resounded throughout the theatre.
>
> The picture seemed to me to be a magnificent achievement as well as a social document that would set a record for the theatre for a long time to come. However, one particular thing in the picture disturbed me so badly that the thrill of seeing it was very nearly neutralized.... I had sacrificed time, money, and reputation to defend my brother and to help him in his battle for vindication. For years I had fought for his freedom, had traveled for him over and over again to Washington, Chicago, Atlanta, La Grange, Springfield and Trenton. In innumerable emergencies I had had to fill the breach, and even at that very moment I was laboring very industriously, pulling every political wire under the sun to insure his sanctuary within the State of New Jersey.... I had hammered the manuscript into shape and had sold it to the publishers. I had assisted in the sale of the motion picture rights.... I was fighting for my brother and in a just cause; *but I was wholly unprepared for the shock that was mine that night!*[6]

Vincent obviously hadn't made the casting cut to portray "himself" in the film. Much to his dismay, he watched Iowa-born playwright and character actor Hale Hamilton play the minister, and he minced no words when later revealing just how he felt during the screening:

> In the picture I was shown as a weak character, largely unaccountable for my brother's leaving home in the first instance; indirectly responsible for his capture in Chicago in 1929; a soft pussy-footing parson who lent little if any real help to his convict brother. It was a bitter pill to swallow. I was so upset about it that I came pretty near jumping up and shaking my fist at the old screen and yelling wildly and ungrammatically:
>
> "That ain't me! You yellow-bellied bunch of two-timing double-crossing cockeyed scriptwriters!"

I cooled off eventually; and sought consolation in the fact that it is "an old Spanish custom" in the making of American motion pictures to portray Protestant ministers in a not-so-attractive light on the screen.... The Catholic priests have always had a fairer and finer interpretation....[6]

A U.S. Army veteran, Vincent can't be faulted for his general reaction to this completely inaccurate depiction of his cinematic counterpart. And his specific comment about the "Catholic vs. Protestant" divide isn't really "politically incorrect," considering that classic Hollywood films feature so many fine actors cast as priests: Spencer Tracy, Pat O'Brien, Bing Crosby and character chameleon Ward Bond, just to name a few. (After all, the Production Code was created, in large part, by the Catholic Legion of Decency, which, in 1932, was working hard on its being enforced by the Hollywood studios.)

During the film's second week in general release, *I Am a Fugitive from a Chain Gang* grossed $64,237 in New York, $30,500 in Boston, $25,000 in Philadelphia, $21,000 in San Francisco, $17,300 in Hollywood, $16,000 in Los Angeles and $12,100 in Cleveland. In some cities, receipts increased further the following week, with Chicago pulling in $19,500, while other large metropolitan areas experienced a typical falloff in ticket sales. After all the receipts were tallied, *Motion Picture Herald* named *I Am a Fugitive from a Chain Gang* the second-highest grossing picture of November 1932.

On Tuesday, November 15, 1932, *I Am a Fugitive from a Chain Gang* had its New Jersey premiere at Newark's Branford Theatre. A Warner Bros. executive had phoned Vincent Burns, asking him to make a personal appearance before the screening, as the studio was counting on a very powerful premiere in the Burns brothers' home state. Vincent believed that it was his duty to do so, and he wanted to make the most favorable public impression possible. New Jersey residents had been reading about his brother, the fugitive, for several months, and expected them to be very sympathetic to his plight.

When Vincent stepped out onto the stage that evening, the Branford was packed to the doors, mostly with the residents of Newark. The theater's manager gave him a warm introduction immediately before the film was scheduled to run. Vincent, who fortunately saved his written speech from that event, spoke seriously and articulately:

> Ladies and Gentlemen, you are going to witness a picture tonight, which is the true life-story of a man who, though a fugitive, lives somewhere in the city of Newark, and even now, at this very moment, may be sitting here in this audience. You will see a great actor, Paul Muni, dramatize the true story in a way that compels the attention and twists the heart as few performances have done. It is a heart-throbbing human document plus a piece of acting that is nothing less than a work of art. But more than

a great story, more than a work of art, this picture is a record of a social wrong, and it will be remembered for its daring exposure of a great injustice. It reveals in all its naked horror the Georgia chain gang, an institution which before the showing of this picture of the writing of this book was thought to be impossible in twentieth century America. I assure you that this picture is mild beside the actual conditions in many Southern chain gangs. When the last scene in this film has been shown and the last flicker has passed from the screen you will walk out of this theatre thrilled and stirred as you never have before. And remember, all of this happened to a man who is even now a fugitive from the prison camps of Georgia and is living right here in the city of Newark....[7]

Among the patrons in the audience for that premiere were Robert Burns and his sweetheart, Bertha Wagner. Also present was Chief James A. McRell of the Newark City Police, who had ordered a cordon of officers to surround the theatre to make certain that the fugitive did not escape. But a man who had pulled off two "impossible" breakouts from Georgia chain-gang camps was not about to be caught outside a New Jersey movie theater. Merely removing his tell-tale, thick-lensed spectacles, he passed right by the cops, with Bertha on his arm, while the officer stopped to question a man wearing a similar pair of glasses. The fugitive had finally seen the film and was well on his way back to his home and store in Newark.

Bertha, who knew Robert as "Richard Crane," had no idea that the cinematic fugitive who had just brought so many tears to her eyes was, in reality, sitting right beside her. She called Muni's exit from the film "unforgettable," and the film "one of the most heart-rending.... I have ever seen in my life. And a true story, too. Oh, how that poor man must have suffered in that chain gang!"

After revealing to Bertha his true feelings about her, and how much she meant to his happiness, he felt great trepidation at telling her the truth that he was the real fugitive on which the film was based. "My name is not Richard Crane," he admitted, "but Robert Elliott Burns. *I am the fugitive from the chain gang*!"[8]

Bertha's amazement was equaled by the massive bear hug she gave Robert. Question after question followed, as she wanted to know all the details that weren't in the film. She had noticed his nervousness while they were in the theater, and Robert attempted to describe to her both the physical and psychological aspects of living a fugitive's existence:

> It's no fun living in hiding. Day and night you've got that fear of capture hanging over your head.... It's maddening. You fear the police wherever you go. The other night I stole into New York under cover of darkness to visit the Plymouth Theatre. In his dressing room I met the man you saw on the screen, Paul Muni. He's playing in *Counsellor-at-Law* and he's one grand guy. I wanted to meet him in Hollywood, but I had

to scram before Muni arrived. You see, I'm not such a good friend, after all. I'm like mercury, always moving.⁹

Now able to call her friend "Bob," rather than "Dick," Bertha assured Robert of her faith and trust in him, and that she would always be there when she needed him. And then her questions turned back to the film. "I think it's going to set the country on fire," she said.

LeRoy Moves On and the Film Goes Nationwide

After wrapping *I Am a Fugitive from a Chain Gang*, Mervyn LeRoy had moved on to directing the James Cagney vehicle *Hard to Handle* (1933) for Warner Bros. before taking a month-long "sabbatical" in New York, where he was interviewed by the major metropolitan newspapers. Claiming that a majority of screen dialogue was too "unsophisticated" for modern moviegoers, he stated, "Never let your audience sit back in their seats." Explaining that he preferred combining simple characterizations and top actors (even in bit parts) with steady directorial pacing, he added that patronizing an audience was not his style, and that "trickery" should be avoided at all costs. He capped off his discussions with praise for Darryl F. Zanuck's "production abilities."¹⁰

Four decades later, LeRoy recalled:

> *Fugitive* caused both myself and Jack Warner plenty of problems. The wardens of the Georgia chain gangs weren't too happy for obvious reasons and tried to stop the picture from being shown. It did one thing, however. The chain gangs were taken off the roads in Georgia. But Warner and I were told not to come there again. I don't think that warning still holds, though.¹¹

On Tuesday, November 15, 1932, *Variety* published a review perceptively summing up both the thematic and box-office aspects of *I Am a Fugitive from a Chain Gang*. "Abel," noted that Warner Bros. presented a "sympathetic, unbiased cinematic transition of the now famous Robert E. Burns autobiography." Pulling no punches, he began his assessment by announcing,

> "I Am a Fugitive from a Chain Gang" is a picture with guts. It took lots of guts to make it, too, considering the apparent minimization of certain essential ingredients. The most necessary elements for the femme trade—the romance angle and a happy ending—are almost totally lacking here. Yet despite their lack, "Fugitive" merits and probably will merit box office recognition. It's a good picture. No dispute as to that. It grips with its stark realism and packs lots of punch.... The women will shudder at its gruesome realism but they'll not be bored.

Following his description of the ending, "Abel" added,

> This comes as such an unexpected finale that it leaves the women limp.... When the sad fade-out eventuates, as the broken fugitive shuffles off into the night, it's a shocker for the average fan.[12]

Indeed, "Abel" and other viewers unfamiliar with the saga of Robert E. Burns and the memoir would not have known that he was still on the lam from "justice" when the film was released, and that Warner Bros. could not have ended it any other way and remained near the truth.

In the same *Variety* issue, the subject of the possible bookings in Georgia was addressed, with only one theater outside Atlanta, the Imperial in Augusta, brave enough to show a picture described as "dynamite" for that state:

> Nothing else has been done in Georgia and probably won't be until after audience reaction is obtained.... Radio had difficulties at first with "Hell's Highway" ... but that film is held up in the trade as a slap on the wrist compared to the sock against Georgia with "Fugitive."[13]

South of the Mason-Dixon line, Paul Short, manager of the Melba Theatre, spared no expense in creating a sensational publicity façade for his building. Placing an enormous billboard-like title above the box-office windows, he added a large cutout of Paul Muni's face in the center. On the

Extensive ballyhoo at the Melba Theatre in Dallas, Texas, for the opening of *I Am a Fugitive from a Chain Gang* (December 1932). The Melba was one of the few theaters whose manager was politically bold enough to exhibit the controversial picture below the Mason-Dixon Line.

marquee, he added the bold statement, "TEN YEARS AGO WE'D BE JAILED FOR SHOWING THIS PICTURE. NOW NOBODY FEARS THE UNVARNISHED TRUTH!"

He exhibited a whipping post, sweat box, ball and chain, and lash. Displaying enlarged prints of the Warner Bros. stills, he described them with such copy as "Sugar Coated? Hell No! "The Story is Brutal and True!" Unfortunately, this sensational promotion of the film didn't last long in Georgia. A few weeks after its release in Atlanta, *I Am a Fugitive from a Chain Gang*, depicting acts and events too close to the truth, was *banned* throughout the state (an act contrasting sharply with later comments from law enforcement officials that Robert Burns' depictions of conditions in the chain-gang camps were all out-and-out lies). Boycotts were also enacted in several other Southern states.

Warner Bros. made sure to appeal in its publicity campaign to potential female viewers, noting that the film balances the brutality of the chain-gang scenes with romantic sequences. The "romance" angle included a merchandising suggestion that department stores display a "Glenda Farrell Gown" based on the alluring attire she wears on screen.

In its December 1932 issue, *Photoplay* selected *I Am a Fugitive from a Chain Gang* as one of the eight "Best Pictures of the Month," and Paul Muni as giving one of the "Best Performances." In its capsule review, the magazine admitted,

> Powerful and timely story, packed with suspense and stark cruelty, that points an accusing finger at the prison chain gang system. Paul Muni gives a strong performance as the returned soldier, anxious to get away from routine, who becomes an accomplice in a crime and is sentenced to ten years on a chain gang. With director Mervyn LeRoy, he has given us a fine, vivid, but depressing picture.[14]

In an interview published in *Picture Play* magazine that month, Muni, who always took his characterizations very seriously, explained his reasons for choosing the role:

> They say that one picture in worth many words. If that's the case, "I am a Fugitive" should be more effective than half a dozen books. The movies bring home great truths to the masses, and it is my hope that I'll be able to expose the convict-camp evil in a manner to force reform. That isn't too much to hope for.
>
> Pictures are the greatest potential force for good that the world has known. They ring the bell with impressive force.

Referring to Robert E. Burns' sudden "disappearance" from the Warner Bros. lot, Muni continued,

> After the film is released, I don't think he'll have anything further to fear. The story tells his personal experiences in a convict hell. And I'm happy to say that before things

got too hot for him, I was able to learn enough to put myself into his character. It wasn't necessary for me to *act* this role![15]

(This comment perhaps explains why Muni arguably gives the most naturalistic screen performance of his career in this film.)

Picture Play reporter Herbert Cruikshank also revealed,

> Because he has had to struggle for everything in his life, the roles that most appeal to him are those of the downtrodden. It has been a hard fight for success, and a harder one to hold it, once won. This is another reason why he is especially enthused over "I Am a Fugitive."[16]

Predicting that Glenda Farrell was going to be Hollywood's "next star," *Motion Picture* reviewed *I Am a Fugitive from a Chain Gang* in their January 1933 issue:

> Here is a sincere and honest expose of a punishment system which seems oddly medieval to modern eyes and yet is in full force in certain sections of the Union today. So painstakingly has this been directed that it hardly seems like a motion picture so much as a photographing of Life itself....
> The close is so poignant that it hurts, with the gradual darkening of the fugitive figure and his bitter cry from the shadows, "I'm going to steal—" It will leave the sensitive onlooker depressed.[17]

The January 1933 *Movie Classic* offered critic Larry Reid's similar appraisal, particularly about the "dramatically intense" climax:

> I warn you to be prepared to grip the arms of your seat. The suspense is terrific. Of the large supporting cast, Glenda Farrell, as the girl who preys on his fears, stands out.[18]

The following month, *Movie Classic* included a letter from Lars Anderson of Los Angeles, offering an observant appraisal from an audience member's viewpoint:

> The truly great actress or actor cannot be measured in greasepaint and grotesque makeup. Rather, it depends upon the degree to which they succeed in submerging "self" for "role."
> Take for example "I Am a Fugitive from a Chain Gang." In that excellent production, one does not consciously see Paul Muni, the actor, but Allen, the flesh-and-blood character of Mr. Burns' book! Why? Because Mr. Muni is a past master at understanding his characterizations—he seems actually to live the part he portrays—thus giving us powerfully real characters.... How much greater some of our stars could be if they could only appear upon the screen as the characters they are portraying rather than as their stereotyped selves. If certain of our big time stars will only realize the truth of this, it will be a big step forward for the entire industry.[19]

In 1933, Anderson was ahead of his time concerning the performance style of screen actors. James Allen remained one of Muni's most "realistic" characterizations for the remainder of his career. When his visage did become buried beneath greasepaint and prosthetics, in *The Story of Louis Pasteur* (1936), *The Life of Emile Zola* (1937) and *Juarez* (1939), the histrionics from his many years on the stage again rose to the fore, although his performances (all in biographical roles) powerfully dominate these fine films.

In *I Am a Fugitive from a Chain Gang*, much of Muni's best acting is nonverbal, facial expressions and bodily gestures that never could be seen by a theater audience but are suited beautifully to the camera. The scene in the camp barracks, during which a prison guard (Harry Woods) intuitively bashes Allen in the forehead with a large ring on the end of a chain, is spine-chilling, even before Muni, who has fallen off his bunk to the floor and grabbed his face, slowly moves his hand to give the audience a look at the mingled agony and anger brewing in his powerful eyes. This is a moment delivered by a truly great actor.

The scholarly film journal *Close Up*, in its March 1933 issue, published a rather lukewarm review of *I Am a Fugitive from a Chain Gang* by H. A. Potamkin, who concluded with a compliment, followed by a pertinent question:

> *I Am a Fugitive* is an advance in American film-content and to that extent its form is shaped. Will it be a jumping-off place for more progressive films or an end-stop?[20]

Perhaps one of the best summations of the power of *I Am a Fugitive from a Chain Gang* is provided by none other than Vincent Burns, whose close connection with the film would make one believe that he couldn't assess the film with any degree of objectivity. Yet, his comments are truly spot-on:

> The picture went sweeping across the country like a prairie fire. Box-office records began to go by the boards. In the South as well as the North, though it was issued in the midst of the worst depression America had ever known, block-long lines waited outside theatres to see this sensational true-life story of chain gang life in the United States. The magazine *Liberty* gave it four stars. The [National] Board of Film Review voted it "the outstanding picture of the year." ... One critic said: "If I could only see one picture a year, this is the kind of picture I'd go to see!"[21]

I Am a Fugitive from a Chain Gang was nominated for three Academy Awards: Best Sound Recording, Best Actor and Best Picture. Though its makers left the Oscars empty-handed, the National Board of Review named it, not only Best Film of 1932, but "one of the best films ever made in this country."[22] Muni eventually would receive a total of five Best Actor nominations (plus a strong write-in for *Black Fury* [1935]), but he won only once, for his (more theatrical) performance in the Warner Bros. prestige biopic *The Story of Louis Pasteur* (1936), directed by William Dieterle.

Glenda Farrell was grateful to share scenes with Muni under LeRoy's direction. Having both come from the theater, she and Muni prepared and rehearsed their roles in a similar fashion. Farrell became so immersed in her character that she didn't realize the truly evil nature of Marie until she finally saw the film on television more than two decades later.

Even the most optimistic Warner Bros. employees were a bit surprised when the film was a box-office smash. Zanuck was proved right in his dedication to the socially relevant material, and he had the foresight to know just how to craft a screen story to capture the attention of a mass audience.

In the 1981 Warner Bros. screenplay book, John E. O'Connor adds,

> There can be no doubt that, although liberals and intellectuals had known about the problem for years, the experience of seeing this film awakened millions of American people to an issue and helped to create the political climate in which real reform could eventually take place.[23]

The film also had a specific effect on its home studio, striking a historic compromise between the economically minded Harry and Abe Warner on the East Coast, and production mogul Jack Warner, who collaborated creatively with Darryl Zanuck, on the West Coast.

Exceptional Cinema

The film, covering 13 years of dramatized biographical material in just 92 minutes, is occasionally episodic, but LeRoy's direction, bolstered by the adroit camerawork of Sol Polito and incisive editing of William Holmes, admirably realizes the overall pacing inherent in the final screenplay polished by Darryl Zanuck and Howard Green. Fast-moving, newsreel-style montages, often including newspaper headlines (a strategy favored by Green), a device used at Warner Bros. throughout the 1930s, are integrated at several key points to indicate a steady flow of events. (These sequences, filmed by a second unit, were done silently, with all the sound dubbed in during post-production.)

Retained in the final screenplay, Holmes and Gibney's "less is more" approach to depicting chain-gang brutality, intending to engage the viewer's imagination, is very successful. More explicit scripted sequences, involving the sweat box and a pick shack, to be used during Allen's second term on the chain gang, were not filmed. A brief prologue, to feature a moving scroll on which would be written a message from Vincent Burns about the authenticity of the material in the film, also was eliminated.

The use of sound, much of which may be attributed to Zanuck, is also a most effective element. The clang of the blacksmith's hammer on the leg shackles, the rhythmic singing of the African American prisoners as they swing their sledgehammers, and Allen's footsteps trailing away into the darkness during the haunting final shot are just a few notable examples.

Except for Hale Hamilton, the supporting cast is impeccable, with Glenda Farrell ably augmented by Allen Jenkins, a ubiquitous character actor with whom she subsequently worked in Warner Bros.' comic delight *Havana Widows* (1933), directed by Ray Enright and costarring Joan Blondell, and other films. Jenkins went on to support every major Warner Bros. star, including Edward G. Robinson, James Cagney, Humphrey Bogart and Errol Flynn. Later at RKO, he played sidekick to the inimitable George Sanders in the early entries in the "Falcon" detective series.

As "Bomber" Wells, 61-year-old Edward Ellis, whose previous experience included an impressive 27 years on Broadway, made his sound feature-film debut in *I Am a Fugitive from a Chain Gang*. Arguably making

I Am a Fugitive from a Chain Gang (1932). Back on the chain gang, the desperate James Allen (Paul Muni) is stopped by "Bomber" Wells (Edward Ellis) from killing a guard with his sledgehammer.

one of the most memorable career entrances by a character actor in Hollywood history, Ellis instinctively knew how to adapt his stage performance style for the motion-picture camera. He manages slyly to underplay the part while still making the most of every word, playing James Allen's only real comrade in the camp, growling forth essential advice that helps his new acquaintance to survive.

When Barney Sykes completes his sentence and shuffles his way out the front gate, Wells informs Allen of the two ways to leave a chain-gang camp: "Work out and *die* out." Later, during Allen's second escape, when "Bomber" is allowed to demonstrate his talent for strategically hurling dynamite from the speeding dump truck, Ellis communicates the character's absolute relish nonverbally, and the pain that registers on his face as Bomber agonizing bids Allen farewell with, "*Getting out* here" (a line *not* in the final screenplay) is one of the film's most moving moments.

Following *I Am a Fugitive from a Chain Gang*, Ellis would work for the next decade at many of the studios. Always noteworthy, he shared the screen with William Powell and Myrna Loy (*The Thin Man* [1934]), Spencer Tracy (*Fury* [1936], directed by Fritz Lang), Burgess Meredith (*Winterset* [1936]) and Shirley Temple (*Little Miss Broadway* [1938]).

Appearing in her fifth film, 25-year-old Helen Vinson, as Allen's real love interest, became one of the key actresses used by Warner Bros. to play sophisticated, upper-class women for the next two years, before she bounced all over Hollywood for the next decade. She benefited by working with many acclaimed directors: Lewis Milestone (*The Captain Hates the Sea* [1934]), Frank Capra (*Broadway Bill* [1934]) and King Vidor (*The Wedding Night* [1935]). She even joined Richard Dix in sailing to England to make the early science-fiction soap opera *Trans-Atlantic Tunnel* (1935), under the direction of Maurice Elvey.

In *I Am a Fugitive from a Chain Gang*, while first getting to know Allen, Helen hears him reveal what he does for a living, a description indicating that he is thoroughly haunted by his experiences on the chain gang. He labors to "build bridges and roads for people to use when they want to get away from things—but they *can't* get away, nobody can."

Like her three actress sisters (Polly Ann, Loretta [Gretchen] and Georgiana Young), Sally Blane (Elizabeth Young) began acting at an early age (seven), but she appears only very briefly at the beginning of *I Am a Fugitive from a Chain Gang* as Allen's (apparent) sweetheart, Alice. Following his rather awkward reception upon returning to his hometown of "Lynndale" from the war, Allen has no further contact with her, and Blane disappears from the film. An entire community dance scene, set shortly after his "homecoming," and featuring other attendees poking fun at Allen's old-fashioned, prewar terpsichorean style, was cut during the first day of shooting.

I Am a Fugitive from a Chain Gang literally brims with Hollywood heavies, several character actors who returned in, not only many more films while under contact to Warner Bros., but productions for other companies as well. Preston Foster (Pete, the man who forces Allen into the holdup) was competent at playing all manner of tough-guy characters, but David Landau (as the sadistic camp warden), Willard Robertson (Prison Board chairman), Douglas Dumbrille (district attorney), Harry Woods (brutal prison guard), Walter Long (blacksmith) and Charles Middleton (train conductor) usually played characters "one loves to loathe." (Long and Middleton even menaced Laurel and Hardy on several occasions!)

More than eight decades after its release, *I Am a Fugitive from a Chain Gang* remains a cinematic tour de force and a monument to—in the words of the Scottish bard Robert Burns—*man's inhumanity to man*. A film that helped lead to actual social awareness and perhaps even legal change, it depicts a litany of deadly sins: lying, chicanery, negligence, greed, blackmail, corruption, brutality, sadism, racism and manslaughter.

5

Out of These Chains

The Continuing Saga of Robert E. Burns and the Warner Bros. Film

> One thing we are sure of: *the old world is gone forever and a new world must follow the end of this great war.* Will it be a world ruled by mighty military dictators or a democratic world where the people will have a voice in their own governments? Will it be a world where the fruits of the earth and the necessities of life will be monopolized and hoarded by giant combines or distributed to and shared by the great masses of the people? Will it be a world poisoned and pauperized by a crude materialism or a world guided by human values and the highest spiritual ideals?
> —Vincent Godfrey Burns, "Preface," *Out of These Chains* (1942)[1]

At the outset of United States' participation in World War II, Vincent G. Burns committed to paper his political viewpoint in no uncertain terms:

> New chains of tyranny are being forged on hapless millions of human beings at this very moment.... We all know how brutal, how barbaric and how inhuman this new slavery is. But can we condemn it so long as our own doorstep is unclean? We must see to it that the actual iron chains of bondage are broken from the bodies of all men who bear them on the American continent. The chain gangs of Georgia, North and South Carolina, of Florida, Texas and Louisiana, of Tennessee, Alabama and Mississippi, are beyond a doubt as flagrant a violation of basic human rights as anything on earth. To tolerate such conditions here in America, while championing the cause of mankind's emancipation elsewhere is not short of base hypocrisy. If we fail to make democracy work here in simple justice, economic equality and social humaneness posterity will condemn us whether we win the war or not. *A magnificent advance in America toward real freedom for all would be immediate federal action to humanize all our prisons and abolish the Southern chain gang forever.*[2]

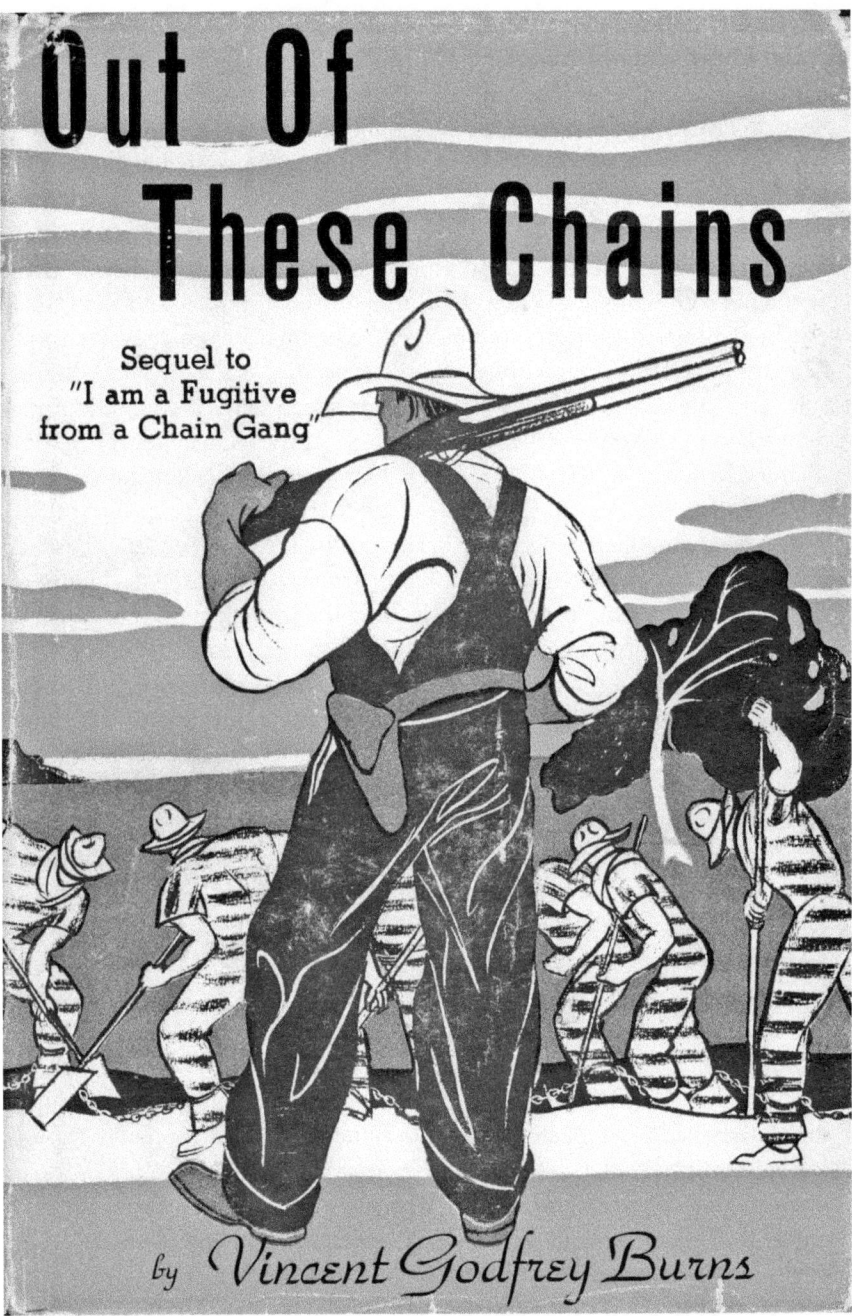

Out of These Chains (1942). The front cover of the dust jacket for Vincent G. Burns' sequel to *I Am a Fugitive from a Georgia Chain Gang!*

In November 1932, Vincent Burns was invited to a lavish party at Trenton's Hotel Hildebrecht by his friend Harold G. Hoffman, then motor vehicle commissioner of New Jersey, for which the guest list included Hollywood heavyweights, notable politicians and chiefs of local law-enforcement agencies. The one favor asked of Vincent: that he be accompanied by his brother, the "fugitive from a chain gang *in the flesh*."

Vincent and Hoffman had been close friends for many years, and a "solemn promise" was given that Robert need fear no possibility of arrest at the party or banquet. When the Burns brothers walked into the Hildebrecht banquet room, they hobnobbed with the likes of Jack Dempsey, Morton Downey, Victor Moore, Warner Bros.' top star Edward G. Robinson, and New Jersey State Police Superintendent, Colonel Norman Schwarzkopf (later the father of General Norman Schwarzkopf, Jr., Commander in Chief of the U.S. Central Command, who led the coalition forces during the Persian Gulf War of 1990–91).

At the luncheon, Robert sat between Philadelphia Athletics baseball star Jimmy Fox and Schwarzkopf, who currently was a popular figure on the *Gang Busters* radio program and leading the investigation into the infamous Lindbergh baby kidnapping, which had occurred on March 1, 1932. Robert had been a bit reticent to make a public appearance, but placed practically in the lap of a formidable lawman like Schwarzkopf was something else indeed. Vincent was very encouraged by Colonel Schwarzkopf, who was friendly toward both of them, and promised that Robert would neither be harassed nor arrested by the State Police.

Following a fabulous floor show in the banquet hall, Harold Hoffman addressed the revelers, announcing that quite a remarkable surprise was in store. He mentioned the magazine serialization and book versions of *I Am a Fugitive from a Georgia Chain Gang!*, the awakening of Americans to the way of life on the Southern chain gangs, and then endorsed the newly released Warner Bros. film. before revealing that the actual Robert E. Burns would be introduced by his illustrious brother.

Vincent rose from his chair and confidently spoke about the great opportunity they had been given to welcome Robert to such a gracious occasion. He emphasized that *I Am a Fugitive from a Georgia Chain Gang!* is a true story, published by *True Detectives Mysteries* and Vanguard Press, and now made as a major motion picture by Warner Bros. He concluded, "I take pleasure in presenting to you the fugitive himself—Robert Elliott Burns."

Robert received a thunderous ovation from the entire gathering. When the roar subsided, he thanked Commissioner Hoffman and all those in attendance before starkly stating:

> The scenes that you will see in the picture are mild beside the truth. To try to reproduce in a movie the actual cruelties that occur in the chain gangs of the South would be a futile and thankless task. It would be too unbelievable, too shocking. Mervyn LeRoy, the director of the picture, wisely understates the chain gang scenes. But you people of New Jersey know how horrible can be the cruelties of a Southern chain gang because you have just read in your newspapers of the shocking death by strangulation in a sweat box, in a Florida chain gang camp, of one of our New Jersey youths, Arther Maillefert. Do not be surprised. It happens every day, somewhere in a Southern chain gang, but nobody ever hears about it.[3]

Robert made it clear that his grievance was not against the people of Georgia, but the "viciously un–American system" of the chain gang and the sadistic administrators and guards, "the cruel arbiters of ignorance and prejudice," who seem to enjoy enforcing its ruthless and brutal practices. He closed his comments about the Draconian penal laws with a very common-sense summation:

> If the officials of Georgia can be furnished with the proof of my reformation, what more should they honestly require? Surely, there is neither sense nor humanity in confining a man to prison who has proven by the test of years that he can become a useful citizen of society.... Colonel Schwarzkopf here has been kind enough to say he will not arrest me. Other policemen and officers in this state have given me the same assurance. But if I am arrested again and Georgia attempts to take me back I will put up a terrible fight for my freedom. In the event of my capture here I know I can count on the sympathetic support of you good people of New Jersey....[4]

Robert's speech was brief but effective, met with lengthy applause by every man at the luncheon. Following the meal, the entire group walked down Trenton's main street to see the marquee of the Stacy-Trent Theatre brightly lit up with the title *I Am a Fugitive from a Chain Gang* bordered by the enormous billboard-sized 24-sheet Warner Bros. posters depicting the fugitive in full flight from the horrors of the prison camp.

Inquiring at the box office about the attendance, the manager responded that the picture had attracted the best business in years and asked Vincent and Robert if they would stay to introduce the second show with a brief explanation of how they collaborated to write the sensational story on which the film was based. Robert merely improvised on his earlier speech, but the crowd roared with applause, impressing the manager into asking them to speak prior to each evening's showing that entire week.

As ticket sales increased each day, the Burns brothers realized that both the film and their added presence were having the positive effect they had been seeking. Following the nights in Trenton, they repeated their act for another week, at the Liberty Theatre in Plainfield, proving to the residents of New Jersey that Robert indeed was no criminal, but a solid, thoughtful citizen who deserved his freedom.

However, as invitations for more public appearances began to pour in from across the state, the brothers agreed that they didn't want to give New Jersey governor Arthur Harry Moore the impression that the Robert E. Burns movement was becoming commercialized in any way. Besides, a Georgia detective impersonating a filmgoer just might stroll into a Jersey theater some evening.

On November 30, 1932, Vincent spoke about the Southern chain gangs to the Rotary Club of Hoboken, New Jersey. During his presentation, he emphasized his belief that Governor A. Harry Moore was a man whose sense of justice might very well lead to a "historical" break in the endlessly trumped-up case against Robert.

Imagine the shock Vincent felt later that day when several New Jersey newspapers carried the following headline:

CHAIN GANG FUGITIVE HAS BEEN PROMISED IMMUNITY BY
GOVERNOR MOORE, BROTHER, PALISADE CLERGYMAN, SAYS.

Vincent had made no such statement to anyone in Hoboken. At noon the following day, he was attending the weekly luncheon of the Fort Lee Rotary Club at an Italian Restaurant on the Palisades above the Hudson, when he received a telephone call. Governor Moore was on the other end of the line, asking if he had seen the newspaper reports.

"Yes, Governor," Vincent replied, "and I assure you that I never made any such statement. What I said was this: I said that I believed you were the kind of man who would stand by your convictions of justice in such a case, I did not say that you had promised immunity. That is fantastic."

"I know how newspapers are, Doctor," Moore affirmed, "but I must ask you to be careful. If your brother is in need, I'll do my very best for you." And, like a wise politician, he added, "But, you know, I can make no promises now."[5]

The following month, as a white blanket of snow began to fall and many of Robert's neighbors had begun to celebrate the Yuletide season, Bertha phoned the gift shop from downtown Newark, asking him if he'd like to join some of her friends who were visiting from Chicago. Resplendent in a new suit, Robert called for her at 8 p.m., and they all enjoyed dinner and dancing at the grill room of the Robert Treat Hotel.

As Bertha's friend, Mrs. Fisher, regaled Robert with her impressions of the film, which she described as a "magnificent experience [she wouldn't] soon forget ... the most gripping thing [she'd] ever seen," he was approached by a rather tough-looking character who summoned him to a quiet corner of the hotel lobby.

Robert recognized the man as a rather well-known Newark newspaper reporter who had expressed interest in his case on more than one occasion. Revealing that he had met with Chief of Police McRell earlier that day, the reporter tipped him off that the Newark police, armed with several telegrams from Georgia, were hot on his trail and, in fact, had detained and questioned a man in East Orange they had mistaken for him only hours before. Informed that it was only a matter of time before he'd be picked up, he was advised to scram as soon as possible.

Around midnight, Vincent was awakened by the ring of his bedroom telephone. "I'm in a tough spot," he heard his brother's voice shake. "The Newark police are hot on my trail.... In East Orange this afternoon, they arrested a man they thought was me. Any minute *I* may be arrested."

Vincent began to grow restless, then a bit frantic.

"We must do something immediately," said Robert. Unless we act at once, they'll get me! You know what that means—friends or no friends—*I'll go back*! This is the crisis. Now is the time when your friends must go to bat for me!"

The success of the film had allowed the brothers' enthusiasm lead to blatant recklessness. Vincent came to realize this fact as his brother grew more and more paranoid. "Keep cool, Ell," he advised. "Everything will be all right. We'll go to Trenton tomorrow to see the governor. I'll meet you in Newark at 10 o'clock tomorrow morning."

Though he tried his best to calm "Ell," as he always called his brother," Vincent didn't sleep a wink, tossing and turning in his rack, the rest of the night, unable to vanquish the vision of the fugitive and him disappearing down a deep, dark hole.

The next day, attempting to avoid sliding about on the December snow while driving though Trenton, Robert's negative attitude continued to drive his thoughts. He admitted that he'd reached a point where he really trusted no one. "What will the governor do if the arrest comes?" he asked.

Vincent reminded "Ell" that, so far, Governor Moore had stood by him every step of the way. "He told you to go ahead with the gift shop, didn't he?" Vincent asked. "And he gave us his word that he'd go along with us in case you were arrested.... *I know we can count on him*!"

At approximately 2:30 p.m. that day, Robert and Vincent were welcomed into the inner office of Governor Moore, who quite frankly, was surprised by the extremely distraught and nearly paranoid behavior of the fugitive, who remained agitatedly silent while his brother did all the talking.

Asked to write a personal letter to the Newark chief of police, Moore responded that, in his role as governor, he did not have jurisdiction over the power of the city of Newark. "In his over-wrought state of mind, I believe your brother is taking this matter too seriously," he informed Vincent. "He is in no immediate danger. Go ahead now and let him take it easy. If the worst comes to the worst, I will go along with you to the very best of my ability. I will decide his case on its merits, and I feel your brother will have nothing to fear in such an eventuality."[6]

Following this disappointing meeting with the governor, Vincent guided Robert directly across the street from the State Capitol to the Motor Vehicle Commissioner's Office. Having enjoyed the wonderful party and banquet Harold Hoffman had held in honor of his brother in December, Vincent figured he would appeal to his longtime friend's willingness to recruit his powerful political allies to support Robert in any approaching calamity.

Inside Hoffman's private office, Vincent barely described the current state of their situation before Hoffman declared, "I think *I* can help you, Vincent." He rattled off the names of commissioners, "fighting Irishmen," reached into his pocket, withdrew a calling-card case, and wrote a personal note on the back of two of the cards:

> This is to introduce Dr. Vincent Burns, one of New Jersey's outstanding ministers. Do what you can for him and it will be considered a personal favor by me.
>
> Harold G. Hoffman

At Newark City Hall, Vincent's first calling card was overturned immediately. Commissioner of Public Safety Eagan had left for the day. While Robert continued to hide out in a nearby bookstore, Vincent walked to Police Headquarters, where he met the very friendly Commissioner Reilly, who took him straight down to Chief McRell's office. Unfortunately, the chief was temporarily out, but perhaps it turned out for the best, after Vincent had a substantive discussion with Deputy Chief Brex, who described his boss as a very by-the-book cop. However, Brex was a supportive and honest man, as well as a good cop, and offered Vincent his own opinion of Robert's ordeal:

> [Y]our brother has done more with his book ... and the motion picture made from it, to reform and renovate the prison systems of America than any other man that I know of. It is one of the finest things ever written in this country and *that picture packs a punch on the side of social reform the like of which this nation has never seen before!* If I had my way, your brother would be as free here in New Jersey as I am. Unfortunately, I haven't any say, but I just want you to know how I feel.[7]

Vincent was impressed by Brex, whom he considered a true gentleman, intelligent and honest, and one of the few totally trustworthy people in law enforcement. He understood that crime is bred at least as much by social forces and living environments as any sort of "hard-wired" biological makeup.

After Brex left the office, Vincent decided to wait for McRell to return. As he sat calmly on a bench, three detectives began administering the third degree to an African American suspect in the outer room. Racial epithets, blows to the face that hurt but leave no mark, and jabbing in the abdomen with a nightstick went on for some time before Vincent walked toward them, politely asking for a little mercy. Laughter from two of the cops was followed by a suggestion from the third: "Get the hell outta here!"

Vincent returned to the bench, but closed the door to the outer room. Soon Commissioner Reilly came strolling back in, reporting that Chief McRell was now in his office on the first floor. During the walk down, the minister described the brutality he'd witnessed during his wait, but Reilly merely replied that the Chief was of "the old school," a remark supported by McRell's expression, described by Vincent as "a face as cold and hard as a granite cliff."

Perhaps unduly influenced by the humane Brex, Vincent made the tragic mistake of even mentioning the ordeal of his brother to McRell, who began his condemnation, speaking with a Southern accent, by promising that Robert would *certainly* be arrested, and then acted as if his crime of being forced to grab $5.80 was one of the most ruthless acts ever perpetrated on society. To McRell, Robert was a liar, a congenital criminal, a subversive, a radical, and the film *I Am a Fugitive from a Chain Gang* "nothing but sheer lies from beginning to end."

As far as Georgia was concerned, there was *no* cruelty, *no* brutality; and even if there were such acts of punishment, they were earned and deserved for any breaking and flaunting of the most trifling law on the books. His tirade concluded, McRell stomped out of the office as a tall, dark-haired man walked in. "I'm Lieutenant White," the young man said to Vincent, speaking in a friendly manner and offering his hand, "*If God Himself should come in here and ask us not to arrest a friend of his, we'd give him the same answer!*"[8]

At the bookstore, Robert was the picture of sweat-soaked anxiety *before* hearing the bad news from his brother. As they left, planning to eat at a restaurant across the street, a large man with a fedora's brim pulled down over his eyes approached. Following an announcement that the Chief would like to see Vincent, the steely-voiced man ordered that he bring his *friend* along.

Just a few blocks down the street, a theater marquee glowed,

I AM A FUGITIVE FROM A CHAIN GANG
the true story written from hiding by Robert Burns
with Paul Muni

In the entrance to the theater, along with Warner Bros. posters, lobby cards and stills, were photos of Robert, Vincent and their mother, including the caption, "Will the chain gang bosses get this man again?"

Following another harangue from McRell, Robert and Vincent were accompanied by an armed detective to the diner across the street, giving them a chance to talk without being overheard. Both brothers knew of an election scandal involving dirty cops in the precinct, plus the reward offered by the Georgia authorities which probably was much higher than the figure published in the newspapers. They theorized that the publicity generated by Robert's capture was a handy smoke screen the police department could use to draw attention away from their acts of corruption.

As Robert was taken to a cell for the night, to await the next morning's arraignment, Vincent telephoned a close friend and colleague who was also the governor's brother-in-law. Within a few minutes, he had, not only affirmative support from the governor, but also a top-flight attorney for Robert, courtesy of Bertha and Ben Martin, one of their closest friends. Fortunately for "Ell," he was able to hear this news from Vincent before he practically collapsed onto his metal bunk. His equally exhausted, crusading brother finally was able to head home, to seek a few hours' sleep.

At 9 a.m., Vincent was back at the courthouse, armed with several newspapers, all of which featured sensationalistic stories about Robert's capture. One Associated Press reporter in Chicago had interviewed Robert's estranged wife, Emily, who had expressed a deep resentment for the way Glenda Farrell played her in the film.

In Georgia, the Prison Commission and Governor Richard B. Russell, Jr., already had extradition proceedings underway. In the Newark courtroom, many local residents who had seen the film were in attendance. When Robert was brought before the bench, and answered truthfully that he had escaped from the La Grange prison camp and was living under an assumed name, Judge Harold Simandl ordered him held for extradition, setting his bail at $25,000—10 times the usual amount—and the highest ever in such a case in the state of New Jersey.

Newspapers across the country printed stories containing "interviews" with other Georgia convicts who supposedly had done time with Robert. Due to Vincent Burns' solid detective work gathering actual facts, often simply using conflicting dates as evidence that the pro–Georgia individuals were lying outrageously; and, in some cases, had never met the men, both prison officials and convicts at various chain-gang camps, that they had praised in their comments, he exposed a whole network of graft, corruption, and deal-making involving sentence-reduction and even pardons.

Sidney George Flagg, one of Robert's major detractors, was proved a flagrant liar by John M. Hampton of Port Arthur, Texas, who wrote a letter describing a 1930 discussion with the ex-convict in Ontario, California, during which he'd heard a story directly belying the one now circulating nationwide. Hampton began his letter by referring to the film as "the most wonderful thing from an eye-opening standpoint to my mind that has ever been put on the silver screen."

Even more damning to Flagg's rambling accusations was a telegram from Atlanta attorney Murphy Halloway, who revealed,

> I appeared as lawyer for Flagg, confederate of Burns, at the original arraignment in this (Fulton) county. I have in my possession facts which will show Governor Moore the truth of this matter and prevent extradition.

Unable to travel to Trenton, Halloway then mailed a letter to Vincent, stating that, at the arraignment, Flagg confessed that Robert had been coerced into participating in the grocery store robbery at the point of his gun. Flagg actually had described Robert as a "total loss" in the act of stealing.[9]

After broadcasting his Friday poetry show on WOR radio, Vincent received a telephone call from Governor Moore and Frank Hague, Mayor of Jersey City, who relayed good news that a hearing on Robert's case would be held in Trenton the following Wednesday afternoon. Hague assured Vincent that they were *in Jersey*, not Georgia, and that no "gorillas" from outside the state would be taking his brother anywhere.

The next morning, Hague asked Vincent to begin a major letter writing campaign to all his New Jersey friends in the clergy, and to prepare an address to give at the hearing on Wednesday. Meanwhile, Mrs. Burns was scheduled to meet with president-elect Franklin D. Roosevelt in Albany to discuss her son's case. FDR had been interested in Robert's ordeal since he first had met Mrs. Burns in Warm Springs, Georgia, in 1929, but he was unable personally to see her on this occasion. However, FDR's secretary, Missy Le Hand, had a long conversation with Mrs. Burns and promised to bring the matter to Roosevelt's attention.

That afternoon, Vincent and his mother met with Judge Crain in the District Attorney's office in Newark, to discuss other, older charges against Robert that had been dismissed but used as propaganda by McRell and his cohorts. Crain said that these dismissals were sound, and then added his opinion of the Georgia extradition effort in straight-shooting terms:

If we can be of any help in giving Robert Elliott Burns a new start in life, with a clean slate, we are at your disposal. As for the State of Georgia and its officials, we no longer count them in the federal union around here. A few months ago we asked Governor Russell for the return of a man from Georgia and we met with a flagrant refusal. In this instance, the man was a notorious swindler, with a long list of crimes against him, and from every standpoint the man should have been returned. As far as I am concerned, Georgia is no longer in the United States, and if I were Governor Moore you may be sure that I'd turn down the Georgia request so quick it would take their breath away. So in your fight for your brother, I am with you wholeheartedly. I wish you all the luck in the world. You have nothing to fear from this office, you may be sure!"[10]

It was at this time, however, that Vincent Burns began to question the very foundations of human brotherhood that had been instilled in him by his mentor, Bill Simpson. In *Out of These Chains*, Vincent writes:

In accord with the great inspiration I had found in my friendship with Bill, I had endeavored to apply literally the basic principle of all religion—*that it was impossible to love God without first loving one's fellowmen, all of them*. And to love one's fellowmen meant being willing to make any sacrifice to bring about a better, happier order in the world. I sought to find ways and means to bring about this better, happier order of things.... Trying to be of help to others became a passion with me. I saw that the tyranny of a blind, heartless economic system was as bad as any other tyranny on earth—and I wanted to do something, however small, to help change it.

However, I began to learn that the path of applied brotherhood, though a joyful way, is paved at times with thorns, and that to follow it faithfully one has to pay a rather large price.... From hard, practical experience I had found that to live the true life of brotherhood was a dangerous, costly and thankless procedure, that it was one thing to talk and sing about loving your neighbor, as so many church people did, but it was a far different thing to stand by the principle in living. I came to see that George Bernard Shaw was right when he said that when you do for people more than they have a right to expect some subtle trait in human nature causes them to hate you for it. I was to find this out more poignantly in my efforts in my brother's case than in any other.[11]

After Warner Bros. released the film, Vincent began to refer to the Southern chain-gang camps during his Sunday sermons. Soon the entire mood of his congregation began to change, with certain members discussing the reverend's "foolishness" in attempting to aid his brother. One particular trustee expressed the view that all mention of the chain gangs be halted lest real trouble, perhaps even violence, erupt against him and the church. One local resident even contacted the Federal Income Tax Bureau, claiming that Vincent had received a large cut from the sale of the film rights to *I Am a Fugitive from a Georgia Chain Gang!* He was visited by income tax agents and even threatened with imprisonment before the federal government realized that he hadn't earned a cent from any aspect of the motion picture's production or commercial success.

Though his unwavering crusade eventually would result in the loss of his pulpit to a "conspiracy" of congregational hypocrites, Vincent, joined by his mother, spoke for 15 minutes on New York's WOR Radio on the Sunday evening preceding Robert's Wednesday hearing. While introducing Vincent, the announcer actually referred to Robert as "the author of the motion picture *I Am a Fugitive from a Chain Gang*."

Katherine first appealed to listeners to write to Governor Moore in Trenton before Vincent emphasized how much worse the actual chain gangs of Georgia were when compared to the descriptions in the book and depictions in the film. Following a brief sermon carefully prepared for the audience, mother and son then headed for Hackensack, where they made another appeal, this time at the invitation of the manager of the Eureka Theatre, who suddenly flashed a spotlight on them *during* the film, just at the point where James Allen is about to accomplish his first escape from the chain gang. Vincent, explaining that Katherine had become too weak to address the audience, refrained from his usual religious fervor while politely asking them to contact the governor by post card, letter or telegram. Though the projectionist restarted the film, the thunderous applause echoing through the auditorium drowned out the Vitaphone sound for several minutes.

A nationwide wave of support followed the WOR broadcast, resulting in the office of Governor Moore being deluged with hundreds of appeals from individuals from all walks of life, as well as many organizations from across the political spectrum. At least one person, William J. Kennefick, an attorney and Robert's commanding officer during the war, traveled by train from Boston to speak face to face with Moore. Conversely, there were the expected propagandistic attempts by the anti–Burns forces to dredge up the same old rumors about the fugitive's "criminal past."

One of the supportive letters received by Moore prior to the hearing was sent by none other than Jack L. Warner, who wrote:

> We had the opportunity of knowing Mr. Burns closely during the time we negotiated for the purchase of the picture rights in his book.
> We can testify from these contacts that he is a man of the most upright and honest intentions and character.
> We beg you in utmost sincerity that in our opinion the cause of justice will be furthered by your refusal to permit the man to be again incarcerated.[12]

At the New Jersey state capitol in Trenton at 2 p.m. on December 21, 1932, snow began to cover the surrounding streets as Robert's public hearing was held in the assembly hall, packed from floor to ceiling with spectators of every stripe. Clarence Darrow had sent a telegram, indicating that only a bad cold could prevent his supportive attendance. Just three blocks from the Essex County Jail, Harold Hardy, warden of the Troup County Chain Gang, and his sidekick, La Grange police chief R. B. Carter, waited at the Newark Hotel, anxious to clap the cuffs back on the fugitive and transport him back to pay "what he still owed" the state of Georgia. In his tiny, dingy cell, Robert, visited only by spectacle-seeking reporters, had become profoundly depressed; and, during his final visit with Vincent on the eve of the hearing, was threatening suicide.

In the front row, to the right of the platform, sat Katherine Burns, Vincent and his wife, attorneys Charles Handler, Arthur Garfield Hays and Harry V. Osborne, Vincent's secretary and several supportive friends. Also in that area were legal eagles from both New Jersey and Georgia, along with Hardy and Carter, ever more anxious to complete what they considered a mere formality so they could take their prisoner back to the chain gang.

Governor Moore entered at 1:30, as press photographers flashed away and newsreel cameramen attempted to capture the most important images of the event. Handler was first called to speak for the defense in calling for a refusal of the extradition warrant, followed by the testimony of two New Jersey physicians who described the details of Robert's poor health, particularly a serious heart condition which made him much too weak for a return to the chain gang. The doctors were supported further by a plea from Hays, who represented the American Civil Liberties Union (ACLU). With Hays' reading of letters from Darrow and George Gordon Battle, Vincent had no reason to believe that his brother would not be permitted to be extradited. Applause and cheers from many New Jersey citizens in attendance lasted so long that Moore had to call for quiet.

Descriptions of the horrendous food and hygiene conditions at the camps were followed by the calling of individual witnesses, including Mrs. Burns, Vincent, and representatives from veterans' organizations, the American Legion and the Veterans of Foreign Wars (VFW), as well as the presentation of a petition signed by 8,000 citizens of the state. But the most surprising witness of all was a grocer called Bernstein, who currently ran a store in Far Rockaway, New York, but formerly was the man held up during the 1922 robbery in Atlanta. Testifying that Robert already had endured far more than was necessary, he supported the defense in every way, including his honest description of what actually had happened during the commission of the crime committed an entire decade earlier. He concluded his remarks by revealing, "I came here today because I thought it was only fair that the truth about the Burns case should be known."

Moore again had to silence the crowd, most of whom were thunderously applauding and cheering the continued defense of the chain-gang fugitive.

"Do you think Burns should go back...?" asked Judge Osborne.

"I certainly do not," replied Bernstein. "I know something about Georgia, and I know what would happen to him if he went back."

One more hurrah from the supportive crowd burst forth as the defense rested.

Merritt Lane, attorney for the state of Georgia, then had the floor. He wasted no time stressing that emotion had no place in the application of *law*, a point which drew a hail of laughter from those who had just issued forth the hurrah. His view that extradition should be an obligatory process, which was objected to by Governor Moore, was then supported by Georgia's assistant solicitor general John L. Kelley, who presented what he considered solid evidence of Robert's heinous crimes against his sovereign state. Kelley also mentioned the "falsehoods" perpetrated by the popular media unleashed by the Brothers Burns:

> This book by Burns is a fraud from cover to cover. The prisoner suffered no such tortures as those described in this book and shown in the motion picture of the same name [sic].... Look at that man, how sullen and rebellious he is! He looks more like a thug or a gangster than Dillinger or Al Capone! What right has such a man to write a book about prisons?[13]

Finally, after four hours had passed, Governor Moore announced that he would *deny* the extradition of Robert Burns to the state of Georgia and a deluge of applause flooded the hall. Aided by Vincent, Mrs. Burns managed to reach Robert as a large portion of the crowd moved to congratulate him. The newsreel cameramen were right on their heels, knowing that Vincent, now widely known for his fiery sermons, would have a speech prepared for them. Greatly relieved, the preacher announced,

> In behalf of my brother ... now no longer a fugitive from a chain gang.... I want to thank the American public for their wonderful kindness to us in this case. I also want to thank Governor Moore.... This will be the happiest Christmas we have ever had. I knew we would win because we were in the right and a Power above and beyond us was working on our side today.

Governor Moore echoed Vincent's emphasis on the importance of public opinion in his decision, and informed Robert that he could remain in New Jersey as long as he led an honest life.

Though a heavy snow continued to fall in Trenton that evening, the temperature was quite warm in Atlanta, where Georgia governor Richard B. Russell, Jr., compared Robert's "crimes" to that of Bruno Hauptmann, who recently had kidnapped and murdered the Lindbergh baby in East

Armwell, New Jersey. Soon after the Georgia House of Representatives passed a resolution condemning any theater exhibiting the film, the *Los Angeles Times* published a letter from a former Georgia resident who also had toiled on the La Grange chain gang. He revealed:

> The motion picture does not tell half of it.... Don't let yourself be misled as to the horrors of those Southern prison camps. They are horrible, brutal, inexcusable, unfair. A man comes out—either a whipped dog, without the courage to meet life, or a sullen rebel against society. That scar on my back still burns when I think of that place.[14]

A large percentage of the letters of support and congratulation that continued to arrive were written by people who first had been shocked by a recent viewing of the film. Perhaps the most famous U.S. citizen to write Vincent was broadcaster Lowell Thomas, who had included a biography of Robert during one of his recent radio broadcasts.

Vincent was especially impressed by the unanimously positive reviews of the film published in newspapers and periodicals nationwide. Perhaps Richard Watts, critic for the "usually conservative" *New York Herald-Tribune*, was his favorite. Watts referred to the picture as a

> grim and devastating biographical account ... [that] recounts with a surprising amount of honest directness the real tragedy of a victim of the futile cruelty of a barbarous penal system, and it is the chief triumph of the work that it actually seems real and honest and direct.... It is, in the best sense of the term, a cinema document...
>
> The acting is excellent, with Paul Muni giving a fine impersonation of the hunted man; with that fine stage actor, Edward Ellis, offering a vivid bit as a sardonic lifer, and with Miss Glenda Farrell playing the convict's betrayer with courageous remorselessness. Mr. LeRoy's direction is admirably vigorous.[15]

After its brief run in Atlanta, *I Am a Fugitive from a Chain Gang* was not only banned in Georgia but also boycotted in several other Southern states. Nonetheless, the film still grossed a total of $5 million during its nationwide exhibition during 1932–33, making a large profit for Warner Bros.

On September 28, 1939, *The Hollywood Reporter* published the results of an essay contest, "The Motion Picture I Liked Best and Why," conducted by five metropolitan New York newspapers which asked filmgoers to pick and describe their number-one Hollywood film from a list of several hundred titles. The winner at a total of 9,000 essays: *I Am a Fugitive from a Chain Gang*, a film released seven years earlier, remained so powerful that it stood head-and-shoulders above every other film these entrants had seen during the ensuing time.

Addressing the fact that *I Am a Fugitive* "was voted ... in 1939 the greatest motion picture of all time," Vincent mentioned discussing the film with Denis Conan Doyle after the son of the famous author of the Sherlock Holmes stories had seen the film in London. Conan Doyle said, "It was to me the biggest thrill I have ever had in a movie theatre. It stirred all England and was probably the most popular picture of the decade there."¹⁶

The film was not only an enormous hit in England but also in Belgium, France, Germany, throughout South America, and in the Soviet Union, where an exhibitor in Moscow reportedly had offered $25,000 for a single print of the film. Back in the States, the Museum of Modern Art in New York selected it as "an outstanding example of a social documentary film," and it drew capacity crowds at the Museum's theater during May, July, September and December 1939.

I Am a Fugitive from a Chain Gang also was added to the permanent film library at the Museum of Modern Art, and prints were issued to be shown at hundreds of colleges and other schools throughout the United States. At the University of Michigan on November 9, 1940, English Professor Kenneth T. Rowe wrote a letter to Vincent Burns, in part to pass on the following information:

> [T]he Art Cinema League Board of the University ... was making up a program of five pictures from a considerable list available for re-showings from the Museum of Modern Art. Having decided to ascertain our own interests just as a straw in the wind for our public we passed the list around for each member to check the five he would most like to see again. When the list came back "I Am a Fugitive" was the only picture which had been checked by all of the seven members.¹⁷

6

The Historic Influence of the Film

> [R]eally very few people act from motives of a truly generous and brotherly sort. There must be some kind of benefit in it for themselves. There are too many Babbitts in this world. The minute they see the color of coin, be it yellow, gold or bright silver, they sell out—lock, stock and barrel—and then rationalize that they are right in doing so. Their ideals, their religion, their deepest convictions never are considered. And if it happens that their fellow being, their own flesh and blood, has to suffer in the process, deep down in their hearts, instead of suffering a twitch of conscience, they'll get a sadistic thrill out of it, too!"
> —Newark, New Jersey, Deputy Chief of Police Brex, December 1932[1]

> "I Am a Fugitive" of Warners broods over the savagery of the Southern Penal system with convincing power and thereby achieves a quality of timelessness and actuality.
> —Richard Watts, Jr., *New York Herald-Tribune*, November 1932[2]

The cinematic influence of *I Am a Fugitive from a Chain Gang* would continue for decades; but what of its effect on the Southern prison camps? Interestingly, in late 1932, soon after the film was released and Robert Burns' extradition was denied, the *Telegraph*, a newspaper published in Macon, Georgia, ran an editorial asking,

> [W]hy cannot something be done about this thing [the chain gang] in Georgia? When our attention is called to our shortcomings and inhumanities which we know exist, we rise up on our hind legs like braying jackasses and say it ain't so.
> Georgia's penal system is outmoded, barbaric and entirely unrepresentative of enlightened sentiment in this state. The cage wagons, the shackles, the stocks, the lash—all these things are representative of an era in the punishment of criminals which has passed in enlightened states. The farming out of prisoners under the present system is little more than the old convict-lease system. The treatment they receive generally is inhumane, committee after committee from the Legislature has reported.

There is every reason we should do something about our prison system, but the attitude of the state officials is largely that of the present Prison Commissioners, an attitude more or less of indifference.³

Several supportive incentives and measures followed. A public statement from former Georgia Democratic governor Hugh M. Dorsey that the state stood indicted before the world prefaced a formal legislative investigation of its prisons by a group of prominent citizens in early 1933. This group, familiar with both the memoir and the film, included attorneys, academics, clergy, social and welfare workers, and former politicians. After making their tour, the members, using stark photographs as visual evidence, recommended a series of reforms to improve prison conditions statewide. On February 9, 1933, a resolution was introduced and passed in both branches of the Georgia Legislature to appoint an official investigative committee.

During the next six months, several state wardens and guards were fired, and one official was indicted for murder. The committee's final report confirmed that actual conditions in the chain-gang camps were far worse than depicted in the book and film. Typically, however, political cronyism and corruption unleashed a quick cover-up, and very little was done about any of the problems for several more years.

Crime and Punishment

There really is no *direct* evidence that Warner Bros.' *I Am a Fugitive from a Chain Gang* had a specific effect on changing penal conditions in the South, but the indirect influence through its effect on public opinion *is inarguable*. Far more people saw the film than read either the book or magazine serialization; and in some areas of the United States, some folks had never heard of a chain gang before seeing the title and Paul Muni's name on theater marquees.

In October 1936, Vincent Burns received a letter from W. T. Anderson, editor of the Macon *Telegraph*, who was eager to report that some major action might finally be taken to deal with the actual camp system:

> I have taken up many suggestions of reform and changes ... but have always met with the argument that there was no money ... a lazy man's excuse because much can be done without money where there is a will to do it.
>
> We are talking about setting up a new prison near Reidsville, Georgia. In fact, the building is almost completed. There is a big farm attached and it is the intention to transfer the able-bodied prisoners from Milledgeville farm ... and I hope it will lead to the elimination of the chain gang system.⁴

Reform continued to crawl on slowly, however, and a September 1937 *New York Times* report that a recent Atlanta meeting of chain-gang wardens had resulted in a reinstatement of the lash, and no-quarter, "shoot-to-kill" orders for all guards to use against prisoners attempting to escape greatly worried many readers in other states.[5] Following a storm of protest from journalists, public servants and clergy members throughout Georgia, the *Times* ran a follow-up story, with the headline "CHAIN GANG SYSTEM TO BE REORGANIZED," claiming that the whole barbaric practice was going to be abolished.[6]

On November 21, 1937, the *Times* then published an incredible report, headlined "END OF CHAIN GANG SLATED IN AMERICA," and including a list of nine specific recommendations for changes involving prisoner classification, rehabilitation, housing, medical care, vocational training and release determined by a special session of the Georgia General Assembly called by Democratic governor Eurith D. Rivers. Referring to this "unbelievable miracle," Vincent Burns wrote,

> [T]he people of Georgia by concerted action had forced the Legislature to a sweeping clean-up and an amazing turnabout in the prison policy of Georgia. Thus, the great humanitarian goal for which we had fought during the years of our struggle, was at last in sight. *I Am a Fugitive from a Chain Gang*, in book, magazine and picture, had aroused the citizenry of Georgia and had planted the dynamite under the chain gang system.[7]

(However, in his 1942 sequel—as the United States became involved in World War II—Burns pointed out that Alabama, Arkansas, Florida, Louisiana, Mississippi, North and South Carolina, Tennessee, Texas and Virginia were still operating chain gangs.)

In *Out of These Chains*, Vincent Burns adds,

> Deliberate torture of human beings is barbaric and wholly out of place among people who make any claim to being civilized...
>
> This was said of the barbarous treatment of political prisoners, as reported by Jan Valtin, in Russia and Germany. Perhaps "deliberate torture of human beings" is even more barbaric and out of place in a country such as ours, where citizens are supposed to have a higher heritage of freedom and democratic rights than anywhere else in the world.[8]

In his conclusion to *Out of These Chains*, Vincent Burns calls the chain gang "the Gestapo of the Swamplands" as he hopes for the essential "spiritual evolution" of humankind. Though his prose often may be purple, his aims are blood red, as he laboriously summarizes his 20-year fight against the chain gangs and what he describes as still-current "Danger Zones in the USA." Referring to both world wars as "symptoms of a deep-seated

6. The Historic Influence of the Film

disease in the very structure of human society," he warns,

> There is no longer any use trying to kid ourselves that complete responsibility for these catastrophes may be laid at the doors of men like the Kaiser in 1914 and Adolf Hitler in 1939. Such an explanation is too simple, too superficial. We know now that we are reaping in sweat and blood what we have sown in stupidity, unbrotherliness and selfishness.[9]

Though revelations of the Nazi Holocaust were yet to come, Burns ably lists the Axis war atrocities of 1937 to 1942 before he again calls for an instatement of his dearly beholden socialism based on the early "Jesus Movement" (also called the "Apostolic Age" by historians, and dated between the years 30 and 100 AD), which included the direct communal followers of Jesus Christ, that preceded the actual establishment of early Christianity:

Vincent Burns' personally-inscribed Christmas card he included with a signed copy of *Out of These Chains* for his friend, W. D. Sedgwick, in December 1947.

> The human world itself is a chain gang and we are all bound by the fetters of ignorance and slavery, until man learns to heed the wisdom of an ancient philosopher—"to do justly, love mercy and to walk humbly with his God!"
> With victory must come dedication to the new world order of economic emancipation for all men in all countries, based on spiritual understanding of the oneness of mankind, and the words of a Great Teacher: "I am come that all men might have Life and have it more abundantly!"[10]

In the meantime, Robert Burns ran his own Newark consulting firm, the New Jersey Tax Adjustment Association, bought a home at 256 Chestnut Street in the town of Union, and happily married Clara (b. April 14, 1909), a college-educated miner's daughter from Scranton, Pennsylvania, with whom he had two children, Frances (b. late 1938) and Robert, Jr. (b. mid–1940). Two more attempts by Katherine and Vincent to obtain a pardon from the state of Georgia were denied, by Democratic governors Eugene Talmadge and Eurith Rivers, respectively.

When he wrote *Out of These Chains,* Vincent lived in—of all places—Hollywood, California. One last-ditch effort by Georgia to extradite Robert, in January 1941, shocked Vincent to the core but ultimately was denied by New Jersey Democratic governor Charles Edison. Press coverage of the case invariably included a mention of the film.

Out of These Chains winds down with Vincent's reminder that his brother, allowed safe haven in New Jersey, "always will be a fugitive in every one of the other 47 States of the Union." With "THE END" just a little further on, he asks the reader,

> *Will Georgia ever be lucky enough, when he is passing through another part of the United States, to spot him and catch him?*[11]

No, the state of Georgia never did. In 1943, Democratic governor Ellis Arnall, having just taken office in Atlanta, was scheduled to address a meeting of the New York Southern Society in the Big Apple. While in the city, he agreed to meet in his suite at the Savoy Plaza with Robert, who—for the first time—personally requested a pardon.

One more time, he was denied. However, in November 1945, at Arnall's request, Robert traveled to Atlanta, where the governor officially served as his attorney. Though he was *not* given a pardon, his sentence was commuted to time served by the state parole board. Returning to New Jersey, he continued to live in Union with his wife and children until his death from cancer on June 5, 1955. The former fugitive from a chain gang was 63 years old, having primarily enjoyed his remaining decade as a free citizen of the United States. He is buried at the Beverly National Cemetery in Beverly, New Jersey. (Clara, nearly 17 years his junior, lived until February 27, 1993, and now rests beside him.)

The Reverend Vincent Burns, ever the crusader for a socialistic, pacifistic Christian world, served in the U.S. Army, studied at Columbia University, held degrees from Penn State, Harvard and Union Theological Seminary, and wrote a total of 20 published works, including several volumes of poetry. In 1962 he was named Poet Laureate of Maryland by Democratic governor

Robert E. Burns' World War II Draft Registration Card, stamped March 17, 1943. Though he was 50 years old at the time, he has written "49" in the corresponding box.

J. Millard Tawes and held the exalted position until his death in February 1979 at age 86.

Though he occasionally became carried away by his own philosophical and oratorical zeal, requiring an actual escort from a public building or court room, he always remained true to his cause. He was a formidably intelligent and committed human being, but his tendency to resort to litigation, suing both Warner Bros. (for the "offensive" characterization of his counterpart in the film) and his own brother's estate (for royalties owned for his part in writing *I Am a Fugitive from a Georgia Chain Gang!*) tarnished his reputation. However, for the most part, in the vernacular of New Jersey, in his own way, he was a "stand-up guy."

Rather than Hale Hamilton, perhaps Warner Bros. should have cast tough, Broadway-trained Thomas Jackson, who was under contract and had taken down Edward G. Robinson in Mervyn LeRoy's *Little Caesar* the previous year, to play Vincent in the film. (LeRoy also had directed Boris Karloff in *Five Star Final* during 1931, but *Frankenstein*, released later that year, had made the highly experienced Anglo-Indian actor a major star at Universal.) Maybe the Reverend wouldn't have sued the studio if

LeRoy had recognized this one weak link in an otherwise superb chain of players.

Film and Television

Universal was the first of Hollywood's other studios to jump onto the *I Am a Fugitive from a Chain Gang* bandwagon, releasing the particularly unpleasant *Laughter in Hell* on January 12, 1933. Based on a book by Jim Tully, this Edward L. Cahn-directed film of murder and mayhem stars Pat O'Brien as Irish mine worker Barney Slaney, sentenced to life on a Tennessee chain gang after killing his adulterous wife, Marybelle (Merna Kennedy) and her lover, Grover Perkins (Arthur Vinton). Repeatedly wronged by Ed Perkins (Douglass Dumbrille), captain of the chain gang (who just happens to be brother of the murdered lothario), and helping to

Heroes for Sale (1933). Warner Bros. lobby card featuring a superb cast: Richard Barthelmess, Robert Barrat, Loretta Young and Aline MacMahon in a bleak World War I "coming home" drama.

stave off an epidemic during a mass escape, Slaney lams it across the state line with a new squeeze, Lorraine (Gloria Stuart, one of Universal's current darlings, who also costarred in two James Whale features, *The Kiss Before the Mirror* and the horror masterpiece *The Invisible Man*, later that year).

Laughter in Hell provoked controversy by including a scene during which several black men are lynched (off camera, as reaction shots depict the horrific responses of guards and other prisoners). While a reporter for *The Motion Picture Herald* expressed concern that the sequence would anger potential African American viewers, black writer Vere E. Johns, in the weekly publication *New Age*, instead praised producer Carl Laemmle, Jr., for drawing attention to the real-life racist atrocities occurring in many Southern states.

During 1933, Warner Bros. followed *I Am a Fugitive from a Chain Gang* with the equally "socially relevant" *Heroes for Sale* and *Wild Boys of the Road*, both directed by William Wellman. These films were included among others closely coinciding with the inauguration of Franklin Roosevelt, whose

Warner Bros. lobby card: A railway worker (a savage Ward Bond) rapes a homeless vagrant (Ann Hovey) in the stark, unforgettable "social problem" drama *Wild Boys of the Road* (1933).

Tough gangster turned juvenile reform-school head Patsy Gargan (James Cagney) in Warner Bros.' "social problem" classic *The Mayor of Hell* (1933).

only major film-industry supporters were the Brothers Warner.

In between these two films, Archie Mayo (and an uncredited Michael Curtiz) directed *The Mayor of Hell* (1933), the first of Warners' "social problem" projects to deal with juvenile delinquency and the punishment and supposed rehabilitation of youths. By this time, the studio was casting James Cagney in roles far more ambiguous than his irredeemable Tom Powers in *The Public Enemy*, usually as a former criminal persuaded by various social forces to mend his ways. Child star Frankie Darro, who also went on effectively to star in *Wild Boys of the Road*, plays the lead juvenile in *The Mayor of Hell*, much as "Dead End" kid Leo Gorcey does in the Lewis Seiler-directed remake, *Crime School* (1938), in which Humphrey Bogart reprises the Cagney role.

On August 12, 1933, Warner Bros. released its own parody of *I Am a Fugitive from a Chain Gang*, a two-reel (20 minute) musical short, *20,000 Cheers for the Chain Gang*, in which four convicts escape, causing a commission to investigate conditions at the camp. Soon after, major reforms include treating the prisoners to steak dinners and lavish live entertainment every day, prompting the escapees to beg the warden to recapture them. Borrowing half the title from another of its hard-hitting prison films, *20,000 Years in Sing Sing* (1933), directed by Michael Curtiz and starring Spencer Tracy and Bette Davis, the studio also pirated the ending: from Fox's *Up the River* (1930), directed by John Ford and featuring the odd convict trio of Spencer Tracy, Humphrey Bogart (both in their feature-film debuts) and comic wise guy Warren Hymer.

The Emperor Jones (United Artists, 1933). Brutus Jones (Paul Robeson) and his pal (Frank R. Wilson), whom he later kills in a bar fight and is sentenced to the chain gang.

The following month, United Artists released the independent film adaptation of Eugene O'Neill's groundbreaking stage success, *The Emperor Jones* (1933), in which African American Renaissance man Paul Robeson transformed his hit theatrical role for the screen. Director Dudley Murphy, who had worked on two 1929 shorts featuring jazz legends—*Black and Tan* (Duke Ellington) and *St. Louis Blues* (Bessie Smith)—shot the entire film at Paramount's East Coast studio in Astoria, Queens, and in Westchester.

One of the film's major scenes involves chain-gang prisoners dragging their shackles through the dust. The voice of Brutus Jones (Robeson) is heard in the background as he sings "John Henry." Robeson's powerful physique is accentuated as he swings a sledgehammer and segues into another African American work song, "Water Boy."

In a sequence with strong slavery overtones, a white guard orders Brutus to remove a prisoner from a sweat box; and when he falls onto the ground, the sadist brandishes a club, hits Brutus for refusing to wake him, and unmercifully beats the unconscious man. Brutus surveys the area, grabs a shovel and swings it at the guard, as the scene cuts to his fellow prisoners sledging rocks. (The Hays Office ordered this killing of a white authority figure by a black man removed.)

Robeson's seemingly invincible physical prowess is demonstrated further as the shackled Brutus scrambles through the rocks, climbs into a dump truck, and orders a bucket load dropped on him. A siren blasts and guards inspect the truck, but the buried Brutus rides toward the possibility of freedom. With its inclusion of the torturous sweat box, *The Emperor Jones*, along with *Hell's Highway*, features a higher degree of chain-gang brutality than *I Am a Fugitive from a Chain Gang*.

In 1934, Warner Bros. reteamed Paul Muni and Glenda Farrell with Mervyn LeRoy for the entertaining newspaper drama *Hi, Nellie!* As in *I Am a Fugitive from a Chain Gang*, Farrell received second billing, behind Muni, and given the female lead. When Muni's Samuel N. ("Brad") Bradshaw, managing editor of the paper and her former beau, falls on hard times as a journalist, tears up his office and goes off on a drunken binge, Farrell's Gerry Crale uses her tough-talking reasoning, telling him he's "short on guts," to help get him back on his feet. LeRoy also cast Farrell, in a quartet with three other top Warner Bros. female stars, Ann Dvorak, Aline MacMahon and Ruth Donnelly, in the gritty *Heat Lightning* (1934), which prefigures in several ways the studio's later *The Petrified Forest* (1936), costarring Leslie Howard, Bette Davis and Humphrey Bogart (as his first cinematic gangster).

John Ford's *Judge Priest* (1934), the film that solidified Will Rogers' status as one of Hollywood's favorite personalities, includes a character, Bob Gillis (David Landau, the sadistic warden in *I Am a Fugitive from a Chain Gang*), who served time on a chain gang prior to fighting for the Confederacy during the Civil War. In casting Landau as a former Robert Burns–like person, Ford and Fox producer Sol M. Wurtzel (probably unknowingly) made quite an ironic move.

Warner Bros. and director Michael Curtiz attacked another "social problem," with Paul Muni again playing the lead role, in *Black Fury* (1935), from a screenplay by Abem Finkel and Carl Erickson depicting the harsh, unhealthy working conditions faced by coal miners based on an actual labor walkout that occurred in Pennsylvania during 1929. Muni's character, Joe Radek, a Slavic immigrant who is beaten severely by private company police officers (one of whom is played by the ubiquitous Ward Bond) is the cinematic version of a striking coal miner who actually was beaten to death during the Pennsylvania incident. Supported by Karen Morley, William

Hi, Nellie! (1934). Warner Bros. re-teamed Glenda Farrell and Paul Muni with Mervyn LeRoy for this exciting and socially relevant news drama (with Farrell in the tough, expertly portrayed "newspaper *man*" role). (This candid was taken on the set by the photographically experimenting Muni.)

Gargan, Barton MacLane, John Qualen and J. Carrol Naish, Muni became a popular write-in vote for Best Actor at the 1936 Academy Awards ceremony.

Beginning on November 12, 1935, John Ford began shooting his first new project for Darryl F. Zanuck, who recently had merged his own

The Prisoner of Shark Island (20th Century-Fox, 1936). Warner Baxter as John Ford's version of Dr. Samuel A. Mudd, the man who set John Wilkes Booth's leg after the Lincoln assassination, and sentenced to the hellish Dry Tortugas for his "crime." This historical drama proved a perfect "successor" to *I Am a Fugitive from a Chain Gang*, and it was cinematically fortunate to have the great Ford throw his often politically-oriented hat into the ring of this growing subgenre.

production company, 20th Century, with Wurtzel's Fox Film Productions to form 20th Century-Fox. Nunnally Johnson's screenplay, *The Prisoner of Shark Island*, was based on the ordeal of Dr. Samuel A. Mudd (Warner Baxter), who was imprisoned for treating the fleeing John Wilkes Booth, following the public assassination of President Abraham Lincoln at Ford's Theatre in Washington, D.C.

Ford's policy of shooting as few takes as possible (often only *one*), then delegating the examination of the printed rushes to his assistant director and editor, enraged Zanuck, who ended up with very little footage (especially the lack of expected "coverage") he could recreate in his own image. The producer didn't care that a man under studio contract had been directing films, most of them *his* way, for two decades, and recently had won a Best Director Academy Award for *The Informer* (1935), made for RKO-Radio.

The Prisoner of Shark Island became one of Ford's first sound films to provide a well-balanced fusion of dramatic realism with his stunning, expressionist-influenced visual style, and fared well both with audiences and reviewers. Warner Baxter is sincere and believable as Dr. Mudd, whose experiences in being imprisoned, brutalized and punished for his attempts to escape parallel those of James Allen in *I Am a Fugitive from a Chain Gang*, but the version of the character created by Johnson, Zanuck and Ford is somewhat fictionalized. The Lincoln assassination is portrayed fairly accurately (though, for dramatic effect, the President dies in his theater seat, rather than across the street at Peterson's boarding house the following morning), but Mudd's actual sociopolitical views and participation in the affair are bowdlerized.

Dr. Mudd did help fight a yellow fever epidemic at the prison where he was incarcerated on the Dry Tortugas, and eventually was pardoned by President Andrew Johnson, but he was not the wholly innocent, heroic figure championed by the film. Warner Baxter's loving family man who develops a touching friendship with Buckingham "Buck" Milford (Ernest Whitman), one of his former slaves, is often a fine testament to Ford's egalitarian values, but a far cry from the historical Mudd, who had met John Wilkes Booth prior to the assassination and believed that slavery was "divinely ordained."

At that point in his career, Ford's positive depiction of blacks reached a new high in *The Prisoner of the Shark Island*, with the expected contemporary stereotypes well-balanced by the major role African Americans play in the narrative. In a film featuring many fine actors, Ernest Whitman (in his second screen role) gives a standout performance, both dramatic and comic.

Frank McGlynn, Sr., who had played the Great Emancipator in John Drinkwater's play *Abraham Lincoln* (1918), several short silent films, and Fox's Shirley Temple vehicle *The Littlest Rebel* (1935), was an inspired choice. After *The Prisoner of Shark Island*, he would portray the 16th President in seven more films, including Republic's *Hearts in Bondage* (1936), the only feature directed by Lew Ayres, and Paramount's *The Plainsman* (1936), directed by Cecil B. DeMille.

Under contract to Warner Bros. from 1936 to 1940, "horror" specialist Boris Karloff starred in one of the most unusual "social problem" films ever concocted by the studio. Blending elements of the innocent man being convicted for a felonious crime with tenets of the then-popular horror genre, producer Louis F. Edelman, with Michael Curtiz on board as director, worked with story specialists Ewart Adamson and Joseph Fields in devising the story of the downtrodden John Elman (Karloff), a man just released from prison, who is framed by racketeers for the murder of Judge Shaw (Joseph King).

Karloff gives in one his finest, most understated, moving performances in this film, in which a scientist, Dr. Beaumont (Edmund Gwenn), miraculously brings him back to life after he is executed in the electric chair. Blending material from *I Am a Fugitive from a Chain Gang* with the innovative, *Frankenstein*-influenced horror screenplay by Ewart Adamson, Peter Milne, Robert Hardy Andrews and Lillie Hayward, *The Walking Dead* is truly a unique and thoughtful entry (the revived Elman seeks revenge against those who framed him, but is driven by a "Higher Power") in the Warner Bros. "social commentary" subgenre.

"They're Fugitives from a ROAD GANG ... and They'll Never Go Back Alive!" announced the Warner Bros. publicity machine, this time drawing attention to a somewhat different type of Southern prison camp, in *Road Gang* (1936), an exciting B-film featuring a notable cast including Donald Woods, Kay Linaker, Henry O'Neill, Charles Middleton, William B. Davidson and Harry Cording. Produced by Brian Foy's unit, the film was written by Dalton Trumbo, who didn't hesitate devoting his script to draw attention to blatant Southern political corruption. In this semi-remake of *I Am a Fugitive from a Chain Gang*, Warner Bros. chose to subject to the torture of a prison farm a journalist (Woods) who suffers due to the hard-hitting exposés he has written about the subject.

The "framed man in prison" subgenre again was blended with horror by master of the macabre Tod Browning for MGM's *The Devil Doll* (1936), in which Lionel Barrymore plays Paul Lavond, a very much Lon Chaney, Sr.–like character (complete with several major old-lady drag scenes), who escapes from Devil's Island to seek revenge upon corrupt colleagues who sent him to the slammer on trumped-up charges. Fleeing with him is Marcel (Henry B. Walthall), a scientific genius, who has developed a way to shrink humans to doll size.

Well done by director of photography Leonard Smith, working with talented special effects and set-design artists, the miniature sequences are expertly juxtaposed with footage using standard-size actors, to depict Lavond's revengeful activities. Unlike *The Walking Dead*, in which the protagonist is guided by a "higher power," thus achieving redemption, here the main character is dead set on vengeance, giving him less sympathetic motives. Barrymore is at his best in the film, perhaps Browning's most impressive sound feature. Another treat is the obsessive performance of the great Henry B. Walthall, who began his prolific film career in 1908, acting with D. W. Griffith (including the starring role in *The Birth of a Nation* [1915]), and making only one more appearance (in Warner Bros.' *China Clipper* [1936]) following *The Devil-Doll*, before passing away, aged only 58, of influenza on June 17, 1936.

Released by RKO Radio in January 1937, Edward Small's morbidly titled *We Who Are About to Die* offers yet another variation on the good man framed by gangsters motif while also, like so many Warner Bros. films, addressing the issue of capital punishment. In New Mexico, John Thompson (John Beal) is an enterprising aircraft designer whose ideas are too experimental for his conservative employer. He quits his job but when returning the next day to collect his paycheck, his car and work lab clothes are commandeered by a criminal, whose gang (led by a mock-Italian J. Carrol Naish and that perpetual wise guy, Russell Hopton) heist the payroll, gun down a guard and accidentally run over the young son (Sonny Bupp) of another employee. (This element is particularly shocking in a 1930s film.)

The local legal system (outwardly represented by a mob mentality in the streets), led by District Attorney Knight (Russell Hicks) and police detective Steven Mathews (Preston Foster), is as quick to convict Thompson and send him to death row as the people were to condemn him. Supported only by his faithful girlfriend, Connie Stewart (Ann Dvorak), Thompson ultimately is freed (literally at the last second) by a second, unbiased investigation by Mathews and the actions of some of his fellow death-row inmates. Though this film ends happily for the framed man, the somber mood of *I Am a Fugitive from a Chain Gang* hangs over much of it.

After *The Petrified Forest* became a major hit in 1936, Jack Warner didn't quite know what to do with Humphrey Bogart, who so effectively had reprised his stage role of gangster Duke Mantee in the Archie Mayo–directed film. Two months before *The Petrified Forest* hit theaters, Bogart had signed a 20-page agreement that wasn't lavish by any means, a sign that Warner wanted to see what his new star could do.

Edward G. Robinson arrived for work on March 16, 1936, playing Johnny Blake, a cop who apparently loses his badge, but stays on the heels of numbers racketeers, in *Bullets or Ballots*, meeting his end from a bullet fired by Bogart's Nick "Bugs" Fenner. The studio was unsure of Bogart's appeal, but the Brian Foy B-unit kept him working constantly, cranking out a programmer every six weeks. Finally Bogart was cast in another of Warners' "social problem" screenplays, *Black Legion* (1937), a completely topical, straightforward look at American fascism, in the form of Detroit-based "night riders" modeled on the Ku Klux Klan who had been terrorizing immigrants in the Midwest.

The script by Abem Finkel and William Wister Haines, based on a story by Robert Lord, dramatizes an actual kidnapping and murder case that had landed the Black Legion in the headlines and the slammer. Reunited with *Petrified Forest* director Archie Mayo, Bogart received top billing as Frank Taylor, a decent working man who turns to a "100-percent American" organization after losing a promotion to Joe Dombrowski (Henry Brandon), an immigrant with less time at the factory. Taylor is told that foreigners are "openly plotting to overthrow our government," and that the Legion is dedicated to keeping the country "free, white, and 100-percent American!" Following a succession of tragic incidents, Taylor confesses in the courtroom, identifying every Black Legion member. All are convicted of murder and sentenced to life in the Big House.

Interestingly, Warner Bros. included a disclaimer at the beginning of *Black Legion*, stating that none of the characters or events had been based on reality. Regardless of this claim, it was the studio's most compelling depiction of a serious social problem since *I Am a Fugitive from a Chain Gang* and *Wild Boys of the Road*. Even without Darryl Zanuck on board, Warners proved that it was still the only Hollywood studio bold enough to expose such unsavory goings-on existing under the "respectable" surface of WASP culture in the United States.

Veteran screenwriter John Bright (*The Public Enemy, Three on a Match*) returned for Warner Bros.' *San Quentin* (1937), collaborating with Robert Tasker, a former inmate at the prison, on a script inspired by recent reform efforts aimed at the corruption and brutality of California's prison system. Director Lloyd Bacon, with his costars Pat O'Brien (as Warden Stephen Jameson) and Bogart (as inmate Joe "Red" Kennedy), were allowed to shoot on location inside the prison, including exteriors and long shots of the yard and cell blocks, under a provision that the faces of actual inmates would not be visible. Bacon, art director Esdras Hartley and cinematographer Sid Hickox did a remarkable job of integrating these shots with their backlot and studio recreations of the Joint.

"Red" Kennedy does escape from a road gang in one scene, but during his flight, is shot, and painfully making his way back to the prison, collapses at the gate, muttering, "Tell Jameson I come back. Tell the cons to play ball with him. He's a swell…" before taking his final dive.

Warner Bros., avoiding any offense to the actual San Quentin, was careful to depict the abuse at the prison, not as a result of the system, but as the work of one unethical individual, and only a lowly lieutenant to boot.

Solitary confinement is never shown, nor is any actual punishment. This choice may also have been budgetary, since costs were held down by using only a few primary sets. Appearing as a convict in one scene is Olympic and football legend Jim Thorpe, who played small parts in 70 films from 1931 to 1950, including *King Kong* (1933), *The Last Days of Pompeii* (1935), Raoul Walsh's *White Heat* (1949), and John Ford's *Wagon Master* (1950), in his final screen performance, as one of the director's beloved Navahos.

Of the three epic biopics Paul Muni starred in for Warner Bros., *The Story of Louis Pasteur* (1936), *The Life of Emile Zola* (1937) and *Juarez* (1939), the second of these also qualifies as a "social problem" film, since much of the film focuses on the famous "Dreyfus Case," during which Zola, the great writer and social crusader, serves as counsel for the French Army Captain Alfred Dreyfus (Joseph Schildkraut), who (being Jewish) quickly has been court-martialed as a traitor and sentenced to Devil's Island. When the new chief of intelligence, Colonel Picquart (Henry O'Neill), discovers proof that the real spy is Walsin-Esterhazy (Robert Barrat), he is ordered to cover up the evidence to avoid any embarrassment to the military.

Years pass and Zola's involvement in attempting to aid Dreyfus brings him much disdain and misery, and he eventually flees to England to continue fighting for the cause. Eventually a new administration takes the reins in France, and Zola is able to exonerate Dreyfus but accidentally dies of carbon monoxide poisoning (from a heating stove) on the evening before a public ceremony is held.

Of all Muni's biopic performances, his bravura turn as Zola may be his finest. Although he won the Best Actor Academy Award for playing the titular role in the handsomely mounted *The Story of Louis Pasteur*, his courtroom defense of Dreyfus in *The Life of Emile Zola* is mesmerizing, and, although it is a more theatrical performance, it's difficult to believe the same actor is portraying the brutalized, working-class James Allen in *I Am a Fugitive from a Chain Gang*. Appearing in a small role is Muni's niece, Dolores Wiesenfreund, born in 1918 in Ottawa, Canada. *The Life of Emile Zola* marked her only screen appearance.

Muni again was nominated for the Best Actor Academy Award for *The Life if Emile Zola*, as were William Dieterle (Best Director), Anton Grot (Best Art Direction), Russ Saunders (Best Assistant Director) and three others. Five nominees won Oscars in three categories for the film: Heinz Herald, Geza Herczeg and Norman Reilly Raine (Best Screenplay), producer Henry Blanke (Best Picture) and Joseph Schildkraut (Best Supporting Actor).

The Life of Emile Zola was a commercial and critical success in 1937 but, in later years, was criticized for failing to stress the anti–Semitism inherent in the persecution of Dreyfus, and the screenplay's failure ever to mention the word "Jew," an aspect some blamed directly on Jack Warner, a Jew himself, who was accused of giving in to pressure from officials at the Production Code Administration who didn't want to antagonize the Nazis. If this was true, Warner would more than make up for it the next year by producing a no-nonsense film aimed directly at the German fascists.

Mervyn LeRoy again sat in the Warner Bros. "social problem" director's chair for *They Won't Forget* (1937), which he also coproduced with Jack Warner. Adapted by Robert Rosson and Aben Kandel from *Death in the Deep South*, a novel by Ward Greene, a fictionalized account of the actual 1913 Atlanta strangulation murder of 13-year-old Mary Phagan and consequent lynching of Leo Frank, a Jew found innocent following subsequent investigations of the case. Claude Rains stars as District Attorney Andrew J. Griffin (he also plays a man named Griffin in his film debut, James Whale's *The Invisible Man* [1933]), a man whose political ambitions drive him to select a scapegoat, Professor Robert Perry Hale (Edward Norris), to take the fall for the Confederate Memorial Day murder of Mary Clay (Lana Turner in her film debut). The screenplay, direction and action brilliantly coalesce to show how hatred and prejudice is created through repeated lies, rhetoric stressing sectional differences, and sheer preying upon the human embracing of a mob mentality.

After Hale is found guilty and condemned to death, his sentence is commuted to life in prison by Governor Thomas Mountford (Paul Everton). However, the townspeople, saturated by the bigotry encouraged by Griffin, satiate their vigilante vengeance by lynching Hale. The film ends with Griffin's apparent apathy over the entire affair.

Poverty Row was responsible for creating a woman's version of the convict escape film, Monogram's *Female Fugitive* (1938), directed by the prolific William Nigh and starring Evelyn Venable in the titular role. Married to the boss of a truck-jacking gang (Craig Reynolds), she is framed for being at the wheel of a getaway car that struck and killed a policeman during the commission of a crime. She escapes, posing as cook for an artist (Reed Hadley) until her husband and a cop recognize her photo on the cover of a magazine.

Having shared the screen with the titular kids of Samuel Goldwyn's hit *Dead End* (1937), Humphrey Bogart was reunited with them (in their Warner Bros. debut) for *Crime School* (1938), a Production Code-friendly remake of *The Mayor of Hell* directed by Lewis Seiler. The boys (Billy Halop,

6. The Historic Influence of the Film

Bobby Jordan, Huntz Hall, Leo Gorcey, Bernard Punsly and Gabriel Dell) are first seen on the streets of the East Side, trying to work some less than honest angles as they are harassed by Mrs. Hawkins (Sibyl Harris) and Officer Hogan (Edward Gargan). At Junkie's Pawn Shop, the gang tries to unload some hot rubbish. Offered only $5 for "the *woiks*," they protest until Spike (Gorcey) hits the proprietor upside the head with a candle stick. When he doesn't move, they all lam out of the joint, but Spike is immediately pinched by the cops.

"If you want to do something for them," the sister of Frankie (Halop), Sue (Gale Page), asks Judge Clinton (Charles Trowbridge), "why don't you clean up the slums?" Replying that many upstanding individuals have emerged from the East Side, Clinton (who cannot get the guilty boy to confess) sentences them all to two years in reform school. Making his first appearance during the hearing, Mark Braden (Bogart) is revealed as the director of a local settlement house.

Late that evening, the boys reach the "school," where their request for supper is refused. Frankie (Halop) is provoked into brawling with another inmate, then chased by guards and, after being caught on a sharp barbed-wire fence, whipped with a cat o' nine tails by the sadistic Superintendent Morgan (Cy Kendall, a specialist at portraying brutal, fascistic authority figures). The next day, Braden, now the Deputy Commissioner, hired to investigate rumors of terrible conditions at the school, is met by Morgan, who defends his beliefs in "law and order" and "patriotism."

In the infirmary, Braden discovers that Frankie's whip cuts have not been treated by the inebriated doctor (Spencer Charters). Braden then fires the guards—ex-cons, disgraced cops and army deserters—and dismisses the doc, whose license had been revoked six months earlier. "This is a school, not a prison," Braden announces. Making a clean sweep, he also gives Morgan the boot. Though Cooper (Weldon Heyburn), the head guard, tells Braden, "I'm with you right from the start," he makes a secret pact with Morgan to bring down the new deputy.

Cooper blackmails Spike, telling Frankie that Braden is making time with his sister in exchange for their decent treatment. Forcing the gang to accompany him, Frankie, armed by Spike, drives into the city to shoot Braden at Sue's apartment. (This sequence is a near-rehash of the climactic scene in *San Quentin*, with Bogart on the other end of the rod this time.) Discovering the set-up, Frankie tries to strangle Spike, who then tells Braden about Cooper's plot to bring the vicious Morgan back to power.

Back at the school, Cooper tries to grab the cooked books from the desk, but Braden arrives to beat him to a pulp. (As Bogie assumes his tough-guy persona, the violence is relegated solely to off-camera sound effects.) "That's just Mr. Braden going over the books with Mr. Cooper," one of the cops explains.

In this 1938 film, Bogart played a role originally created by James Cagney five years earlier. Unlike Cagney's interpretation, however, Bogie's version is not a former criminal, but a social worker with a sense of humor. Unlike *The Mayor of Hell*, *Crime School* is leavened by a lighter tone, and the ending requires a less violent resolution. Back in Judge Clinton's chambers, all the boys, now dressed in nice new suits, are paroled, and Braden (in typical Hollywood fashion) ducks out with Sue, his future wife.

Directed by Arthur Lubin, the exciting B-film drama *Prison Break* had three working titles ("State Prison," "Prison Walls" and "Walls of San Quentin") prior to its release on July 15, 1938. Initially planned as the first of four Universal projects to costar *I Am a Fugitive from a Chain Gang*'s

Prison Break (Universal, 1938). Glenda Farrell costars with Ward Bond and Barton MacLane in this "penal reform" picture.

Glenda Farrell with Barton MacLane (who worked together at Warner Bros.), *Prison Break* was the only film actually produced.

Ward Bond's career criminal, "Big Red" Kincaid, provides the only real physical presence in *Prison Break*, both with his athletic build and menacing, understated performance. Kincaid is a stone killer who looms as a legend in the minds of all the yard birds, except for Joaquin Shannon (MacLane), a Portuguese-Irish tuna fisherman, sent to the Big House after being framed for a manslaughter rap by the bigoted father (Victor Kilian) of his fiancée, Jean Fenderson (Farrell).

Farrell and MacLane proved their collective acting prowess by giving good performances while saddled with the clumsy dialogue of screenwriter Dorothy Reid, who adapted Norton S. Parker's story "Walls of San Quentin." However, in the best tradition of *I Am a Fugitive from a Chain Gang*, she was able (without becoming preachy) to work in a few swipes at antiquated criminal laws.

Innocent, abused prison escapee Dr. Charles Gaudet (Boris Karloff, whose ability to express pain with his eyes was nearly cinematically peerless) on his way to the guillotine in Warner Bros.' controversial *Devil's Island* (1939).

During his four-year contract with Warner Bros., Boris Karloff again got into the "social problem" act (something dear to the actor's own heart) while making *Devil's Island*, directed by William Clemens, and influenced by the early scenes in the studio's own pirate adventure classic *Captain Blood* (1935), which introduced Errol Flynn to U.S. audiences. In June 1938, Karloff reported to Warners to star in the film, inspired by the French government's closing of the notorious penal colony the previous year.

Originally selecting George Raft (who sabotaged his career by turning down lead roles in nearly every film between 1938 and 1942, including *High Sierra*, *The Maltese Falcon* and *Casablanca*, which all went to Bogart, catapulting him to stardom) to play Dr. Charles Gaudet, a physician incarcerated and severely abused after treating a political revolutionary, producer Brian Foy instead turned to Karloff when the decline of the horror genre killed off the proposed thriller "Witches' Sabbath." Shot quickly by Clemens, the film was ready for release in September, but was delayed by a French propaganda campaign. By the time the embassy gave Warner Bros. the word to release the film in January 1939, *Devil's Island*, in which Gaudet and a few companions make a daring escape from the hellish prison colony, the film had languished on a studio shelf for four months.

Warner Bros.' Michael Curtiz-directed masterpiece *Angels with Dirty Faces* (1938), starring James Cagney in one of his greatest performances, as gangster William "Rocky" Sullivan, includes a socially relevant element in its depiction of the "Dead End" Kids' initial hero worship that turns to disbelief after the once-invincible criminal turns "yellow" while walking the last mile to the electric chair. (Curtiz already had tackled the controversial and morbid subject of capital punishment, especially of the electrocution variety, in *The Walking Dead*, with Karloff going to the chair.) When commenting on his powerful, unforgettable performance, Cagney said,

> I think in looking at the film it is virtually impossible to say which course Rocky took—which is just the way I wanted it. I played it with deliberate ambiguity so that the spectator can take his choice. It seems to me it works out fine in either case. You have to decide.[12]

For his performance as the indefinable "Rocky" Sullivan, Cagney won the New York Critics Best Actor Award, and was nominated for an Oscar, but lost to a Catholic Priest characterization (and not that of Pat O'Brien in *Angels with Dirty Faces*): Spencer Tracy as Father Flanagan, in MGM's sentimental favorite, *Boys Town* (1938). *Angels with Dirty Faces* is arguably the best film Warner Bros. had released since enforcement of the Production Code began four years earlier.

Perhaps Warner Bros.' most obvious, and dangerous, "social problem"

James Cagney, in one of his finest performances, as Rocky Sullivan in Warner Bros.' *Angels with Dirty Faces* **(1938), director Michael Curtiz's masterpiece dealing with the "social problems" of juvenile delinquency and capital punishment.**

film began as an adaptation of Leon Torrou's book *The Nazi Spy Conspiracy in America*. The earlier entries in this subgenre were all confined to conditions in the United States, but this film would tackle world politics head on, and Jack Warner at first had been lukewarm about confronting the Third Reich directly. However, the recent murder of a Jewish studio representative in Germany spurred him to produce a major film exposing the German-American Bund and its connections to Berlin.

Like Paul Muni, Edward G. Robinson was using his chameleonic acting abilities to graduate to big-budget biopics and, guaranteed the titular role in the upcoming *Dr. Ehrlich's Magic Bullet*, a "prestige picture" to be directed by William Dieterle, he also agreed to star in *Confessions of a Nazi Spy* (1939), the first film to take a direct hit at Adolf Hitler's fascist regime of hate.

There were extensive legal problems (including a $500,000 lawsuit filed by the Bund) that needed to be solved before the Nazi project could reach its pre-production stage. Fortunately for Jack Warner, Edward G.

Robinson signed a new, three-year contract for two films per year (at $85,000 each). For his Warner Bros. projects, he was to consider three scripts each May and September, giving him the power to select the principal male role in each, a clause assuring his stardom, rather than reducing him to the rank of character actor.

With his role in *Dr. Ehrlich's Magic Bullet* confirmed, Robinson agreed to star in *Brother Orchid*, a seriocomic gangster picture also to feature Humphrey Bogart, at a later date, and the temporarily titled "Storm Over America," which would be released as *Confessions of a Nazi Spy*. During his off-work hours, Robinson became more involved with the Anti-Nazi League, an organization intending to wage a personal appearance and radio campaign to persuade President Roosevelt to get tough with Hitler.

Robinson, the former gangster, began playing an FBI agent on the *Confessions of a Nazi Spy* set on February 13, 1939, and immediately received threatening phone calls at his home. Jack Warner and his wife, Ann, also heard death threats, so the mogul quickly hired bodyguards to accompany him to and from the studio. German officials made protests to the U.S. State Department, but Warner stood his ground, refusing to be intimidated by the Third Reich's threats to make its own film exposing "American corruption."

Hal Wallis and director Anatole Litvak were dedicated to making *Confessions of a Nazi Spy* a powerful work, and allowed Robinson to change dialogue passages in Milton Krims and John Wexley's screenplay, which brings his character, Edward Renard, into the action at mid-point. "Eddie" had completed the film by March, when Wallis asked if he would approve a plan to pitch the film as a pseudo-documentary, featuring no "star billing" in the film credits nor advertising campaign. Though his contract insured the billing, Robinson told him to forgo such ego-massaging.

The plot was based on an actual case involving the German-American Bund, a fascist organization popular in Wisconsin and on Long Island (but no competition for that native group, the KKK, which had a general hold on hate). At one point, Wexley saw Texas congressman Martin Dies, the first chairman of the Special Committee Investing Un-American Activities, leaving Jack Warner's office, having just warned the mogul not to malign a "friendly country" like Germany. Apparently the notorious witch-hunter also had requested that the script place some equally feared "Commies" alongside the Nazis, but Wexley characteristically refused.

The first anti–Nazi propaganda feature produced in the United States (James Whale's *The Road Back* [1937], an epic sequel to *All Quiet on the Western Front*, had been butchered by Universal after threats from Third

Reich officials; and Charles Chaplin's daring *and* funny *The Great Dictator* [1940] was yet to be released), *Confessions of a Nazi Spy* premiered on April 21, 1939, when policeman and plainclothes detectives were stationed throughout the theater.

Jack Warner and Hal Wallis demonstrated sheer guts in giving the green light to the project, directly intended to alert U.S. citizens to the evils of fascism on a worldwide level. The power of the film was proved when the Third Reich banned it, followed by a denunciation from the German ambassador in Washington. Despite Hitler's own threat to "execute" the cast and crew, the film did very well at the box office and with the critics, who praised its frank, hard-hitting approach. Not even the frivolous Bund lawsuit could stop the film, especially after its leader, Fritz Kuhn, was arrested for embezzling the organization's funds.

Warner Bros. had "inaugurated" the "social problem" film with *I Am a Fugitive from a Chain Gang*. Since its bringing this cinematic version of one *individual's* mistreatment by a bigoted society in 1932, *Confessions of a Nazi Spy* became the next most effective Warners film to depict a societal

Blackmail (MGM, 1939). Ruth Hussey and Edward G. Robinson in a suspenseful semi-remake of *I Am a Fugitive from a Chain Gang*.

wrong, and this time on a *grand scale* that eventually would escalate to a level of sheer horror and cruelty the modern world had never seen.

The middle third of MGM's *Blackmail* (1939), directed by H. C. Potter, is a virtual remake of *I Am a Fugitive from a Chain Gang* (with some screenplay material supplied by the earlier film's treatment writer Brown Holmes), starring Edward G. Robinson (on loan-out from Warner Bros.) as John Ingram, Oklahoma oil-field firefighter and unfortunate victim of wily extortionist William Ramey (Gene Lockhart, in one of his most obsequious performances), who railroads him back to a chain gang from which he had escaped nine years earlier. A truly chameleonic actor during his day, Robinson superbly depicts Ingram's agony while toiling in the blazing sun, suffering the claustrophobia of the prison wagon and while scampering through the woods with the bloodhounds nipping at his heels. Though episodic and uneven, *Blackmail*, like most of the MGM films directed by Potter during this period, is entertaining and very well acted.

Paramount's *Sullivan's Travels* (1941), written and directed by Preston Sturges, features Joel McCrea as the ridiculously named John L. Sullivan, a Hollywood director of purely escapist fare, who shocks his studio boss (Robert Warwick) by deciding to hit the road, disguised as a downtrodden hobo, to examine personally the conditions of "real life." Universally considered a comic masterwork, this film cleverly examines the very nature of the "social problem" film *supposedly* pioneered by Warner Bros.

(Did the Warner brothers and Darryl Zanuck make pictures like *I Am a Fugitive from a Chain Gang*, *Heroes for Sale* and *Wild Boys of the Road* as social crusaders or, more simply, because the themes were topical: "ripped from the headlines" in Zanuck's own words? The answer arguably involves a blend of both.)

After his truly terrible experiences during his eye-opening journey, which include incarceration in a labor camp, John L. Sullivan (who has been deemed dead by the populace) decides that making a "socially relevant" film adaption of the (fictitious) novel *O Brother, Where Art Thou?* would only depress people further. In the end, he returns to the "reel" world of Tinsel Town to direct truly laugh-inducing, joyful comedies.

Mervyn LeRoy, at his personal request, directed Glenda Farrell one more time, persuading her to work into her busy stage career a brief but unforgettable performance in MGM's much-praised *Johnny Eager* (1942). A commanding gangster drama which tests the nature of true friendship, the film costars Robert Taylor, Lana Turner and Van Heflin, in an electric performance that (very rightfully) earned him a Best Supporting Academy Award.

6. The Historic Influence of the Film

Johnny Eager (MGM, 1942). Mervyn LeRoy *insisted* on using Glenda Farrell one more time in this compelling, well-acted (particularly by an electric, Oscar-winning Van Heflin) gangster drama (here seen with Henry O'Neill in this on-set candid).

The British cinema contributed a suspenseful film noir, *They Made Me a Fugitive* (1947), also known as *I Became a Criminal*, directed by Alberto Cavalcanti, featuring Trevor Howard as "Clem," a jaded former RAF flyer, framed as the driver of a getaway car that strikes and kills a policeman. After escaping from prison, he makes his way to London, where he seeks revenge against those who set him up. Produced by Alliance Films in England, the film was released in the United States by Warner Bros. on March 6, 1948.

B-film workhorse Lew Landers made *Chain Gang* (1950) for Columbia, where he was a prolific house director for a decade, churning out mysteries, thrillers, horror films and comedies, always in short order. This 70-minute programmer, for which Columbia astutely recruited *I Am a Fugitive from a Chain Gang* screenwriter Howard J. Green, depicts investigative journalist Cliff Roberts (Douglas Kennedy) infiltrating a chain-gang camp armed with a cigarette containing a small camera, with which he documents

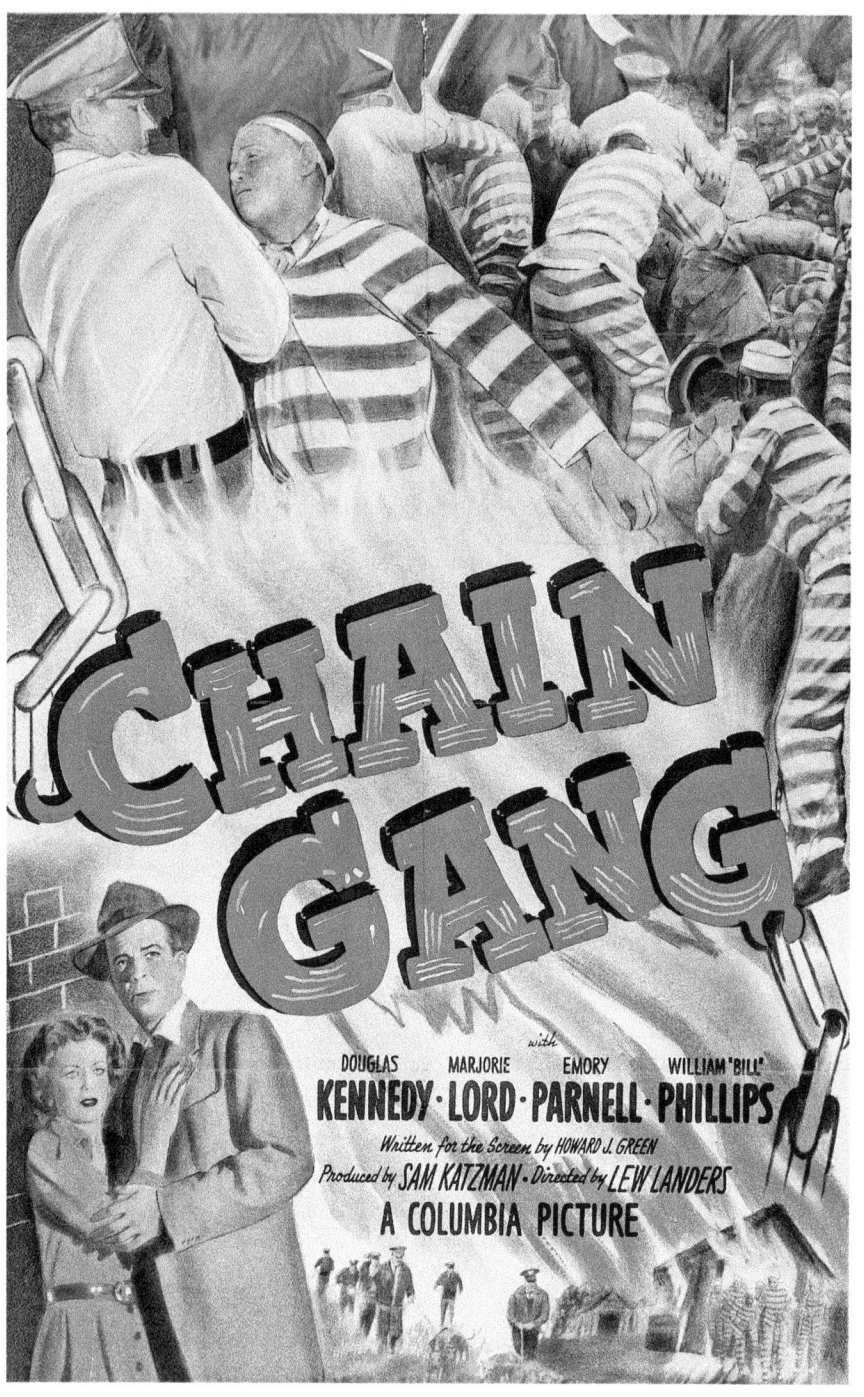

Chain Gang (Columbia, 1950). Douglas Kennedy and Marjorie Lord star in this "B" crime thriller directed by the prolific Lew Landers.

the brutality occurring under the iron fist of Duncan (Emory Parnell), sadistic Captain of the Guard. Following his escape, Roberts exposes the atrocious conditions in an expose resulting in sweeping reforms.

James Stewart stars as moonshiner-turned-M1 rifle inventor David Marshall Williams in MGM's fact-based *Carbine Williams* (1952), directed by Richard Thorpe. Sentenced to 30 years' hard labor for the death of a deputy sheriff that occurred during a raid on his hooch-distilling operation in 1921, the real-life Williams, while working in a prison tool shop, built the carbine gas system, was released in 1929 and went to work for Winchester Firearms, where he helped develop the M1 used by U.S. troops during World War II.

The Caledonia State Prison Farm (in North Carolina) in which Williams was held did involve a chain gang, and James Stewart's "Marsh" begins his sentence on such a crew before being transferred to a prison farm where warden Captain H. T. Peeples (Wendell Corey) notices his gifts, which are put to good use in the shop. The Williams character's ability to exhibit redeeming qualities and "make good" parallels the qualities of Robert E. Burns (and the cinematic James Allen). With the well-cast Stewart in the lead, *Carbine Williams* was a solid hit throughout North America, earning a $500,000 profit for MGM producer Armand Deutsch.

Commander Films Corporation, a production company established by producer John C. Champion, completed only one picture, *Hellgate*, filmed from March 25 to mid–April 1952, partially in Los Angeles' Bronson Canyon. This low-budget affair, distributed by Lippert Pictures, was co-written by Champion and Charles Marquis Warren, who also directed.

Based loosely on Ford's *The Prisoner of Shark Island*, *Hellgate*, set in 1867 Kansas, stars Sterling Hayden as Gilman Hanley, a veterinarian and ex-Confederate soldier, who treats a stranger proving to be the notorious guerrilla leader Verne Brechene, who has been looting and burning homes, killing innocent women and children in the process. Wrongly convicted of aiding and abetting the gang, Hanley is sentenced to Hellgate Prison, a subterranean series of cells located in the New Mexican desert, run by Lieutenant Vorhees (Ward Bond, at his quietly sly and sarcastic best), whose own wife and child were roasted by guerrillas.

Vorhees is assisted by even more sadistic guards (including the ever-unpleasant Robert Wilkie as a taunting sergeant) and ferocious members of a Pima tribe, who track down escapees in the surrounding desert, earning $25 for a living captive and $50 for a dead one. Deprived of even basic necessities, Hanley endures a tortuous session in the "oven," a metal box sunk into the burning sands, before heroically making his way across the

Hellgate (Lippert Pictures, 1952). Sterling Hayden and Ward Bond in this Western prison camp film influenced by *I Am a Fugitive from a Chain Gang* and John Ford's *The Prisoner of Shark Island*.

desert to bring a load of water to the typhus-wracked prison. Although a new prisoner who could have cleared Hanley dies before Vorhees can speak with him, the Lieutenant, finally overcoming his hatred, frees him.

This solid variation on *I Am a Fugitive from a Chain Gang* and *The Prisoner of Shark Island* has other John Ford connections, including actors James Arness and Mickey Simpson in supporting roles, and the contributions of Andrew V. McLaglen (son of Ford leading man and character favorite Victor McLaglen) as assistant director.

In 1956, *I Am a Fugitive from a Chain Gang* was reissued to theaters for the first and only time before it began to be shown on television. Though Warner Bros. officially had re-released both *Little Caesar* and *The Public Enemy* in 1954, *I Am a Fugitive from a Chain Gang* fell to this lesser independent distributor, who also ran theatrical prints of the Pat O' Brien-Humphrey Bogart B-feature *San Quentin* (1937) during 1956.

Using the book *Captain Dreyfus: The Story of a Mass Hysteria* by Nicholas Halasz as his source material, Gore Vidal wrote the screenplay

6. The Historic Influence of the Film

The Defiant Ones (United Artists, 1958). Tony Curtis and Sidney Poitier are bigoted escaped convicts chained together in Stanley Kramer's "Civil Rights-era message film."

for *I Accuse!* (1958), director Jose Ferrer's version of the Dreyfus Case, featuring an all-star European supporting cast including Anton Walbrook, Viveca Lindfors, Leo Genn, Emlyn Williams, Donald Wolfit and Herbert Lom. Placing less emphasis on Emile Zola (Williams) than the 1937 Warner Bros. classic, Ferrer and Vidal focus more explicitly on Dreyfus himself, presenting a very powerful and convincing version of the flagrant injustices committed against the loyal soldier until his ultimate exoneration and release from imprisonment on Devil's Island.

Perhaps the king of the 1950s and 1960s "message film," producer-director Stanley Kramer contributed a Civil Rights-era convict classic, *The Defiant Ones* (1958), costarring Tony Curtis and Sidney Poitier as mutually bigoted white and black prisoners shackled together who, after escaping from a wrecked truck, must develop tolerance in order to survive. Gradually they wake up to life's realities and develop a true friendship. The supporting cast, including Theodore Bikel, Charles McGraw, Lon Chaney, Jr. (in one of his best performances), King Donovan and Lawrence Dobkin, is as impressive as the star duo.

Though the characters don't actually work on a chain gang, their being shackled together (a problem they eventually must eliminate), the prolonged escape and the overt "social problem" elements more than qualify *The Defiant Ones* as a cinematic descendant of *I Am a Fugitive from a Chain Gang*. Nominated for ten Academy Awards, the film won two, for Best Story and Best Screenplay. Continuing on his issue-related filmmaking path, Kramer immediately followed *The Defiant Ones*, as producer and director, with *On the Beach* (1959), *Judgment at Nuremburg* (1960) and *Inherit the Wind* (1961). In 1967, he also wore both hats for *Guess Who's Coming to Dinner*, again directing Sidney Poitier.

On October 20, 1958, the *Westinghouse Desilu Playhouse* television anthology program broadcast "The Case for Dr. Mudd," a one-hour dramatization of the "Shark Island" story written by Don Brinkley and Joseph Landon, and directed by Allen H. Miner. Cast in the titular role, Lew Ayres was supported by Donald Harron (as John Wilkes Booth), Jack Weston and Henry Brandon. Hosted by Desi Arnaz, the show was aired on the CBS network.

The Western became one of the most popular genres on television from the late 1950s throughout the 1960s, with early, well written, directed and acted efforts such as *Gunsmoke* (1955–1975), starring James Arness, *Wagon Train* (1957–1965), originally starring Ward Bond, *Have Gun, Will Travel* (1957–1963), featuring Richard Boone, and *Bonanza* (1959–1973), headed by Lorne Greene, spawning dozens of lesser imitations that endlessly recycled the same few stories. Some of these series, particularly *Gunsmoke*, which relied on repeating spare variations on a small handful of plots, and whose acting became either tedious (Milburn Stone's "Doc") over the top (in the case of Ken Curtis), arguably overstayed their welcome.

Nearly every show included an episode in which one of the lead characters is kidnapped and forced to work in a mining operation, usually a cave, sometimes on a guarded work gang, but often chained, as well. Like Clint Eastwood in *Rawhide* (1959–1965), a television Western unfortunately marred by the one-note, grimaced acting of series lead Eric Fleming, Steve McQueen became a star in the top-flight series *Wanted: Dead or Alive* (1958–1961). In the December 12, 1959, episode, "Chain Gang," McQueen's Josh Randall, captured by a corrupt deputy (Chris Alcaide), is forced to join a chain gang overseen by Sheriff Blore (James Burke), in cahoots with mine owner George Winters (Ted de Corsia), who adds time to a prisoner's sentence every time he breaks one of the rules. Usually emerging triumphant, the

Desire in the Dust **(20th Century-Fox, 1960). Raymond Burr and Martha Hyer in this drama about a drunk-driving death and an innocent man sentenced to a Southern prison farm.**

wily Randall devises a plan to free the prisoners and end the local corruption.

20th Century-Fox's *Desire in the Dust* (1960), adapted by Charles Lang from the Harry Whittington novel and directed by William F. Claxton, focuses on an innocent man, Lonnie Wilson (Ken Scott), bribed by Colonel Ben Marquand (Raymond Burr) to take the rap for the drunk-driving death of his son, Davey Marquand, actually committed by his daughter, Melinda (Martha Hyer), who had been involved with Lonnie. Following a six-year sentence on the chain gang, Lonnie returns to his hometown, where the truth eventually emerges after the Colonel attempts to have Sheriff Wheaton (Kelly Thordsen) "eliminate" him.

From 1963 to 1967, David Janssen starred as *The Fugitive* for Quinn Martin Productions and broadcast for four seasons on the ABC Television network. As Dr. Richard Kimble, an innocent man convicted and sentenced to death for the brutal murder of his wife, he escapes when the train carrying him to prison crashes, and he continues to elude the law, mainly in the person of Lieutenant Philip Gerard (Barry Morse), who pursues him relentlessly across the nation, as he seeks a "one-armed man" he witnessed fleeing the crime scene.

Cleverly maintaining the suspense for a majority of its 120 episodes, *The Fugitive* production team included creator Roy Huggins, directors Lewis Allen, Abner Biberman, Richard Donner, Jerry Hopper, Christian Nyby, Leo Penn, Joseph Pevney, Sydney Pollack, Mark Rydell and James Sheldon, writers John D. F. Black, Don Brinkley, Alan Caillou, Lee Loeb and John Meredyth Lucas (who also directed), and narrator William Conrad. Among the dozens of top guest stars were Edward Asner, Richard Carlson, Ruby Dee, Bruce Dern, Angie Dickinson, Ivan Dixon, Robert Duvall, James Edwards, Dianne Foster, Jack Klugman, John Larch, J. Pat O'Malley, Lois Nettleton, Warren Oates, Susan Oliver, Mickey Rooney, Janice Rule, William Shatner, Nita Talbot and *I Am a Fugitive from a Chain Gang*'s Glenda Farrell, who appeared in the episode "Fatso" (directed by Ida Lupino and aired on November 19, 1963). Nominated for five Emmy Awards, it won one for Outstanding Dramatic Series in 1966.

Spanish auteur Luis Bunuel's Mexican spiritual classic *Nazarin*, which won the international prize at the 1959 Cannes Film Festival (but not released in the United States until 1968), bears a host of elements paralleling those of *I Am a Fugitive from a Chain Gang*. For *Nazarin*, Bunuel benefited greatly by collaborating with cinematographer Gabriel Figueroa, one of Mexico's true artistic treasures, whose extensive study of painting and a 1936 "master class" in Hollywood with Gregg Toland led to an arguably peerless visual style. After he formed a Mexican stock company with a group of artists including Dolores del Rio and Pedro Armendariz, he shot John Ford's religious allegory, *The Fugitive* (1947), perhaps "Pappy's" most strikingly beautiful film. Unfortunately, Ford's subsequent attempt to sign Figueroa to a contract with his own Argosy Productions was shot down by the blacklist, and the Mexican master was denied entry into the United States.

From the sublime to the ridiculous, the utterly atrocious *Girl on a Chain Gang* (1966), a no-budget independent exploitation exercise shot on Long Island by writer-director Jerry Gross (and distributed by his own Jerry Gross Productions), features Julie Ange as Jean Rollins, a young woman framed by Southern redneck cops and sentenced to an all-male chain gang.

Often cited as one of the greatest Vietnam-era antiestablishment films, *Cool Hand Luke* (1967), made by Warner Bros., stars Paul Newman as an early 1950s rebellious chain-gang convict who continually escapes, temporarily becoming a hero to his fellow prisoners before being gunned down at the end. Occasionally weighed down by its obvious thematic and visual parallels to the Christ story, the film nonetheless is considered a classic, featuring one of Paul Newman's most acclaimed performances in an acting career that spanned 54 years.

Cool Hand Luke was nominated for nine Academy Awards, but only supporting actor George Kennedy walked away a winner, for his portrayal of "Dragline," the prisoners' official leader. One of the most celebrated scenes in the film involves the use of the infamous sweatbox, but the terrible shock of this device already had been effectively depicted in *Hells Highway* and *The Emperor Jones*, both made more than three decades earlier.

A thoroughly blatant attempt to capitalize on the success of MGM's *The Dirty Dozen* (1967), American International's *The Devil's 8* (1969), costars Christopher George and Sixties pop sensation Fabian as two of the titular characters, chain-gang convicts offered pardons in return for their agreement to combat a Southern moonshining syndicate. Arguably the film's saving grace is the welcome cameo offered by Ralph Meeker.

Released on August 18, 1969 (exactly two months after *The Devil's 8*), writer-director-actor Woody Allen's first "solo" feature, *Take the Money and Run*, is a brilliant and *very* funny "mockumentary" about the life of incompetent bank robber Virgil Starkwell. Including a parody of John Dillinger's infamous 1934 breakout from an "escape-proof" jail using a carved imitation pistol, as well as dozens of other hilarious escapades, the film features a section during which Starkwell is sentenced to a chain gang where he is

130   The Making and Influence of *I Am a Fugitive from a Chain Gang*

Cool Hand Luke (Warner Bros., 1967). Paul Newman as the seemingly indomitable Luke in this powerful chain-gang classic.

served a bowl of *steam* before suffering the unspeakable horror of sharing a "steam box" with an insurance salesman!

"Chained like animals—treated like trash—even the filth and sweat couldn't stop their primitive cravings!" crowed the publicity campaign for Crown International's exploitation potboiler *Chain Gang Women* (1971). A prime example of the "drive-in" genre of the period, the film includes

6. The Historic Influence of the Film

Take the Money and Run (Cinerama Releasing Corporation, 1969). In his first "solo" film as writer, director and star, Woody Allen briefly, hilariously winds up on a chain gang.

escaped chain-gang convicts who become involved in such unpleasantness as jail-bait marriage, kidnapping, home invasion and rape.

More unsavory activities occur in the "Blaxploitation" film *Sweet Sugar* (1972), featuring Phyllis Davis as Sugar Bowman, a prostitute framed by an unscrupulous politician, who waves jail time in favor of working on a sugar cane plantation, which actually is a front for a chain gang operated by the maniacal racist Dr. John (Angus Duncan). This 90-minute exercise in sadism includes such horrors as prisoners locked in wooden cages, floggings, rapes and even a burning at the stake.

Papillon (1973), with its powerhouse costarring duo of Steve McQueen and Dustin Hoffman, is one of the most famous, fact-based prison films ever made. Directed by Franklin J. Schaffner from a screenplay by the formerly blacklisted Dalton Trumbo (who also appears in the small role of a commandant), Lorenzo Semple, Jr., and William Goldman, this often grueling experience literally pushed McQueen (who at times resembles Boris Karloff in *Devil's Island*) and Hoffman (as wrongly convicted killer Henri Cherierre and forger Louis Dega, respectively) to the limits (especially the scenes with Cherierre spending seven years in solitary confinement, with McQueen's method acting reportedly leading him actually to consume a cockroach in one scene), featuring some of the most exciting, suspenseful escape scenes ever filmed.

If ever there was a blues and folk singer, musician and composer who had experienced much of the material he performed, it was Huddie William Ledbetter (1888–1949), publicly known more often as "Lead Belly." The early years of this legendary African American artist's adventurous and troubled life are dramatized in director Gordon Parks' epic film, *Leadbelly*, released by Paramount in 1976. Written by prolific radio, television and screenwriter Ernest Kinoy, coproduced by David Frost and starring Roger E. Mosley in the lead role, the film includes ample coverage of Lead Belly's Louisiana chain-gang experiences, including time in the sweat box, while serving an attempted homicide sentence for taking part in a 1930 knife fight with a white man. Kinoy's admirable screenplay also includes depictions of the unique blues musician Lemon Henry ("Blind Lemon") Jefferson (Art Evans) and groundbreaking historian-documentarian John Lomax (James Broadhead).

Bing Crosby Productions and American International Pictures were responsible for *Mean Dog Blues* (1978), directed by television documentarian Mel Stuart (whose feature documentaries include *Wattstax* [1972]). Gregg Henry stars as Paul Ramsey, a country singer who takes the rap for a friend after he hits a small girl while driving drunk. Sold out by a shyster, Ramsey

6. *The Historic Influence of the Film*

Papillon (Allied Artists, 1973). Devil's Island convicts Henri (Steve McQueen) and Louis (Dustin Hoffman) are unforgettable in Franklin Schaffner's prison epic written by Dalton Trumbo, Lorenzo Semple, Jr., and William Goldman.

is sentenced to five years on a Southern prison farm, where he is subjected to hard labor on a chain gang. The diverse supporting cast is impressive, with Kay Lenz, Scatman Crothers, Tina Louise, Gregory Sierra and William Windom joined by George Kennedy in another of his hard-edged chain-gang film appearances.

39 Stripes (1979), a title referring to a line (based on a traditional Jewish

Leadbelly (Paramount, 1976). Roger E. Mosley as the controversial, innovative singer-songwriter-musician Huddie Ledbetter in director Gordon Parks' epic "biopic."

law) spoken by the Apostle Paul in *Corinthians*—"*Five times I received at the hands of the Jews the forty lashes less one*"—is based on the true story of Ed Martin, a chain-gang convict who, in 1944, converted to Christianity, forming the "HopeAglow Prison Ministries," with which he attempted to aid his fellow inmates. The film was produced and directed by Ron Ormond, who cast as Martin his brother, Tim, with whom he also co-wrote the screenplay. Having previously worked in a variety of genres, including horror and exploitation, Ron Ormond made only Christian-based projects following his survival of a plane crash in 1968. Produced on a low budget with primarily his own money, *39 Stripes* also was distributed by Ron's own company, The Ormond Organization.

The successful comic duo of Gene Wilder and Richard Pryor (who had struck box-office lightning in *Silver Streak* [1976]), briefly appear in chain-gang regalia during a scene in the Sidney Poitier-directed *Stir Crazy* (1980). Truly innocent New Yorkers framed by Southwestern rednecks, they are sentenced to 125 years for armed bank robbery. While hopping from the department of corrections bus toward the prison fence, Wilder brilliantly improvises dialogue referring to being shackled from head to toe as "from the middle ages" and "probably illegal." Another sequence involves Wilder chained, Spartacus-style, in his cell. The result: A long-standing spine ailment is cured! The film includes a spoof of nearly every conceivable incarceration element, and Wilder even mentions "prison movies" at one point. Although overlong, the film features enough outrageous incidents, realized by the equally adept improvisational skills of both actors, to maintain viewer interest.

Chain Gang (1984) is a no-budget, exploitation gore-fest directed by Worth Keeter, who co-wrote the screenplay with Todd Durham. In this exercise existing primarily to depict as much gratuitous violence, brutality and on-screen torture as possible, Earl Owensby plays Mac McPherson, an unfortunate traveler passing through a redneck town in the Carolinas where, after attempting to save a young woman from the horrors of a local strip joint, is framed for her murder and sentenced to 15 years' hard labor at the Black Creek Correctional Facility.

Mac's "innocent" nature is definitely called into question as time wears on. During an escape, he shoots to death several guards, and the final scenes feature quite a bloodbath as other prisoners follow suit. Other than the initial premise of an innocent man being convicted for a crime he didn't commit, very little of this film can be traced back to the "social problem" nature of *I Am a Fugitive from a Chain Gang*.

On Halloween 1987, Home Box Office (HBO Films) broadcast *The*

Man Who Broke 1,000 Chains, the only other direct adaptation of the Burns book *I Am a Fugitive from a Georgia Chain Gang!* (and borrowing the title from one of Vincent Burns' later books). Using the real-life individuals' actual names, the Michael Campus-written script benefits from an excellent cast including Val Kilmer (Robert Burns), James Keach (Vincent Burns), Sonia Braga (Emily Del Pino Pacheo), Kyra Sedgewick (Lillian Salo), Charles Durning (Warren Hardy), Clancy Brown (Flagg) and an 83-year-old Elisha Cook, Jr. (in his final feature role as "Pappy Glue"). Others in small supporting and bit roles are Taj Mahal, Paul Benjamin and a pre–*Sling Blade* (1995) Billy Bob Thornton (though unfortunately his scenes were deleted).

Veteran, Sanford Meisner-educated stage, film and television director Daniel Mann, whose impressive feature credits include *Come Back, Little Sheba* (1952), starring Burt Lancaster and Shirley Booth, *The Rose Tattoo* (1955), featuring Anna Magnani and Burt Lancaster, *I'll Cry Tomorrow* (1955), casting Susan Hayward (in her Oscar-winning performance) opposite Richard Conte, *The Teahouse of the August Moon* (1956), with Marlon Brando and Michiko Kyo, and *The Last Angry Man* (1959), graced by an excellent Paul Muni in his final screen role, made his filmmaking bow with *The Man Who Broke 1,000 Chains*. At 115 minutes, the film runs a bit longer than *I Am a Fugitive from a Chain Gang*, including a few more events from the Burns book, as well as more details about the real-life figures. Though obviously not having the overall effect and historically significant influence of the original adaptation, it provides an entertaining and useful companion piece to the Warner Bros. classic. Nominated for seven Cable ACE Awards, it won one for the work of director of photography Mikael Salomon.

The year after his successful television series *Magnum P.I.* (1980–1988) ended, small-screen star Tom Selleck became *An Innocent Man* (1989) for a theatrical feature film directed by Peter Yates. As Jimmie Rainwood, a victim of corrupt cops who mistakenly break into the wrong home, expecting to find a notorious drug dealer, he is framed, convicted on the perjured testimony of a narcotics informant. In a prison environment where so many convicts claim they are innocent, Rainwood finds it nearly impossible to find sympathetic support. Selleck holds his own in this well-made film, but is outshined by the great, Uta Hagen-trained character actor F. Murray Abraham (*Amadeus* [1984]) as fellow inmate Virgil Caine.

The NBC television series, *Quantum Leap*, created by Donald P. Bellasario, was a popular hit from 1989 to 1993. In the November 27, 1991, episode, "Unchained—November 2, 1956," series star Scott Bakula, as Dr. Sam Beckett, journeys back in time to leap into the body of chain-gang convict Chance Cole. Cole is chained to Jazz Boone (Basil Wallace), an innocent African American man unjustly convicted of a jewel store robbery. The two men escape but are captured and locked in a "punishment pit" (a direct connection to *The Prisoner of Shark Island*, with its relationship between an incarcerated white man [Warner Baxter] and a black [Ernest Whitman]). The situation becomes more complicated when Rear Admiral Al Calivicci, the project observer at Quantum Leap (Dean Stockwell, also a series regular) reports to Sam that the real jewel thief, who has visited the chain-gang camp, is still perpetrating his robbery racket.

In 1993, Warner Bros. released a feature-film remake of *The Fugitive* TV series, starring Harrison Ford as Dr. Richard Kimble, the role originally played by David Janssen, and Tommy Lee Jones as Deputy Samuel Gerard. As in the original television version, Kimble conducts his own investigation in an effort to track down the "one-armed man" who actually murdered his wife (Sela Ward).

The following year, writer-director Frank Darabont adapted the Stephen King novella *Rita Hayworth and Shawshank Redemption* into a screenplay, abbreviating the title to *The Shawshank Redemption* (1994), a film that fared poorly during its theatrical run but, after its release to video and cable television, became one of the most popular films ever made. Populated by an impressive ensemble cast including Tim Robbins, Morgan Freeman, David Proval and James Whitmore, the film deals with how a banker convicted of two life sentences (for murdering his wife and her lover) deals with penitentiary life, always insisting that he is innocent of the crimes. Abused by a prison gang led by Bogs Diamond (Mark Ralston) and enduring solitary confinement, Andy Dufresne (Robbins) benefits from his friendship with fellow inmate Ellis Boyd ("Red") Redding (Freeman) and is protected by guards after the corrupt Warden Norton (Bub Gunton) uses his knowledge of financing for a money-laundering racket. In the end, "Red" is paroled and Dufresne tunnels his way out of the Shawshank State Penitentiary (a fictional institution) after 17 years of brutal work, and they are happily reunited in Mexico. Like many other prison films (even though the stories are fictitious), the elements of the innocent man suffering torturous abuse and the often life-saving aid gained by his friendship with another incarcerated individual, link *The Shawshank Redemption* to *I Am a Fugitive from a Chain Gang*.

The often hilarious "buddy" comedy *Life* (1999), directed by Ted Demme, features the innate improvisational chemistry of costars Eddie Murphy and Martin Lawrence. As two early 1930s African American would-be bootleggers wrongfully convicted of the murder of a redneck law

Life (Universal, 1999). Eddie Murphy and Martin Lawrence costar in this often hilarious comedy about two would-be bootleggers sentenced to a Mississippi prison camp in 1932. Thanks to some very impressive makeup effects, they age convincingly for decades, unsuccessfully attempting to escape numerous times in the most harebrained of schemes. (Some of the funniest moments are contributed by the late Bernie Mac, who left us way too soon.)

officer in the South, they serve a total of 65 years, not on a chain gang, but at Mississippi's hard-labor "Camp 8" (now Mississippi State Penitentiary), from which they ineptly, unsuccessfully attempt to escape innumerable times. A scene featuring Nick Cassavetes (son of John Cassavetes and Gena Rowlands, and a director in his own right) as Sergeant Dillard, a guard who explains the purpose of an invisible "gun line" to the prisoners, is a comic high point, climaxing with a litany of reasons why a man (not necessarily attempting to escape) "*will be shot!*" Elements tying this sometimes outrageous parody to *I Am a Fugitive from a Chain Gang* include hard times, bigotry, wrongful incarceration, escape attempts and a much prolonged stay in a Southern prison camp rife with corruption. (After loading this R-rated film with his Richard Pryor-inspired trademark, improvisational profanity [the "F-word" is used 63 times], Murphy shifted his career into a more "family friendly" course.)

Another 1999 release, the outrageous comedy *Happy, Texas* involves three chain-gang escapees, two (Steve Zahn, Jeremy Northam) of whom hide out in the titular town, where they pose as gay representatives of a beauty pageant. Complications arise when Sheriff Chappy Dent (William H. Macy) actually proves to be gay and develops an attachment to Harry (Northam). This Miramax release, directed by Mark Illsley, also includes Ally Walker, Illeana Douglas and Ron Perlman in the cast.

The Man Who Broke 1,000 Chain's Charles Durning also plays a supporting role (stand-up politician Pappy O'Daniel) in *O Brother, Where Art Thou?* (2001), writer-director-producer sibling duo Joel and Ethan Coen's modern comic takeoff on Homer's *Odyssey* titled by the fictitious literary tale used by Joel McCrea's character in *Sullivan's Travels*. With this film, a clear lineage from *I Am a Fugitive from a Chain Gang* to *Sullivan's Travels* to *O Brother* (a span of nearly 70 years) can clearly be recognized.

George Clooney, John Turturro and Tim Blake Nelson costar as three escaped chain-gang convicts in 1930s Mississippi who attempt to reach the home of Ulysses Everett McGill (Clooney), where he has buried a fortune in loot from a previous bank robbery. Their own odyssey involves a series of bizarre and menacing characters who pose consistent threats to their intentions fueled by greed. John Goodman (Big Dan Teague) and Michael Badalucco (George "Baby Face" Nelson) are notable in top supporting roles.

In one scene, the convicts perform at a radio studio as "The Soggy Bottom Boys," a traditional three-part harmony trio whose recording becomes a surprise popular hit. Produced by T-Bone Burnett, the soundtrack album, including period folk, religious and African American gospel

O Brother, Where Art Thou? (Universal, 2001). George Clooney, Tim Blake Nelson and John Turturro star in the Coen Brothers' wild realization of the film conceived in *Sullivan's Travels* (1941). Memorable, very effective supporting turns are contributed by John Goodman as "Big Dan Teague," Michael Badalucco as a nickname-loathing version of the notorious bandit George "Baby Face Nelson" (most real-life gangsters detested the sobriquets created by the media), and Chris Thomas King, the New Orleans-based blues and hip-hop musician and record producer.

music, features Dan Tyminski (longtime member of the bluegrass band led by vocalist and fiddler Alison Krauss), Harley Allen and Pat Enright (whose collaboration as the Soggy Bottom Boys on "Man of Constant Sorrow" proved a considerable hit), Tim Blake Nelson (who sings "I'm in the Jailhouse Now"), Krauss and Gillian Welch, the acapella gospel group the Fairfield Four, singer-guitarist Norman Blake, singer-banjoist-fiddler John Hartford, New Orleans blues and hip-hop singer-songwriter Chris Thomas King (who plays real-life blues musician Tommy Johnson in the film) and others. Most of the posters and other advertising material for the film features the three convicts, clad in their striped prison garb, taking it on the lam—images highly reminiscent of the *I Am a Fugitive from a Chain Gang* Paul Muni of seven decades before.

As long as innocent individuals and victims of an imperfect and corrupt justice system wind up behind bars, some of them forever or even awaiting the walking of that "last mile," well-made films like *I Am a Fugitive from a Chain Gang* and others will remain relevant, timeless works of cinematic art, regardless of the original intentions of the people who produced them. In an era permeated by television "cop" and forensically saturated Crime Scene Investigation programs, and scores of theatrical feature films with endless (and mostly archaic) good-versus-evil plots (which necessitate as much computer-generated, digitally produced special-effects violence as possible), perhaps, at some point, even another chain-gang picture will slip in between the ever-tightening Hollywood cracks.

Wouldn't it be wonderful if the world could be just a *wee* bit more like the utopian one envisioned and definitely recommended by Vincent Godfrey Burns, and less like the one endlessly suffered through by his brother, Robert?

Well, peace, harmony and love—if even possible within this current human species—just isn't nearly as much fun, now, is it? But Warner Bros.' Roy Del Ruth, who passed up directing *I Am a Fugitive from a Chain Gang*, was proved wrong by the filmgoers of 1932 and those who have come after. His idea that people already would be too depressed by their lots in life to watch such a dark, reality-based picture was way off the mark. Perhaps they, like us, sometimes need a work of stark cultural art to provide a catharsis, suggesting that no matter *how bad* conditions become in our own existences, they always can get much, much *worse*. And you can place your money—or lack of it—down on the names of the *Brothers Burns* on that bet...

Appendix A
Credits and Cast of *I Am a Fugitive from a Chain Gang*

Credits: Director: Mervyn LeRoy; Executive Producer: Hal B. Wallis; Screenplay: Howard J. Green, Brown Holmes and Sheridan Gibney; Based on the book *I Am a Fugitive from a Georgia Chain Gang!* by Robert E. Burns (and Vincent G. Burns); Director of Photography: Sol Polito; Film Editor: William Holmes; Musical Score: Bernhard Kaun; Art Director: Jack Okey; Costume Designer: Orry-Kelly; Silks: Cheney Brothers; Assistant Director: Al Alleborn; Camera Operator: Robert H. Wagner; Costume Jeweler: Eugene Joseff; Musical Conductor: Leo F. Forbstein; Musicians: The Vitaphone Orchestra; Technical Director: S. H. Sullivan; Consultant: Robert E. Burns; General Press Agent: S. Charles Einfeld; Technical Director: Jack Miller; Locations: Bronson Canyon, Pasadena, Chatsworth and Griffith Park, Los Angeles, California; Production Dates: July 29–September 7, 1932; Warner Bros.–First National Pictures; Budget: $195,845; New York Premiere: October 11, 1932; Released November 19, 1932; Running Time: 92 minutes.

Cast: Paul Muni (James Allen), Glenda Farrell (Marie Woods), Helen Vinson (Helen), Noel Francis (Linda), Preston Foster (Pete), Allen Jenkins (Barney Sykes), Berton Churchill (The Judge), Edward Ellis (Bomber Wells), David Landau (The Warden), Hale Hamilton (Reverend Robert [aka "Clint"] Allen), Sally Blane (Alice), Louise Carter (James Allen's Mother), Willard Robertson (Prison Board Chairman), Robert McWade (W. E. Ramsey), Robert Warwick (Fuller), William Le Maire (A Texan), Erville Alderson (Police Chief), Irving Bacon (Bill, Barber), Reginald Barlow (Mr. Parker), James Bell (Red), Everett Brown (Sebastian T. Yale), Frederick Burton (Southern Prison Official), A. S. ("Pop") Byron (Cop in Barber Shop), Eddy Chandler (Job Foreman), Spencer Charters (C. K. Hobb), Wallis Clark (Chicago Lawyer), G. Pat Collins (Wilson), George Cooper (Vaudevillian), Jack Curtis (Prison Guard), Douglass Dumbrille (District Attorney), J. Frank Glendon (Arresting Officer), C. Henry Gordon (District Attorney), William Janney (Sheriff's Son), Lew Kelly (Mike, Diner Cook), Jack La Rue (Ackerman), Edward LeSaint (Chamber of Commerce),

Walter Long (Blacksmith), Jack Low (Big Prisoner), John Marston (Prison Commissioner), Edward McNamara (Second Warden), Charles Middleton (Train Conductor), Dennis O'Keefe (Café Chateau Dancer), William Pawley (Doggy), Dewey Robinson (Blacksmith), Charles Sellon (Hot Dog Stand Owner), Allen D. Sewell (Train Station Guard), Lee Shumway (Arresting Officer), William H. Strauss (Pawnbroker), Sheila Terry (Allen's Secretary), Fred ("Snowflake") Toones (Marine on Ship), Jack Wise (Tailor), Harry Woods (Prison Guard), John Wray (Nordine), Sam Baker, Russell Simpson, Morgan Wallace (Bits).

Appendix B
Film Precursors

The following are films, both documentary and narrative, with content dealing with social issues and scenes featuring prison, particularly chain-gang, brutality and escapes, distributed before November 19, 1932, the nationwide theatrical release date of *I Am a Fugitive from a Chain Gang*.

"Charleston Chain Gang" (1902) [documentary]
Credits: Filming Location: Charleston, South Carolina; Edison Manufacturing Company; Released April 1902; Running Time: 1 minute.
Cast: Chain-Gang Prisoners (Themselves).

"The Chain Gang" (1917) [documentary]
Credits: Directed and Screenplay by Robert C. Bruce; Bruce Scenics–Educational Film Exchanges; Released 1917; Running Time: 20 minutes.
Cast: Chain-Gang Prisoners (Themselves).

Master of the Range (1928) [Western–prison road gang]
Credits: Directed by B. Frank Wilson; (black and white / 1.33:1 ratio); Morris R. Schlank Productions–Anchor Film Distributors, Incorporated; Released in 1928.
Cast: Cliff ("Tex") Lyons, Ione Reed, Al Ferguson (Bits).

Hallelujah (1929) [chain gang]
Credits: Directed by King Vidor; Produced by King Vidor and Irving Thalberg; Screenplay by Wanda Tuchok, Richard Schayer and Ransom Rideout; Story by King Vidor; Titles (silent version) by Marian Ainslee; Directors of Photography: Hugh Wynn, Gordon Avil (black and white / 1.20:1 ratio); Film Editors: Anton Stevenson, Hugh Wynn; Musical Direction: Eva Jessye; Art Director: Cedric Gibbons; Assistant Directors: Robert A. Golden, Harold Garrison; Sound Engineer: Douglas Shearer; Still Photographer: Ruth Harriet Louise; Assistant to Director: Fred M. Wilcox; Locations: Memphis, Tennessee, and Arkansas;

Metro-Goldwyn-Mayer Pictures–Loew's Incorporated; New York Premiere: August 20, 1929; Released August 29, 1929; Running Time: 109 minutes.

Cast: Daniel L. Haynes (Zeke), Nina Mae McKinney (Chick), William Fountaine (Hot Shot), Harry Gray (Parson), Fanny Belle DeKnight (Mammy), Everett McGarrity (Spunk), Victoria Spivey (Missy Rose), Milton Dickerson, Robert Couch, Walter Tait (Johnson Kids), Dixie Jubilee Singers (Themselves), Matthew ("Stymie") Beard (Child), Evelyn Pope Burwell, Eddie Connors, Eva Jessye (Singers), William Allen Garrison (Heavy), Sam McDaniel (Adam), Blue Washington (Church Member), Georgia Woodruff (Singer).

"The Chain Gang" (1939) [chain gang cartoon]

Credits: Directed by Burt Gillet; Walt Disney Productions–Columbia Pictures; Released August 18, 1939; Running Time: 8 minutes.

Cast: Pinto Colvig (Voice of the Hounds, including Pluto), Walt Disney (Voice of Mickey Mouse).

Hell's Highway (1932) [chain gang]

Credits: Directed by Rowland Brown; Produced by David O. Selznick; Screenplay by Samuel Ornitz, Robert Tasker and Rowland Brown; Director of Photography: Edward Cronjager (black and white / 1.37:1 ratio); Film Editor: Edward Hamilton; Music: Clarence Muse; Musical Director: Max Steiner; Art Director: Carroll Clark; Assistant Director: James H. Anderson; Fill-in Director: John Cromwell; Sound Recordist: John H. Tribby; Assistant Cameras: James Daly, Harold E. Wellman; Camera Operator: Harry J. Wild; Still Photographer: Fred Hendrickson; RKO Radio Pictures; Released September 23, 1932; Running Time: 62 minutes.

Cast: Richard Dix (Duke Ellis), Tom Brown (Johnny Ellis), Rochelle Hudson (Mary Ellen), C. Henry Gordon (Skinner), Oscar Apfel (Billings), Stanley Fields (Whiteside), John Arledge (Carter), Warner Richmond (Pop-Eye), Charles Middleton (Matthew), Clarence Muse (Rascal), Louise Carter (Mrs. Ellis), Sandy Roth (Maxie), Fuzzy Knight (Society Red), Louise Beavers (Rascal's Sweetheart at Visitors Center), Allan Cavan (Hunt Club Manager on Telephone), The Etude Ethiopian Chorus (The Singers of the Spirituals), Eddie Hart (Turkey Neck Burgess, Cook), Robert Homans (Sheriff), John Lester Johnson (Blubber Mouth), Jed Kiley (Romeo Schultz), Frank Marlowe (Convict), Bob Perry (Spike), Harry Smith (Buzzard), Bert Starkey (Hype).

Appendix C
Film and Television Successors

These "progeny" following in the wake of *I Am a Fugitive from a Chain Gang* (1932) fall into one of three basic categories, and sometimes in a combination of them: [1] the "social problem" film; [2] films involving either chain gangs or similar work gangs, farms or prisons from which (often innocent or framed though convicted) convicts attempt to escape; or [3] films that reunited director Mervyn LeRoy with his lead actors from the original film. They are indicated as either ["social problem"]; [chain, work or prison gang]; or [reunion] in each listing.

(These credits and cast listings have been updated to include information gleaned from the most recently discovered research materials available at the time of publication.)

Laughter in Hell (1933) [chain gang]

Credits: Directed by Edward L. Cahn; Produced by Carl Laemmle, Jr.; Screenplay by Tom Reed; Based on the Novel *Laughter in Hell* by Jim Tully; Director of Photography: John Stumar (black and white / 1.37:1 ratio); Film Editor: Philip Cahn; Sound Supervisor: Gilbert Kurland; Dialogue Director: Russell Hopton; Presenter: Carl Laemmle; Universal Pictures; Production began September 26, 1932; Released January 13, 1933; Released Running Time: 70 minutes.

Cast: Pat O'Brien (Barney Slaney), Tommy Conlon (Barney as a Boy), Merna Kennedy (Marybelle Evans), Berton Churchill (Mike Slaney), Gloria Stuart (Lorraine), Tom Brown (Martin), Lew Kelly (Mileaway), Arthur Vinton (Grover Perkins), Clarence Muse (Abraham Jackson), Douglas Dumbrille (Ed Perkins), Dick Winslow (Ed Perkins as a Boy), Rollo Lloyd (Zeb), Noel Madison (Brownfield), Tom Ricketts (Judge), William H. Turner (I. N. Tree), Richard Alexander (Construction Boss), Ted Billings (Chain Gang Member), Bob Burns (Sheriff with Posse), Charles K. French (Townsman), Mary Gordon (Townswoman), Pat Harmon (Avery, Chain Gang Guard), Jane Keckley (Maude, Zeb's Wife), Fred Koehler, Jr. (Chain Gang Member), Gus Leonard (Townsman), Walter Long (Chain Gang Member), Michael Mark (Convict), Russ Powell (Jailer), Bob Reeves (Sheriff's Deputy), Blackie Whiteford (Chain Gang Member).

Appendix C

Heroes for Sale (1933) ["social problem"]

Credits: Directed by William A. Wellman; Produced by Hal B. Wallis; Screenplay by Robert Lord and Wilson Mizner; Director of Photography: James Van Trees (black and white / 1.37:1 ratio); Film Editor: Howard Bretherton; Musical Director: Bernhard Kahn; Musical Conductor: Leo F. Forbstein; Musicians: Vitaphone Orchestra; Art Director: Jack Okey; Costume Design: Orry-Kelly; Second Camera Operator: Louis Jennings; Assistant Camera: James Van Trees, Jr.; Warner Bros.–First National Pictures; Released June 17, 1933; Running Time: 76 minutes.

Cast: Richard Barthelmess (Tom Holmes), Aline MacMahon (Mary), Loretta Young (Ruth), Gordon Westcott (Roger), Robert Barrat (Max), Berton Churchill (M. Winston), Grant Mitchell (George Gibson), Charley Grapewin (Pa Dennis), Robert McWade (Dr. Briggs), G. Pat Collins (Leader of Agitators), James Murray (Blind Soldier), Edwin Maxwell (Laundry Company President), Margaret Seddon (Jeanette Holmes), Arthur Vinton (Captain Joyce), Robert Elliott ("Red" Squad Policeman #1), Charles C. Wilson ("Red" Squad Policeman #2), John Marston (Judge [voice]), Willard Roberston (The Sheriff [scenes deleted]), Ward Bond (Red), Eddy Chandler (Henderson, Soldier), Ronnie Cosby (Young Bill Holmes), Frank Darien (Announcer at Roger's Reception), James Donlan (Laundry Cashier), Lee Phelps (Ed Brady, Angry Laundry Worker), Mike Donlin, Larry McGrath, John ("Skins") Miller, Bob Perry, Leo White (Angry Laundry Workers), Douglass Dumbrille (Jim, Chief Engineer), Hans Feurberg (Lefner, German Prisoner), Eddie Graham (Man Attending Roger's Reception), Pat Harmon (Policeman with Constable), Arthur Hoyt (Gibson's Secretary), George Irving (Gibson's Lawyer), Milton Kibbee (Harry, Bank Teller), Henry Otho (Policeman Phoning for Riot Squad), Inez Palange (Mrs. Bonicelli), Lorin Baker (Bank Employee), Dewey Robinson (Arguer), Landers Stevens (Laundry Executive), Guy Usher (Constable), Tammany Young (Drug Peddler).

The Mayor of Hell (1933) ["social problem"–work gang]

Credits: Directed by Archie Mayo and Michael Curtiz; Produced by Edward Chodorov and Lucien Hubbard; Screenplay by Edward Chodorov and Islin Auster; Directors of Photography: Barney McGill and Merritt B. Gerstad (black and white / 1.37:1 ratio); Film Editor: Jack Killifer; Musical Score: Bernhard Kahn; Musical Conductor: Leo F. Forbstein; Musicians: Vitaphone Orchestra; Art Director: Esdras Hartley; Costume Design: Orry-Kelly; Makeup Artist: Perc Westmore; Assistant Director: Frank Shaw; Second Camera Operators: Kenneth Green, David Harris, Ben White; Still Photographer: William P. Whitley; Costume Jeweler: Eugene Joseff; Warner Bros.–Vitaphone Pictures; Released June 24, 1933; Running Time: 90 minutes.

Cast: James Cagney (Patsy Gargan), Madge Evans (Dorothy), Arthur Byron (Judge Gilbert), Allen Jenkins (Mike), Dudley Digges (Thompson), Frankie Darro (Jimmy), Sheila Terry (Blonde with Mike), Robert Barrat (Fred Smith), Allen "Farina" Hoskins (Smoke), Harold Huber (Joe), Dorothy Peterson (Mrs. Smith), G. Pat Collins (Brandon), Edwin Maxwell (Louis Johnson), John Marston (Hopkins), William V. Mong (Mr. Walter), Mickey Bennett (Butch), Sidney Miller (Izzy), Hobart Cavanaugh (Mr. Gorman), George Humbert (Mr. Carmonotti),

Raymond Borzage (Johnny Stone), George Offerman, Jr. (Charlie), Charles E. Cane (Tommy), Beaudine Anderson (Boy), James Donlan (Sam), Sam Finn, Huey White, Harry Wilson (Joe's Henchmen), Ben Hendricks, Jr. (Guard Taking Jimmy to Thompson), Gladden James (Car Owner Paying 25 Cents), Wilfred Lucas (Bill), Wallace MacDonald (Man in Johnson's Office), Larry McGrath (Johnson's Assistant), Jack McHugh (Boy Prosecutor), Bert Moorhouse (Joe's Henchman Playing Cards), Adrian Morris (Car Owner Refusing to Pay), Frank O'Connor (Cop in Court), Henry Otho (Guard in School Armory), Bob Perry, Charles Sullivan (Collectors), Hector V. Sarno (Hollis), Andy Shuford (Boy Judge), William H. Strauss (Mr. Horowitch), Ben Taggart (Sheriff), Fred ("Snowflake") Toones (Mr. Hemingway), Sailor Vincent (Guard), Charles C. Wilson (Wilson), Dorothea Wolbert (Mrs. Burns).

20,000 Cheers for the Chain Gang (1933) [chain gang parody]

Credits: Directed by Roy Mack; Story by Cyrus Wood and A. Dorian Otvos; Director of Photography: Edwin B. DuPar (black and white / 1.37:1 ratio); Choreography: Harry Crosley; Warner Bros. Pictures; Released August 12, 1933; Running Time: 20 minutes.

Cast: Jerry Bergen (Himself), The Rollickers (Themselves), Novia, The Pickens Sisters (Helen, Jane and Patty), The Vitaphone Boys and Girls (Themselves), James Baskett (Vocalist), Harry Shannon (bit).

The Emperor Jones (1933) [chain gang–innocent man]

Credits: Directed by Dudley Murphy and William C. DeMille; Produced by Gifford Cochran and John Krimsky; Screenplay by Dubose Heyward; Based on the Play *The Emperor Jones* by Eugene O'Neill; Director of Photography: Ernest Haller (black and white / 1.37:1 ratio); Film Editor: Grant Whytock; Musical Score and Direction: Frank Tours; Vocal Arranger: J. Rosamond Johnson; Music Synchronization: Max Manne; Art Director: Herman Rosse; Production Managers: J. Edward Shugrue, George Knafka; Assistant Director: Joseph H. Nadel; Sound Engineer: Joseph Kane; Still Photographer: Jack Shalitt; Cast Associate: Fritz Pollard; Presenters: Gifford Cochran, John Krimsky; Supervisor: William C. DeMille; United Artists Pictures; Production Dates: May 25–Late July 1933; Released September 29, 1933; Running Time: 72 minutes.

Cast: Paul Robeson (Brutus Jones), Dudley Digges (Smithers), Frank H. Wilson (Jeff), Fredi Washington (Undine), Ruby Elzy (Dolly), George Haymid Stamper (Lem), Brandon Evans (Carrington), Taylor Gordon (Stick-man), Rex Ingram (Courtcrier), Jackie ("Moms") Mabley (Marcella), Billie Holliday (Extra in Night Club Scene), James P. Johnson (Pianist), Fritz Pollard, Lorenzo Tucker (Extras in Nightclub Scene), Harold Nicholas (Young Tap Dancer), Blueboy O'Connor (Treasurer).

Wild Boys of the Road (1933) ["social problem"]

Credits: Directed by William A. Wellman; Produced by Robert Presnell, Sr.; Screenplay by Earl Baldwin; Based on the Story "Desperate Youth" by Daniel Ahern; Director of Photography: Arthur L. Todd (black and white / 1.37:1 ratio);

Film Editor: Thomas Pratt; Musical Score: Bernhard Kahn; Musical Conductor: Leo F. Forbstein; Art Director: Esdras Hartley; Makeup Artist: Perc Westmore; Property Master: Scotty Moore; Sound Recording Engineer: Robert B. Lee; Key Grip: Charles Davis; Chief Electrician: Claude Hutchinson; Still Photographer: Mac James; Assistant Camera: Vernon Larson; Second Camera Operator: William Schurr; Warner Bros.–First National Pictures; Released October 7, 1933; Running Time: 68 minutes.

Cast: Frankie Darro (Eddie), Edwin Phillips (Tommy), Rochelle Hudson (Grace), Dorothy Coonan Wellman (Sally), Sterling Holloway (Ollie), Arthur Hohl (Dr. Heckel), Ann Hovey (Lola), Minna Gombell (Aunt Carrie), Grant Mitchell (Dr. James Smith), Claire McDowell (Mrs. Smith), Robert Barrat (Judge R. H. White), Beaudine Anderson (Boy), Ward Bond (Red, the Raping Brakeman), Wade Boteler (Policeman in Court), Eddy Chandler (Brakeman Throwing Stones), John R. Coonan (Youth in Lineup), George Cooper (Man Near Columbus), Shirley Dunstead (Harriet Webster), Charley Grapewin (Mr. Cadman), Alan Hale, Jr. (Boy), Buddy Messinger (Boy), Sidney Miller (Boy Selling Letter), Adrian Morris (Buggie Maylin, a Gangster), Louis Natheaux (Buggie's Pal), George Offerman, Jr. (Boy), Lee Phelps (Movie Theater Patron), Lee Shumway (Mike, Policeman), Edwin Stanley (Merchant).

Hi. Nellie! (1934) [reunion]

Credits: Directed by Mervyn LeRoy; Produced by Robert Presnell, Sr., Hal B. Wallis and Jack L. Warner; Screenplay by Abem Finkel and Sidney Sutherland; Director of Photography: Sol Polito (black and white / 1.37:1 ratio); Film Editor: William Holmes; Musical Score: Bernhard Kahn, Ray Heindorf; Musical Conductor: Leo F. Forbstein; Musicians: Vitaphone Orchestra; Art Director: Robert M. Haas; Costume Designer: Orry-Kelly; Warner Bros.–Vitaphone Pictures; Released January 20, 1934; Running Time: 75 minutes.

Cast: Paul Muni (Brad), Glenda Farrell (Gerry Crale), Ned Sparks (Shammy), Robert Barrat (Brownell), Berton Churchill (Graham), Kathryn Sergava (Grace), Hobart Cavanaugh (Fullerton), Douglass Dumbrille (Dawes), Edward Ellis (O'Connell), Paul Kaye (Helwig), Donald Meek (Durkin), Dorothy Libaire (Rosa Marinello), Marjorie Gateson (Canfield), George Meeker (Sheldon), Harold Huber (Leo), Allen Vincent (Nick Grassi), Pat Wing (Susie), Frank Reicher (Danny), George Chandler (Sullivan), George Humbert (Mike Marinello), Nina Campana (Italian Woman), James Donlan (Evans), Antonio Filauri (Merry Go Round Headwaiter), Howard C. Hickman (Dr. John W. Wilson), Milton Kibbee (Charlie Dwyer), Frank Marlowe (Henchman), Ralph McCullough (Poker Player), Harold Miller (Graham's Secretary), Sidney Miller (Louie), Bob Montgomery (Henchman), Bert Moorhouse (Extra at Merry Go Round Club), John Qualen (Steve), Gus Reed (Mac), Harry Seymour (Drunk at Bar), Sidney Skolsky (Skolsky), Renee Whitney (Telephone Operator), Jack Wise (Vital Statistics Clerk).

Heat Lightning (1934) [reunion]

Credits: Directed by Mervyn LeRoy; Produced by Samuel Bischoff; Screenplay by Brown Holmes and Warren Duff; Based on the Play *Heat Lightning* by Leon

Abrams and George Abbott; Director of Photography: Sid Hickox (black and white / 1.37:1 ratio); Film Editor: Howard Bretherton; Musical Score: Bernhard Kahn; Musical Direction: Leo F. Forbstein; Musicians: Vitaphone Orchestra; Art Director: Jack Okey; Costume Designer: Orry-Kelly; Costume Jeweler: Eugene Joseff; Warner Bros.–Vitaphone Pictures; Production began November 20, 1933; Released March 3, 1934.

Cast: Aline MacMahon (Olga), Ann Dvorak (Myra), Preston Foster (George), Lyle Talbot (Jeff), Glenda Farrell (Mrs. Tifton), Frank McHugh (Frank), Ruth Donnelly (Mrs. Ashton-Ashley), Theodore Newton (Steve Laird), Willard Robertson (Everett Marshall), Harry C. Bradley ("Popsy," a Businessman), James Durkin (The Sheriff), Jane Darwell (Gladys, the Wife), Edgar Kennedy (Herbert, the Husband), Muriel Evans (Blonde Cutie), Jill Dennett (Girl with Black Bangs), Sam Hayes (Voice of Radio Announcer), Chris-Pin Martin (Mexican Husband with Family), Margareta Montez (Mexican Wife), Eddie Shubert (The Last Traveler).

Judge Priest (1934) [chain gang]

Credits: Directed by John Ford; Produced by Sol M. Wurtzel; Screenplay by Dudley Nichols and Lamarr Trotti; Based on Stories by Irvin S. Cobb; Director of Photography: George Schneiderman (black and white / 1.37:1 ratio); Film Editor: Paul Weatherwax; Musical Score: Cyril J. Mockridge, Samuel Kaylin; Musical Orchestrations: Emil Gerstenberger; Musical Direction: Samuel Kaylin; Song Lyrics: Dudley Nichols, Lamar Trotti; Set Decorator: William S. Darling; Costume Design: Royer; Assistant Director: Edward O'Fearna; Sound: Albert Protzman; Still Photographer: William E. Thomas; Wardrobe Supervisor: Sam Benson; Assistant Editor: John Pommer; Fox Film Corporation; Production Dates: Early June–July 18, 1934; Released September 28, 1934; Running Time: 80 minutes.

Cast: Will Rogers (Judge Priest), Tom Brown (Jerome Priest), Anita Louise (Ellie May Gillespie), Henry B. Walthall (Reverend Ashby Brand), David Landau (Bob Gillis), Rochelle Hudson (Virginia Maydew), Roger Imhof (Billy Gaynor), Frank Melton (Flem Talley), Charley Grapewin (Sergeant Jimmy Bagby), Francis Ford (Juror No. 12), Hattie McDaniel (Aunt Dilsey), Stepin Fetchit (Jeff Poindexter), Melba Brown, Thelma Brown, Vera Brown (Black Singers), Grace Goodall (Mrs. Maydew), Winter Hall (Judge Floyd Fairleigh), Pat Hartigan (Townsman in Saloon), Si Jenks (Juror No. 10), Beulah Hall Jones (Black Singer), Lillian Lawrence (Townswoman at Trial), Duke R. Lee (Deputy), Margaret Mann (Governess), Louis Mason (Sheriff Birdsong), Paul McAllister (Doc Lake), Matt McHugh (Gabby Rives), Paul McVey (Trimble), Hyman Meyer (Herman Feldsburg), Frank Moran (Townsman in Saloon), Robert Parrish (Taffy Puller at Festival), Vester Pegg (Joe Harringer), George Reed (Black Servant), Constantine Romanoff (Townsman in Saloon), Mary Rousseau (Guitar Player), Ernest Shields (Milan), Harry Tenbrook (Townsman in Saloon), Gladys Wells (Black Singer), Harry Wilson (Townsman in Saloon).

*Remade by John Ford as ***The Sun Shines Bright*** for Republic Studios in 1953, with Stepin Fetchit reprising the character of Jeff Poindexter, and his brother, Francis

Ford, appearing in his final screen role. (One of cinema's true pioneers, Francis passed away, aged 72, on September 5, 1953.)

Black Fury (1935) ["social problem"]

Credits: Directed by Michael Curtiz; Produced by Hal B. Wallis and Jack L. Warner; Screenplay by Abem Finkel and Carl Erickson; Based on the Story "Jan Volkanik" by Judge Michael A. Musmanno and the Play *Bohunk* by Harry R. Irving; Director of Photography: Byron Haskin (black and white / 1.37:1 ratio); Film Editor: Thomas Richards; Musical Score: Bernhard Kahn, Howard Jackson; Musical Direction: Leo F. Forbstein; Art Director: John Hughes; Makeup Artist: Perc Westmore; Hair Stylist: Emily Moore; Unit Manager: Frank Mattison; Assistant Director: Russell Saunders; Second Assistant Director: Carroll Sax; Props: Emmett Emerson; Gaffer: Charles Alexander; Grip: Harry Barnhouse; Still Photographer: John Ellis; Assistant Camera: Ted Hayes; Wardrobe: Dan Brown (men); Mary Dery (women); Assistant Wardrobe: Hugh Blair; Dialogue Director: Frank McDonald; Script Assistant: Fred Applegate; Supervisor: Robert Lord; Stand-in: Harry Raven; Warner Bros.–First National Pictures; Production began October 20, 1934; Released May 18, 1935; Running Time: 94 minutes.

Cast: Paul Muni (Joe Radek), Karen Morley (Anna Novak), William Gargan (Slim), Barton MacLane (McGee), John Qualen (Mike), J. Carrol Naish (Steve), Vince Barnett (Kubanda), Tully Marshall (Poole), Henry O'Neill (Hendricks), Joseph Crehan (Farrell), Mae Marsh (Mrs. Mary Novak), Sara Haden (Sophie Shemanski), Willard Robertson (Mr. J. J. Welsh), Effie Ellsler (Bubitschka), Wade Boteler (Mulligan), Egon Brecher (Alec Novak), G. Pat Collins (Lefty, Company Policeman), Ward Bond (Mac, Company Policeman), Akim Tamiroff (Sokolsky), Purnell Pratt (Henry B. Jenkins), Eddie Shubert (Butch), Wally Albright (Willie Novak), John Bleifer (Ivan, a Miner), Ferike Boros (Wife of Hospitalized Winer), Don Brodie (Newsreel Man), Glen Cavender (Worried Miner), Eddy Chandler (Security Policeman Stopping Anna), Nick Copeland (McGee's Policeman at Party), Harry Cording (Louie, a Miner), Jane Eberling (Tessie Novak), Edith Fellows (Agnes Shemanski), Dick French (Orderly), Dorothy Gray (Mary, Tessie's Young Friend), Henry Hastings (Mose, a Miner), Oscar ("Dutch") Hendrian (Security Force Applicant), Herbert Heywood (Charlie, the Bartender), Samuel S. Hinds (Judge), Mitchell Ingraham (Lawyer), Milton Kibbee (Union Man Checking Badges), Michael Mark (Miner at Meeting), Mike Mazurki (Security Force Applicant), Claire McDowell (Nurse), Pat Moriarty (Pat, a Miner), Bobby Nelson (Johnny Novak), George Offerman, Jr. (Pete Novak), Henry Otho (Locked-Out Miner), Inez Palange (Mrs. Morova), Pedro Regas (Tony, a Miner), Mickey Rentschler (Chris Shemanski), Addison Richards (Government Man), Constantine Romanoff (Security Force Applicant), Jack Roper (Security Force Applicant), Christian Rub (Hospitalized Miner), Mary Russell (Mary, Lefty's Girl), Floyd Shackleford (Black Miner at Meeting), Harry Tenbrook (Security Force Applicant), William H. Turner (Watchman), Kathrin Clare Ward (Mrs. Clancy, Croner's Landlady), Leo White (Miner at Meeting), Jack Wise (Miner at End).

The Prisoner of Shark Island (1936) [prison gang–innocent man]

Credits: Directed by John Ford; Produced by Darryl F. Zanuck and Nunnally Johnson; Screenplay by Nunnally Johnson; Based on Research by Darryl F. Zanuck; Director of Photography: Bert Glennon (black and white / 1.37:1 ratio); Film Editor: Jack Murray; Musical Score: R. H. Bassett, Hugo Friedhofer; Art Director: William S. Darling; Set Decorator: Thomas Little; Costume Design: Gwen Wakeling; Assistant Director: Edward O'Fearna; Sound: W. D. Flick, Roger Heman, Sr.; Wardrobe Supervisor: Sam Benson; Assistant Editors: Harvey Manger, Thomas Vincent; Presenter: Joseph M. Schenck; A Darryl F. Zanuck Twentieth Century Production; 20th Century-Fox Pictures; Production Dates: November 12, 1935–Early January 1936; Released February 28, 1936; Running Time: 96 minutes.

Cast: Warner Baxter (Dr. Samuel Alexander Mudd), Gloria Stuart (Mrs. Peggy Mudd), Claude Gillingwater (Colonel Jeremiah Milford Dyer), Arthur Byron (Mr. Erickson), O. P. Heggie (Dr. MacIntyre), Harry Carey (Commander of Fort Jefferson), Francis Ford (Corporal O' Toole), John McGuire (Lieutenant Lovett), Francis McDonald (John Wilkes Booth), Douglas Wood (General Ewing), John Carradine (Sergeant Rankin), Joyce Kay (Martha Mudd), Ernest Whitman ("Buck" Milford), Paul Fix (David Herrold), Frank Shannon (Judge Advocate General Joseph Holt), Frank McGlynn, Sr. (President Abraham Lincoln), Leila McIntyre (Mary Todd Lincoln), Etta McDaniell (Aunt Rosabelle Milford), J. M. Kerrigan (Judge Maiben), Arthur Loft (Frank J. Thomas, Carpetbagger), Paul McVey (General David Hunter), Maurice Murphy (Orderly), Matthew ("Stymie") Beard (Boy Seeking Dr. Mudd), Robert Dudley (Druggist at Trial), Jan Duggan (Actress at Ford's Theatre), Earl Eby (Usher), Dick Elliott (Actor at Ford's Theatre), Bess Flowers (Woman Sitting Behind Lincoln in Theatre Box), Bud Geary (Sergeant), Charles Haefeli (Prisoner), Robert Homans (Sergeant), John Lester Johnson (Black Soldier at Prisoner), Beulah Hall Jones (Blanche), Paul Kruger (Soldier), Duke R. Lee (Sergeant), Wilfred Lucas (Testifying Colonel), Murdock MacQuarrie (Edman Spangler), James A. Marcus (Blacksmith), Paul McAllister (Doctor), Merrill McCormick (Commandant's Aide), J. P. McGowan (Ship's Captain), Wedgwood Nowell (Court-Martial Member), Vester Pegg (Soldier), Jack Pennick (Corporal), George Reed (Black Man Giving Booth Directions), Paul Stanton (Agitating Orator), Tom Steele (Trooper), Harry Strang (Ship's Mate), Cyril Thornton (Michael O'Laughlin), Ray Turner, Blue Washington (Black Guards at Prison), Cecil Weston (Mary Surratt), Lloyd Whitlock (Major Rathbone), Frank Baker, Stanley Blystone, Stanley Bordagary, Whitney Bourne, Arthur Millett, Robert Parrish (bits).

The Walking Dead (1936) ["social problem"–framed man–horror]

Credits: Directed by Michael Curtiz; Produced by Louis F. Edelman; Screenplay by Ewart Adamson, Peter Milne, Robert Hardy Andrews and Lillie Hayward; Story by Ewart Adamson and Joseph Fields; Director of Photography: Hal Mohr (black and white / 1.37:1 ratio); Musical Score and Orchestrations: Bernhard Kahn; Musical Director: Leo F. Forbstein; Film Editor: Thomas Pratt; Art Director: Hugh Reticker; Costume Design: Orry-Kelly; Makeup Artist: Perc

Westmore; Assistant Director: Russell Saunders; Costume Jeweler: Eugene Joseff; Dialogue Director: Irving Rapper; Warner Bros.–Vitaphone Pictures; Production began December 23, 1935; Released March 14, 1936; Running Time: 66 minutes.

Cast: Boris Karloff (John Elman), Ricardo Cortez (Nolan), Edmund Gwenn (Dr. Beaumont), Marguerite Churchill (Nancy), Warren Hull (Jimmy), Barton MacLane (Loder), Henry O'Neill (Werner), Joseph King (Judge Shaw), Addison Richards (Prison Warden), Paul Harvey (Blackstone), Robert Strange (Merritt), Joseph Sawyer (Trigger), Eddie Acuff (Betcha), Kenneth Harlan (Stephen Martin), Miki Morita (Sako), Ruth Robinson (Mrs. Shaw), Brandon Beach (Second Guest), George Beranger (Nolan's Butler), Wade Boteler (Cellist's Guard), Tom Brower (Guard), James P. Burtis (Guard Who Answers Phone too Late), Edwin J. Carlie, James Pierce, Tom Schamp (Prisoners), Glen Cavender (Man in Courtroom), Lucille Collins (Courtroom Woman Dodging "Betcha"), Frank Darien (Cemetery Caretaker), Sarah Edwards (Female Doctor, Guest at Party), Bill Elliott (First American Radio Announcer), Carl Faulkner (Warden at Execution), Edward Gargan (Guard Sitting Outside Warden's Office), Malcolm Graham (Third Guest), Earle Hodgins (Trial Reporter), Harry Hollingsworth (Bailiff), Fred Hueston (Fourth Guest), Paul Irving (First Guest), Boyd Irwin (British Doctor), John Kelly (Joe, Merritt's Bodyguard), Craufurd Kent (British Radio Announcer), Larry Kent, Milton Kibbee, Charles Marsh, Eddie Shubert (Reporters), Richard Kipling (Court Clerk), Isabel La Mal (Sob Sister), Alphonse Martell (Florist), Nick Moro (Convict), William H. O'Brien (Juror), Spec O'Donnell (Copy Boy), Paul Panzer (Man in Courtroom), Jean Perry (French Radio Announcer), Lee Phelps, Lee Prather (Bailiffs), Harrington Reynolds (English Doctor), Sam Rice (Counterman), John J. Richardson (Man Leaving First Trial), Syd Saylor (Courtroom Reporter), Charles Sherlock (Man in Courtroom Dodging "Betcha"), Edgar Sherrod (Prisoner Chaplain), Billy Wayne (Trusty), Leo White (Man in Courtroom).

Road Gang (1936) [work–prison gang]

Credits: Directed by Louis King; Produced by Brian Foy and Hal B. Wallis; Screenplay by Dalton Trumbo; Story by Abem Finkel and Harold Buckley; Director of Photography: L. William O'Connell (black and white / 1.37:1 ratio); Film Editor: Jack Killifer; Musical Score: Heinz Roemheld; Musical Direction: Leo F. Forbstein; Art Director: Hugh Reticker; Warner Bros.–First National Pictures; Released March 28, 1936; Running Time: 61 minutes.

Cast: Donald Woods (James ["Jim"] Larrabie), Kay Linkaer (Barbara Winston), Carlyle Moore, Jr. (Robert ["Bob"] Gordon), Joseph Crehan (Harry Shields), Henry O'Neill (George Winston), Joe King (J. W. Moett), Addison Richards (Warden Parmenter), Charles Middleton (Mine Warden Grayson), Olin Howard (Doctor), William B. Davidson (Attorney General Marsden), Harry Cording (Sam Dawson, Guard), Marc Lawrence (Pete, Convict), Eddie Shubert (Buck Draper), Edward Van Sloan (Mr. Dudley, Lawyer), Ben Hendricks, Jr. (Jake, Motorcycle Cop), George Lloyd (Hymie Seeball, the Gorilla), Ernie Adams (Jeff, Convict with Bad Leg), Ted Billings, Frank Bruno, Charles Graham (Convicts), Eddy Chandler (Ed, Guard No. 1), Jack Cheatham, Jack Curtis, Harry

Hollingsworth, Lee Prather (Guards), Nick Copeland (Second Guard at Farm), Don Downen (Western Union Messenger), Frank Fanning (Frank, Guard), Frank Faylen (Police Radio Dispatcher), Douglas Gordon (Chuckler at Blackfoot), Sol Gorss, Henry Otho, Lee Phelps (Guards in Blackfoot Mine), Herbert Heywood, Sailor Vincent (Convicts at Blackfoot), Stuart Holmes (Guard at Farm), John Irwin (Old Convict), Milton Kibbee (Convict Warning Larrabee), Paul Kruger (Engineer), Edward LeSaint (Judge), Tom Manning (W. B. Heffin, Jailer), Rex Moore (Boy Sent to Blackfoot), Edward Peil, Sr. (Guard in Sleeping Quarters), Bernice Pilot (Lucinda, Winston's Maid), Sam Rice (Convict Withholding Fork), John J. Richardson (Smokey, Safecracking Convict), Constantine Romanoff (Tangle-Eye, Convict at Farm), Albert Russell (Expressionless Convict), Frank Shannon (Chaplian), Leo White, Jack Wise (Convicts at Farm), Tom Wilson (Bull, Guard at Blackfoot).

The Devil Doll (1936) [prison gang–horror]

Credits: Directed by Tod Browning; Produced by Tod Browning and E. J. Mannix; Screenplay by Garrett Fort, Guy Endore and Erich von Stroheim; Story by Tod Browning; Based on the Novel *Burn, Witch, Burn* by Abraham Merritt; Director of Photography: Leonard Smith (black and white / 1.37:1 ratio); Film Editor: Frederick Y. Smith; Musical Score: Franz Waxman, Edward Ward; Musical Orchestrations: Wayne Allen, Paul Marquardt, Clifford Vaughan; Art Director: Cedric Gibbons; Makeup Artist: Robert J. Shiffer; Assistant Director: Harry Sharrock; Associate Art Directors: Stan Rogers, Edwin B. Willis; Recording Director: Douglas Shearer; Production Sound Mixer: James Brock; Sound Effects Editors: T. B. Hoffman, Michael Steinore; Sound Re-recording Mixers: Standish J. Lambert, Ralph A. Pender, R. L. Stirling, Don T. Whitmer; Music Mixer: M. J. McLaughlin; Additional Photographer: Willard Vogel; Wardrobe: Dolly Tree; Dance Director: Val Raset; Double (for Arthur Hohl): Paul Foltz; Metro-Goldwyn-Mayer Pictures; Production Dates: Late March–April 29, 1936; Released July 10, 1936; Running Time: 78 minutes.

Cast: Lionel Barrymore (Paul Lavond), Maureen O'Sullivan (Lorraine Lavond), Frank Lawton (Toto), Rafaela Ottiano (Malita), Robert Greig (Emile Coulvet), Lucy Beaumont (Madame Lavond), Henry B. Walthall (Marcel), Grace Ford (Lachna), Pedro de Cordoba (Charles Matin), Arthur Hohl (Victor Radin), Juanita Quigley (Marguerite Coulvet), Claire Du Brey (Madame Coulvet), Rollo Lloyd, Christian J. Frank, Sherry Hall, Mahlon Hamilton (Detectives), E. Alyn Warren (Commissioner), Jean Alden, Paul Foltz (Apache Dancers), King Baggot (Detective Pierre), Egon Brecher (Detective), Robert Du Couedic (Policeman), Billy Gilbert (Matin's Butler), Robert Graves, Sidney Jarvis, Edward Keane (Gendarmes), Gus Leonard (Eiffel Tower Elevator Operator), Eily Malyon (Laundry Proprietress), Evelyn Selbie (Flower Woman), Nick Thompson (Police Sergeant), Wilfred Lucas (Off-Screen Voice).

We Who Are About to Die (1937) [framed man]

Credits: Directed by Christy Cabanne; Produced by Edward Small; Executive Producer: Samuel J. Briskin; Screenplay by John Twist, Paul Perez and William

N. Robson; Based on the Novel by David Lamson; Director of Photography (black and white / 1.37:1 ratio): Robert H. Planck; Musical Score: Bernhard Kahn, Max Steiner, Roy Webb; Film Editor: Arthur Roberts; Art Director: Van Nest Polglase; Costume Designer: Edward Stevenson; Assistant Director: James H. Anderson; Assistant Art Director: Field M. Gray; Sound Recordist: Denzil A. Cutler; Edward Small Productions-RKO Radio Pictures; Released January 8, 1937; Running Time: 81 minutes.

Cast: Preston Foster (Steven Mathews), Ann Dvorak (Miss Connie Stewart), John Beal (John E. ["Johnny"] Thompson), Ray Mayer (Bright Boy Schultz), Gordon Jones (Slim Tolliver), Russell Hopton ("Mac" MacAndrews), Paul Hurst (Nick Trotti), Frank Jenks (Clyde Beasly), John Wray (Jerry Daley), Frank M. Thomas (M. L. Thomas), Barnett Parker (John Parker), Willie Fung (Kwong), John Carroll (Joe Donahue), DeWitt Jennings (Mike Brannigan), Landers Stevens (Warden Lawton), John ("Skins") Miller (Macy), Howard C. Hickman (Prison Chaplain), Robert Emmett O'Connor (Detective Mitchell), Oscar Apfel (Mr. Armitage), William Bailey (Policeman Passenger), Willie Best (Airport Porter), Stanley Blystone (Plainclothesman with Rifle), Harry Bowen (Agitated Citizen in Mob), Ed Brady (Angry Aircraft Worker Throwing Stone), Lynton Brent, Jerry Fletcher, Al Herman (Reporters), Sonny Bupp (Hit and Run Victim), William Burress (Charlie Gaunt, Cashier), Ralph Byrd (Police Lab Technician), Eddy Chandler (Prison Guard Sergeant), Wallis Clark (Dr. Hedges), Frank Fanning (Guard in Vistor's Room), Jim Farley (Police Officer Johnson), Eddie Hart (Police Driver), Dell Henderon (Blake's Associate), Oscar ("Dutch") Hendrian, Sailor Vincent (Convicts), Russell Hicks (District Attorney Knight), Arthur Hoyt (Governor's Secretary), Edward Keane (Ed Stanley), Donald Kerr (Agitated Citizen at Shoeshine Stand), Edward LeSaint (Judge), Wilfred Lucas (Prison Yard Captain), Frank Marlowe (Prison Lab Technician), Tom McGuire (Death Row Captain Harris), Bruce Mitchell (Prison Guard with Machine Gun), Philip Morris (Guard Escorting Kwong to Gallows), Carrol Nye (Police Radio Dispatcher), Frank O'Connor, Dick Rush (Detectives), Jack Perry (Convict Making Noise with Cup), George Reed (Black Convict), Larry Steers (Man in District Attorney's Office), Jack Stoney (Aircraft Mechanic), Brick Sullivan (Policeman), Charles Sullivan, Max Wagner (Cell Block E Convicts), Richard Tucker (Defense Attorney), Monte Vandergrift (Plainclothesman Finding Gun), Emmett Vogan (Prison Lieutenant), Ethel Wales (Travel Bureau Customer), Walter Walker (The Governor), Bryant Washburn (Martin Blake).

Black Legion (1937) ["social problem"]

Credits: Directed by Archie Mayo and Michael Curtiz; Produced by Robert Lord, Hal B. Wallis and Jack L. Warner; Screenplay by Abem Finkel and William Wister Haines; Story by Robert Lord; Director of Photography: George Barnes (black and white / 1.37:1 ratio); Film Editor: Owen Marks; Musical Score: Bernhard Kahn, W. Franke Harling; Art Director: Robert M. Haas; Costume Designer: Milo Anderson; Unit Manager: Frank Mattison; Assistant Director: Jack Sullivan; Sound Recordist: C. A. Riggs; Special Effects: Fred Jackson, Jr., Hans Koenekamp; Assistant Camera: Gene Davenport; Second Camera Operator: George Gordon Nogle; Warner Bros. Pictures; Production Dates: Late August–October 5 and December 2–3, 1936; Released January 30, 1937; Running Time: 83 minutes.

Cast: Humphrey Bogart (Frank Taylor), Dick Foran (Ed Jackson), Erin O'Brien-Moore (Ruth Taylor), Ann Sheridan (Betty Grogan), Helen Flint (Pearl Davis), Joe Sawyer (Cliff Moore), Clifford Soubier (Mike Grogan), Alonzo Price (Alf Hargrave), Paul Harvey (Billings), Dickie Jones (Buddy Taylor), Samuel S. Hinds (Judge), Addison Richards (Prosecuting Attorney), Eddie Acuff (Metcalf), Dorothy Vaughan (Mrs. Grogan), John Litel (Tommy Smith), Henry Brandon (Joe Dombrowski), Charles Halton (Osgood), Pat C. Flick (Nick Stumpas), Francis Sayles (Charlie), Paul Stanton (Barham), Harry Hayden (Jones), Egon Brecher (Dombrowski), Robert Barrat (Brown), John Berkes (Convicted Black Legion Member), Ted Bliss (Radio Announcer), John Butler (Jenkins, Auto Salesman), Eddy Chandler, Robert Homans (Motorcycle Cops), Larry Emmons (Man in Drugstore), John Hiestand (First Radio Announcer Breaking Story), Milton Kibbee (Reporter), Charles Frederick Lindsley (March of Time Announcer), Wilfred Lucas (Bailiff), Fred MacKaye (Third Radio Announcer Breaking Story), Carlyle Moore, Jr. (Reporter), Dennis Moore (Reporter at Jail), Jack Mower (Court Clerk), Frank Nelson (Radio Announcer), Lee Phelps (Guard at Jail), Sam Rice (Extra on Bus), Frank Sully (Truck Driver's Helper), Emmett Vogan (News Commentator), Max Wagner (Truck Driver in Diner), Billy Wayne (Jim, Diner Counterman), Don Barcley Joseph Crehan, Paul Graetz (scenes deleted).

San Quentin (1937) [work–prison gang]

Credits: Directed by Lloyd Bacon; Produced by Samuel Bischoff, Hal B. Wallis and Jack L. Warner; Screenplay by Peter Milne and Humphrey Cobb; Story by Robert Tasker and John Bright; Director of Photography: Sid Hickox (black and white / 1.37:1 ratio); Film Editor: William Holmes; Musical Score: Charles Maxwell, Heinz Roemheld, David Raksin; Musical Director: Leo F. Forbstein; Musical Orchestrations: Ray Heindorf, Joseph Nussbaum; Songs: "How Could You," Music and Lyrics by Harry Warren and Al Dubin; "I'm Forever Blowing Bubbles," Music and Lyrics by Jean Kenbrovin and John William Kellette; Art Director: Esdras Hartley; Costume Designer: Howard Shoup; Assistant Director: Richard Maybery; Special Effects: James Gibbons, Hans Koenekamp; Stunts: Sol Gorss, Eddie Parker, Harvey Parry, Allen Pomeroy; Second Unit Photographer: Tony Gaudio; Additional Photographer: Hans Koenekamp; Still Photographer: S. C. Manatt; Grip: Dudie Maschmeyer; Warner Bros.-First National Pictures; Production Dates: October 5–November 19, 1936, mid–January 1937 and March 5, 1937; Released August 7, 1937; Running Time: 70 minutes.

Cast: Pat O'Brien (Captain Stephen Jameson), Humphrey Bogart (Joe "Red" Kennedy), Ann Sheridan (May), Barton MacLane (Lieutenant Druggin), Joe Sawyer ("Sailor Boy" Hansen), Veda Ann Borg (Helen), Archie Robbins (Mickey Callahan), Gordon Oliver (Captain), Garry Owen (Dopey), Marc Lawrence (Venetti), Emmett Vogan (Lieutenant), William Pawley, Al Hill, George Lloyd,

Noble ("Kid") Chissell, Sidney D'Albrook, Lalo Encinas, Allen Fox, Jack Kenney, John Northpole, Harvey Parry, Doc Stone, Leo Sulky, Brick Sullivan, Elliott Sullivan, Jim Thorpe, Sailor Vincent, Douglas Williams (Convicts), Wax Wagner (Prison Runner), Ernie Adams (Fink), Jimmy Aye (Nightclub Patron), George Beranger (Lorenz Review Headwaiter), Glen Cavender (Hastings), Eddy Chandler, Hal Craig, Alexander Cross, Bruce Mitchell (Guards), Jack Chefe (Reporter), Davison Clark (Guard in Visiting Room), Gino Corrado (Lorenz Review Waiter), Joe Cunningham (Doctor), Gennaro Curd (Nightclub Proprietor), John Webb Dillon (Plainclothesman), Ralph Dunn (Head Cell Block Guard), Frank Fanning, Ray Flynn, Claude Payton, Lee Prather (Cops), Frank Faylen (Convict Envying Hoffman), Pat Flaherty (Cop Clearing May), James Flavin (Guard Announcing Jailbreak), Jerry Fletcher (Hoffman), Charles K. French (Nightclub Patron), Jack Gardner (Young Gardner), Edward Gargan ("Captain" Road Gang Guard), Sol Gorss (Clerk), Eddie Gribbon (Singing Convict 51310), Gordon Hart (Second Prison Board Member), Ben Hendricks, Jr. (Guard Holding Kennedy), Herbert Heywood (Pop), Max Hoffman, Jr. (Wall Guard Dropping Rifle), Harry Hollingsworth (First Guard), George Humbert (Truck Driver Picking Up Red), John Ince (Old Convict), Edward Keane (Second Detective), Leonard Lord (Dorgan), Jack Low (Office Guard), Herman Marks (Dorgan), Frank Marlowe, George Offerman, Jr. (Young Convicts), Charles McAvoy (Cop at Nightclub), Frank Meredith (Yard Guard), Dennis Moore (Simpson), Jack Mower (Man in Car), Hal Neiman (Convict 38216), Wedgwood Nowell (First Prison Board Member), Pat O'Malley (Bunkhouse Road Gang Guard), Ted Oliver (Hank), Frank Orth (Convict in Bunkhouse), Ted Osborne (Police Radio Announcer), Paul Panzer (Casey), Eddie Parker (Guard in Jameson's Office), Edward Peil, Sr. (Deputy Guard), Jack Perrin (Hank), Bob Perry (Convict in Prison Yard), Lee Phelps (First Detective), John J. Richardson (Convict Knowing How to Make Bed), Lee Shumway (Machine Shop Guard), Harry Stafford (Nightclub Patron), Michael Stark (Cop at Nightclub), Dick Wessel (Trusty), Claire White (Woman in Car), Robert J. Wilke (Young Convict in Yard), William A. Williams (Bill Conklin), Harry Wilson (Marching Convict), Jack Wise (Convict in Fight), Douglas Wood (Prison Board Chairman), Ernest Wood (Fink's Attorney), Ralph Byrd, Lane Chandler, Jim Farley, Kenneth Harlan, Ethan Laidlaw, Cliff Saum (scenes deleted).

The Life of Emile Zola (1937) ["social problem"–innocent man]

Credits: Directed by William Dieterle; Produced by Henry Blanke, Hal B. Wallis and Jack L. Warner; Screenplay by Norman Reilly Raine, Heinz Herald and Geza Herczeg; Story by Heinz Herald and Geza Herczeg; Based on the Book *Zola and His Time* by Matthew Josephson; Director of Photography: Tony Gaudio (black and white / 1.37:1 ratio); Film Editor: Warren Low; Musical Score: Max Steiner; Musical Direction: Leo F. Forbstein; Musical Orchestrations: Hugo Friedhofer; Art Director: Anton Grot; Set Decorator: Albert C. Wilson; Costume Designers: Milo Anderson, Ali Hubert; Makeup Artists: Perc Westmore, Gordon Bau, Norbert A. Myles; Assistant Directors: Irving Rapper, Russell Saunders; Set Designer: Harper Goff; Costume Jeweler: Eugene Joseff; Dialogue

Director: Irving Rapper; Press Representative: S. Charles Einfeld; Warner Bros. Pictures; Released October 2, 1937; Running Time: 116 minutes.
Cast: Paul Muni (Emile Zola), Gale Sondergaard (Lucie Dreyfus), Joseph Schildkraut (Captain Alfred Dreyfus), Gloria Holden (Alexandrine Zola), Donald Crisp (Maitre Labori), Erin O'Brien-Moore (Nana), John Litel (Charpentier), Henry O'Neill (Colonel Picquart), Morris Carnovsky (Anatole France), Louis Calhern (Major Dort), Ralph Morgan (Commander of Paris), Robert Barrat (Major Walsin-Esterhazy), Vladimir Sokoloff (Paul Cezanne), Grant Mitchell (Georges Clemenceau), Harry Davenport (Chief of Staff), Robert Warwick (Major Henry), Charles Richman (M. Delagorgue), Gilbert Emery (Minister of War), Walter Kingsford (Colonel Sandherr), Paul Everton (Assistant Chief of Staff), Montagu Love (M. Cavaignac), Frank Sheridan (M. Van Cassell), Lumsden Hare (Mr. Richards), Marcia Mae Jones (Helen Richards), Florence Roberts (Madame Zola), Dickie Moore (Pierre Dreyfus), Rolla Gourvitch (Jeanne Dreyfus), Arthur Aylesworth (Chief Censor), Egon Brecher (Brucker), Iphigenie Castiglioni (Madame Charpentier), Robert Cummings, Sr. (General Gillian), Frank Darien (Albert), Holmes Herbert (Commander of Paris), Paul Irving (LaRue), Alexander Leftwich (Major D'Oboville), Eric Mayne, Alexander Novinsky (Members of the Court), Frank Mayo (Mathieu Dreyfus), Moroni Olson (Captain Guignet), Frank Reicher (Frank Perrenx), Walter O. Stahl (Senator Scheurer-Kestner), Wilhelm Von Brincken (Schwartzoppen), Pierre Watkin (Prefect of Police), Harry Worth (Lieutenant), Maurice Black, Stanley Blystone, Franklin Farnum, Dolores Weisenfreund (bits).

They Won't Forget (1937) ["social problem"]

Credits: Directed by Mervyn LeRoy; Produced by Mervyn LeRoy and Jack L. Warner; Screenplay by Robert Rossen and Aben Kandel; Based on the Novel *Deep in the Deep South* by Ward Greene; Director of Photography: Arthur Edeson (black and white / 1.37:1 ratio); Film Editor: Thomas Richards; Musical Score and Arrangements: Adolph Deutsch; Musical Direction: Leo F. Forbstein; Art Director: Robert M. Haas; Costume Designer: N'was McKenzie; Makeup Artist: Al Bonner; Hair Stylist: Helen Turpin; Assistant Director: Lee Katz; Props: Lloyd S. Edwards; Grip: James Hicks; Technical Advisor: Dalton S. Raymond; A Mervyn LeRoy Production; Warner Bros.–First National Pictures; Production began Early March 1937; Released October 9, 1937; Running Time: 95 minutes.
Cast: Claude Rains (Andy Griffin), Gloria Dickson (Sybil Hale), Edward Norris (Robert Hale), Otto Kruger (Gleason), Allyn Joslyn (Bill Brock), Lana Turner (Mary Clay), Linda Perry (Imogene Mayfield), Elisha Cook, Jr. (Joe Turner), Cy Kendall (Detective Laneart), Clinton Rosemond (Tump Redwine), E. Alyn Warren (Carlisle P. Buxton), Elisabeth Risdon (Mrs. Hale), Clifton Soubier (Jim Timberlake), Granville Bates (Detective Pindar), Ann Shoemaker (Mrs. Mountford), Paul Everton (Governor Mountford), Donald Briggs (Harmon), Sibyl Harris (Mrs. Clay), Trevor Bardette (Shattuck Clay), Elliott Sullivan (Luther Clay), Wilmer Hines (Ransom Clay), Eddie Acuff (Drugstore Clerk), Frank Faylen (Reporter), Leonard Mudie (Judge Moore), Harry Davenport,

Harry Beresford, Edward McWade (Confederate Soldiers), Al Bridge (Mob Leader Outside Governor's Mansion), Tom Brower (First Turnkey), Raymond Brown (Colonel Foster, Redwine's Lawyer), Claudia Coleman (Dolly Holly, Reporter), Robert Cummings, Sr. (Whipple, Banker), John Dilson (Detective Briggs), Earl Dwire (Jury Foreman), Jerry Fletcher, Eddie Foster, Peter Potter, John Ridgely (Boys in Pool Room), Roger Gray (Barbershop Customer), George Guhl (Bartender), Henry Hall, I. Stanford Jolley, Kenner G. Kemp, Charles Morton (Courtroom Spectators), Harry Hollingsworth (Turnkey), Thomas E. Jackson, George Lloyd (Detectives on Train), Owen King (Flanagan), Paul Maxey (Man in Saloon Smoking Pipe), Howard M. Mitchell (Police Captain), Forbes Murray (Dougherty, Publisher), Psyche Nibert (Hazel, Imogene's Friend), Robert Porterfield (Jimmy Harrison, Dissenting Juror), Frank Rasmussen (Detective Tucker), Dick Rich (Cop Guarding Hale), Adele St. Mauer (Mrs. Timberlake), Maidel Turner (Stout Lady on Train), Tom Wilson (Farmer in Courtroom), Walter Young (Mr. Mimms), Addison Richards (Trailer Narrator Voice).

Female Fugitive (1938) [prison gang]

Credits: Directed by William Nigh; Produced by E. B. Derr and Frank Melford; Screenplay by Bennett Cohen and John T. Neville; Director of Photography: Arthur Martinelli (black and white / 1.37:1 ratio); Film Editor: Finn Ulback; Musical Direction: Abe Meyer; Art Director: Frank Dexter, Sr.; Assistant Director: Theadore Joos; Sound Recordist: Karl Zint; Crescent Pictures Corporation-Monogram Pictures; Production Dates: March 2–Week of March 18, 1938; Released April 15, 1938; Running Time: 58 minutes.

Cast: Evelyn Venable (Peggy Mallory), Craig Reynolds (Jim Mallory), Reed Hadley (Bruce Dunnung), John Kelly (Red, Dunning's Chauffeur), John Merton (Henchman Mort), Ray Bennett (Henchman Burke), Emmett Vogan (Investigator Tom Leonard), Lee Phelps (Investigator Steve Roberts), Sam Flint (Edward J. Howard); Martha Tibbetts (Claire Bannister), Charlotte Treadway (Mrs. Bannister), Reginald Sheffield (Dr. Richardson), Fern Emmett (Cook Who Quits), Lynton Brent (The Medic).

Crime School (1938) ["social problem"]

Credits: Directed by Lewis Seiler; Produced by Brian Foy, Hal B. Wallis and Jack L. Warner; Screenplay by Crane Wilber and Vincent Sherman; Director Photography: Arthur L. Todd (black and white / 1.37:1 ratio); Film Editor: Terry O. Morse; Musical Score: Max Steiner; Musical Direction: Leo F. Forbstein: Musical Orchestrations: Hugo Friedhofer, George Parrish; Art Director: Charles Novi; Costume Designer: N'was McKenzie; Unit Manager: Lee Hugunin; Assistant Director: Fred Tyler; Sound: Francis J. Scheid; Dialogue Director: Vincent Sherman; Warner Bros.–First National Pictures; Production Dates: Late January–Early March 1938; Released May 28, 1938; Running Time: 85 minutes.

Cast: Humphrey Bogart (Mark Braden), Gale Page (Sue Warren), Billy Halop (Frankie Warren), Bobby Jordan (Squirt), Huntz Hall (Goofy), Leo Gorcey (Spike), Bernard Punsly (Fats), Gabriel Dell (Bugs), George Offerman, Jr. (Red),

Weldon Heyburn (Cooper), Cy Kendall (Morgan), Charles Trowbridge (Judge Clinton), Spencer Charters (Old Doctor), Donald Briggs (New Doctor), Fred Jacquet (Commissioner), Helen MacKellar (Mrs. Burke), Al Bridge (Mr. Burke), Sibyl Harris (Mrs. Hawkins), Paul Porcasi (Nick Papadopolos), Frank Otto (Junkie), Edward Gargan (Officer Hogan), James B. Carson (Schwartz), Glen Cavender (Policeman Outside Judge Clinton's Office), Loia Cheaney (Nurse), Hal E. Chester, Paul Nichols (Boys), Harry Cording (Jim, the Second Guard), Sol Gorss, George Magrill (Guards), Eddie Graham, Stuart Holmes (Reporters), Herbert Heywood (Boiler Room Supervisor), Ethan Laidlaw (Guard Peterson), Vera Lewis (Aunt Liz), Clayton Moore, John Ridgely (Reporters Covering "Escape"), Jack Mower (John Brower, Judge's Assistant), David Newell (Dormitory Guard), Frank O'Connor (Court Policeman), Eddie Parker (State Trooper), Cliff Saum (Cliff Brandon, First Guard), Harry Tenbrook (Clerk Outside Morgan's Office), Dorothy Vernon (Neighbor), Tom Wilson (Washroom Guard).

Prison Break (1938) ["social problem"–prison gang–framed man]

Credits: Directed by Arthur Lubin; Produced by Trem Carr and Paul Malvern; Screenplay by Dorothy Davenport; Story by Norton S. Parker; Director of Photography: Harry Neumann (black and white / 1.37:1 ratio); Film Editor: Jack Ogilvie; Musical Score: Hayes Pagel, Frank Sanucci; Musical Direction: Frank Sanucci; Art Director: Charles Clague; Assistant Director: Glen Cook; Sound Supervisor: Bernard B. Brown; Sound Technician: Robert Pritchard; Production Dates: May 23–mid–June 1938; Universal Pictures; Released July 12, 1938; Running Time: 72 minutes.

Cast: Barton MacLane (Joaquin Shannon), Glenda Farrell (Jean Fenderson), Paul Hurst (Soapy), Constance Moore (Maria Shannon, Joaquin's Sister), Edward Pawley (Joe Fenderson), Edmund MacDonald (Chris Nelson, Maria's Bridegroom), Ward Bond (Big Red Kincaid), Guy Usher (Warden), Victor Kilian (Old Man Fenderson), Frank Darien (Joaquin's Cellmate), George Cleveland (Ding, Fisherman with Joaquin), Johnny Russell (Jackie, Jean's Son), Thomas Louden (The Priest), Paul Everton (Judge at Joaquin's Trial), Roy Barcroft (Captain of the Prison Guard), Horace B. Carpenter, Charles McAvoy, Jack O'Shea, Harry Semels (Tuna Fishermen at Party), Ralph Dunn (Detective), John Elliott, Lloyd Ingraham (Parole Board Members), Jack Kirk (Fisherman at Unemployment Office), George Lloyd, Frank O'Connor (Dock Policemen), Walter Long (Convict), Belle Mitchell (Party Woman), Bruce Mitchell (Detective), Monte Montague (Hiring Boss), Hal Price (Detective Arresting Joaquin for Parole Violation), Jason Robards, Sr. (Note-Finding Prison Guard), Constantine Romanoff (Convict), Cy Schindell (Party Waiter), John Sheehan (Bartender), Jack C. Smith (Cannery Manager), Glenn Strange (Tough Hit by Joaquin at Bachelor's Party), Forrest Taylor (Shannon's Parole Officer), Al Thompson (Party Waiter), Carleton Young (Prisoner).

Angels with Dirty Faces (1938) ["social problem"]

Credits: Directed by Michael Curtiz; Produced by Samuel Bischoff, Hal B. Wallis and Jack L. Warner; Screenplay by John Wexley, Warren Duff, Ben Hecht and

Charles MacArthur; Story by Rowland Brown; Director of Photography: Sol Polito (black and white / 1.37:1 ratio); Film Editor: Owen Marks; Musical Score: Max Steiner; Musical Direction: Leo F. Forbstein; Musical Orchestrations: Hugo Friedhofer; Art Director: Robert M. Haas; Costume Designer: Orry-Kelly; Makeup Artist: Perc Westmore; Unit Manager: Frank Mattison; Second Unit Director: Sterling Campbell; Assistant Director: Sherry Shourds; Second Assistant Director: Emmett Emerson; Props: Herbert Plews; Sound: Everett Alton Brown; Sound Effects Editor: Peter Berkos; Stunts: Harvey Parry; Assistant Camera: Frank Evans; Gaffer: Frank Flanagan; Second Camera: Al Green; Best Boy: William Harrington; Grip: Harold Noyes; Costume Jeweler: Eugene Joseff; Wardrobe: Charley Mark; Dialogue Director: Jo Graham; Technical Advisor: J. J. Devlin; Script Clerks: Frank Kowalski, Jack Lucas; Warner Bros.–First National Pictures; Production Dates: June 27–Early August 1938; Released November 26, 1938; Running Time: 97 minutes.

Cast: James Cagney (Rocky Sullivan), Pat O'Brien (Jerry Connelly), Humphrey Bogart (James Frazier), Ann Sheridan (Laury Martin), "Dead End" Kids (Billy Halop, Bobby Jordan, Leo Gorcey, Gabriel Dell, Huntz Hall, Bernard Punsly), Joe Downing (Steve), Edward Pawley (Edwards), Adrian Morris (Blackie), Frankie Burke (Rocky as a Boy), William Tracy (Jerry as a Boy), Marilyn Knowlden (Laury as a Child), Robert Mitchell Boys Choir (St. Brendan's Church Choir), Harris Berger (Basketball Captain), Sidney Bracey, Brian Burke, Oscar ("Dutch") Hendrian, George Taylor, Dan Wolheim (Convicts), Edwin Brian (Newsboy), Sonny Bupp, Jack Eggar, Frank Kowalski, Vince Lombardi, Roger McGee, A. W. Sweatt (Boys), Gary Carthew, Bill Cohee, Le Val Lund, Jr., Bobby Mayer, Norman Wallace (Church Basketball Team Players), Lane Chandler, Ben Hendricks, Jr. (Guards), Frank Coughlan, Jr., David Durand (Boys in Pool Room), William Crowell (Whimpering Convict), Joe Cunningham (Managing Editor), Steve Darrell, Joe Devlin (Gangsters), John Dilson (Chronicle Editor), Mike Donovan, Bud Geary, Jack Perrin, Michael Stark (Death Row Guards), Earl Dwire (Priest), William Edmunds (Italian Storekeeper), Jim Farley (Railroad Yard Watchman), Galan Galt, Robert Homans (Policemen), Jack A. Goodrich, Earl Gunn, Donald Kerr, Al Lloyd, Alexander Lockwood, Charles Marsh, Carlyle Moore, Jr., Jeffrey Sayre (Reporters), Mary Gordon (Mrs. Patrick McGee), Frank Hagney (Sharpie), John Hamilton (Police Captain), John Harron (Sharpie), Harry Hayden (Pharmacist), Thomas E. Jackson (Press City Editor), Vera Lewis (Soapy's Mother), Wilfred Lucas (Police Sergeant), Wilbur Mack (Croupier), John Marston (Well-Dressed Man), Billy McClain (Janitor), Belle Mitchell (Mrs. Maggione), Jack Mower, Lee Phelps (Detectives), Spec O'Donnell (Inquisitive Youth in Pool Room), Pat O'Malley, Jack C. Smith (Railroad Guards), Oscar O'Shea (Kennedy), George Offerman, Jr. (Older Boy), Emory Parnell (Officer McMann), William Pawley (Bugs), Theodore Rand (Gunman No. Three), Dick Rich (Gangster), Ralph Sanford (Policeman on El Toro Club Phone), George Sorel (Headwaiter), James Spottiswood ("Record" Editor), Chuck Stubbs (Red), Charles Sullivan (Ed), Elliott Sullivan (Cop), Eddie Syracuse (Maggione Boy), Charles Trowbridge (Norton J. White), Dick Wessel (Man in Pool Room Slugged by Father Connelly), Leo White (Man with Baby), Poppy Wilde (Girl at Gaming Table), Lottie Williams (Onlooker at Drug Store), Charles C. Wilson (Police Lieutenant Buckley), Claude Wisberg (Hanger-on in Pool Room), William Worthington (Warden), Al Hill, George Mori (bits).

Devil's Island (1940) ["social problem"–prison gang–innocent man]
Credits: Directed by William Clemens; Produced by Brian Foy; Screenplay by Kenneth Gamet and Don Ryan; Story by Anthony Coldeway and Raymond L. Schrock; Director of Photography: George Barnes (black and white / 1.37:1 ratio); Film Editor: Frank Magee; Musical Score: Howard Jackson, Max Steiner; Art Director: Max Parker; Makeup Artist: Ray Romero; Assistant Director: Arthur Leuker; Sound: Robert B. Lee; Stunts: Sol Gorss, Don Turner; Dialogue Director: John Langan; Technical Advisor: Louis Van Den Ecker; Warner Bros. Pictures; Production Dates: Late June–Early August 1938; Released January 7, 1939; Running Time: 62 minutes.
Cast: Boris Karloff (Dr. Charles Gaudet), Nedda Harrigan (Madame Lucien), James Stephenson (Colonel Armand Lucien), Adia Kuznetzoff (Pierre), Rolla Gourvitch (Collette), Will Stanton (Bobo), Edward Keane (Dr. Duval), Robert Warwick (Demonpre), Pedro de Cordoba (Marcal), Tom Wilson (Emil), John Harmon (Andre), Richard Bond (Georges), Earl Gunn (Leon), Sidney Bracey (Soupy), George Lloyd (Dogface), Charles Richman (Governor Beaufort), Stuart Holmes (Gustav LeBrun), Leonard Mudie (Advocate General), Egon Brecher (Debriac), Frank Reicher (President of Assize Court), James Blaine, Galan Galt, Frank Hagney, Stanley King, Douglas Williams (Guards), Dick Botiller (Pilot of Escape Boat), Al Bridge (Captain of the Guards), Nat Carr (Court Clerk), Glen Cavender (Gendarme on Train), Davison Clark (Captain of Gendarmes), Neil Clisby (Jules), Harry Cording (Guard Accepting Bribe), Gino Corrado (Man Escaping Gendarmes with Debriac), Earl Dwire (Priest), Eddie Foster (Supply Clerk), Sol Gorss, Don Turner (Guards Escorting Gaudet After Operation), John Hamilton (Captain of Second Convict Ship), Ben Hendricks, Jr. (Francois, Sergeant of the Guards), Vera Lewis (Gaudet's Housekeeper), Billy McClain (Governor's Servant), Henry Otho (Guard Handcuffing Pierre), Paul Panzer (Jury Foreman), Alonzo Price (Captain Edward Ferreau of the First Convict Ship), Dick Rich (Guard Drugged by Gaudet), Cliff Saum (Uniformed Gendarme), Francis Sayles (Boatman Taking Madame Lucien to Mainland), Earl Smith (Madame Lucien's Servant), Walter Soderling (Wagon Driver), Elliott Sullivan (Gate Guard).

Confessions of a Nazi Spy (1939) ["social problem"]
Credits: Directed by Anatole Litvak; Produced by Robert B. Lord, Hal B. Wallis and Jack L. Warner; Screenplay by Milton Krims and John Wexley; Based on Articles in *The New York Post* by Leon G. Turrou; Directors of Photography: Sol Polito, Ernest Haller (black and white / 1.37:1 ratio); Film Editor: Owen Marks; Musical Score: Max Steiner; Musical Direction: Leo F. Forbstein; Musical Orchestrations: Hugo Friedhofer; Art Director: Carl Jules Weyl; Costume Designer: Milo Anderson; Makeup Artists: Robert Cowan, Joe Stinton; Hair Stylist: Ruby Felkner; Unit Manager: Louis Baum; Second Unit Director:

Claude Archer; Assistant Director: Chuck Hansen; Props: M. Goldman; Assistant Props: Harry Goldman; Sound: Robert B. Lee; Stunts: Jimmie Dundee, Sol Gorss, Fred Graham, Gil Perkins; Best Boy: William Conger; Montage Cameraman: Archie R. Dalzell; Still Photographer: Mack Elliott; Assistant Camera: Frank Evans; Gaffer: Frank Flanagan; Grip: Harold Noyes; Second Camera Operator: John Polito; Wardrobe: Cora Lobb, Dick Moder; Montages: Don Siegel; Dialogue Director: Ted Thomas; Technical Advisor: Leon G. Turrou; Publicist: Fred Heacock; Script Clerk: Jean McNaughton; Warner Bros.-First National Pictures; Production Dates: February 1–March 18, 1939; World Premiere, Beverly Hills, California, April 27, 1939; Released May 6, 1939; Running Time: 104 minutes. (Banned in The Third Reich.)

Cast: Edward G. Robinson (Edward Renard), Francis Lederer (Schneider), George Sanders (Schlager), Paul Lukas (Dr. Kassell), Henry O'Neill (Attorney Kellogg), Dorothy Tree (Hilda Kleinhauer), Lya Lys (Erika Wolf), Grace Stafford (Mrs. Schneider), James Stephenson (British Military Intelligence Agent), Hedwiga Reicher (Mrs. Kassell), Joe Sawyer (Werner Renz), Sig Ruman (Krogman), Lionel Royce (Hintze), Henry Victor (Wildebrandt), Hans Heinrich Von Twardoski (Helldorf), Wolfgang Zilzer (Westphal), Frederick Vogeding (Captain Richter), Willy Kaufman (Greutzwald), Rudolph Anders (Captain Straubel), Wilhelm von Brincken (Captain von Eichen), George Rosener (Klauber), Frederick Burton (U.S. District Court Judge), Eily Malyon (Mrs. McLaughlin), Bodil Rosing (Passenger on Boat), Fred Aldrich (Nazi at Bund Meeting), Sherwood Bailey (Newsboy at End), Ward Bond (American Legionnaire), Walter Bonn (Naval Officer Seeing Renard at Seaplane), Egon Brecher (Fritz Muller, German Agent), Tommy Bupp (Shoeshine Boy), Glen Cavender (Man in Montage Stuffing Mailboxes), John Conte (Voice of Radio Announcer), Alec Craig (McGregor, Scottish Postman), Jimmie Dundee, Sol Gorss (Nazi Goons at Bund Meeting), Frederick Giermann (German-American at Bund Meeting), Lisa Golm (Mrs. Anna Westphal), William Gould, Edward Keane (FBI Agents), Fred Graham (American Legionnaire at Bund Meeting), Creighton Hale, Stuart Holmes (Draftsmen), John Hamilton (FBI Chief), John Harron (Man in Montage with Propaganda), Eddie Hart (Nazi Agent), Adolf Hitler (Himself [archival footage]), Max Hoffman, Jr. (Soldier at Renz's Arrest), Arthur Stuart Hull (U.S. Government Agent), Selmer Jackson (Customs Official), Robert Emmett Keane (Harrison, Passport Official), Milton Kibbee (Man Greeting Waiter Bill), Martin Kosleck (Joseph Goebbels), Frank Mayo (FBI Agent Phillips), Ray Miller (Bill, Coffee Shop Proprietor), Walter Miller (Bill, Waiter with Coffee), Jack Mower (FBI Agent "Mac" MacDonald), George Offerman, Jr. (Western Union Messenger), Lotte Palfi Andor (Kassel's Nurse), Gil Perkins (Goebbel's Aide), Norman Phillips, Jr. (Gottfried Simmons, Nazi Youth), Lucien Prival (Kranz), Otto Reichow (Driver of Nazi Car That Crashed), John Ridgely (Army Hospital Clerk), Hans Shumm (Bismark Officer with Crew List), Charles Sherlock (FBI Agent Fred Young), Edwin Stanley (U.S. Official), Robert R. Stephenson (Fritz, von Eichen's Aide), Regis Toomey (Tom, in Coffee Shop), Frederic Tozere (FBI Agent Staunton), Charles Trowbridge (Major Williams), Emmett Vogan (Hotel Desk Clerk), Louis Aldon, Jack Egger, Lon McCallister, Tempe Piggot, Ferdinand Schumann-Heink, Lester Sharpe, Rudolf Steinboeck, Dave Wengren (bits), John Deering (Narrator).

Blackmail (1939) [chain gang–framed man]

Credits: Directed by H. C. Potter; Produced by John W. Considine, Jr., and Albert E. Levoy; Screenplay by David Hertz and William Ludwig; Story by Endre Bohem and Dorothy Yost; Additional Writers: Nathanie Bucknall and Brown Holmes; Director of Photography: Clyde De Vinna (black and white / 1.37:1 ratio); Film Editor: Howard O'Neill; Musical Score: David Snell, Edward Ward; Musical Orchestrations: Wally Heglin, Leonid Raab; Art Director: Cedric Gibbons; Set Decorator: Edwin B. Willis; Second Unit Director: Charles Dorlan; Second Unit Director (Chase Inserts): Charles T. Trego; Assistant Director: Gilbert Kurland; Associate Art Director: Howard Campbell; Recording Director: Douglas Shearer; Wardrobe: Dolly Tree; Metro-Goldwyn-Mayer Pictures–Loew's Incorporated; Production Began June 5, 1939; Released September 8, 1939; Running Time: 81 minutes.

Cast: Edward G. Robinson (John R. Ingram), Ruth Hussey (Helen Ingram), Gene Lockhart (William Ramey), Bobs Watson (Hank), Guinn ("Big Boy") Williams (Moose McCarthy), John Wray (Diggs), Arthur Hohl (Rollins), Esther Dale (Sarah), Trevor Bardette (Southern Deputy), Willie Best (Bunny, the Janitor), Stanley Blystone, Harry Fleischmann, Ethan Laidlaw (Oil Workers), Wade Boteler (Police Sergeant), Ed Brady (Prisoner Worrying About Dick Tracy), Everett Brown (Black Prisoner), Eddy Chandler (Prisoner Boss Brown), George Cooper (Released Prisoner Hawley), Joseph Crehan (Mr. Blaine), Jack Daley (Policeman), Frank Darien (Ramey's Oil-Well Watchman), Hal K. Dawson (Hotel Desk Clerk), Joe Dominguez (Pedro), Robert Homans (Cooper), Cy Kendall (Southern Sheriff), Victor Kilian (Warden Frank Miller), Robert Middlemass (Desk Sergeant), Charles Middleton (Southern Deputy), Art Miles (First Truck Driver), Ivan Miller (Detective Webber), Ed Montoya (Juan), Philip Morris (State Trooper), James C. Morton (Second Policeman Arresting John), Gil Perkins (Kearney, Oil Worker Blown Up), Bob Reeves (Chain Gang Guard), Cyril Ring (Ramey's Butler), Harry Strang (First Policeman), Harry Tenbrook (Truck Driver at Gas Station), Leo White (Prisoner), Joe Whitehead (Oil Worker Anderson), Lew Harvey, Mitchell Lewis, Louis Natheaux, Ted Oliver, Lee Phelps (scenes deleted).

Johnny Eager (1942) [reunion]

Credits: Produced and Directed by Mervyn LeRoy; Screenplay by John Lee Mahin and James Edward Grant; Story by James Edward Grant; Director of Photography: Harold Rosson (black and white / 1.37:1); Film Editor: Albert Akst; Musical Score: Bronislau Kaper, Daniele Amfitheatrof; Musical Orchestrations: Lennie Hayton, Wally Heglin, Leonid Raab; Art Director: Cedric Gibbons; Set Decorator: Edwin B. Willis; Costume Designer: Robert Kalloch; Unit Manager: William H. Cannon; Assistant Director: Al Shenberg; Associate Art Director: Stan Rogers; Recording Director: Douglas Shearer; Camera Operator: Harkness Smith; Publicity Director: Howard Dietz; Metro-Goldwyn-Mayer Pictures–Loew's Incorporated; Production Dates: September 2–October 28, 1941; Released January 17, 1942; Running Time: 107 minutes.

Cast: Robert Taylor (Johnny Eager), Lana Turner (Lisbeth Bard), Edward Arnold (John Benson Farrell), Van Heflin (Jeff Hertnett), Robert Sterling (Jimmy

Courtney), Patricia Dane (Garnet), Glenda Farrell (Mae Blythe), Henry O'Neill (Mr. Verne), Diana Lewis (Judy Sanford), Barry Nelson (Lew Rankin), Charles Dingle (Marco), Paul Stewart (Julio), Cy Kendall (Halligan), Don Costello (Billiken), Lou Lubin (Benji), Joseph Downing (Ryan), Connie Gilchrist (Peg), Robin Raymond (Matilda), Leona Maricle (Miss Mines), Byron Shores (Officer No. 711), Hooper Atchley (Gambler Who Made Eight the Hard Way), Arthur Belasco, Larry Clifford, James C. Morton (Card Players), Sheldon Bennett (Headwaiter at Luce's), Gladys Blake (Receptionist at Verne's Office), Joyce Bryant (Woman with Gambler Who Made Eight the Hard Way), Jack Carr (Cupid, Halligan's Guard at Card Game), Georgie Cooper (Wife Who Wants a New Car), Jules Cowles (Man on Betting Line in Front of Mr. Verne), Cliff Danielson (Floyd Markham), John Dilson (Pawnbroker), Mike Donovan (Switchman), Edward Earle (Man No. Two Watching Dog Run at Track), Franklyn Farnum (Racetrack Spectator), Harrison Greene (Card Player Who Says, "It's Getting Late"), Alice Keating (Ella, Lisbeth's Maid), Richard Kipling (Husband Who Lost More Than $2,000), Art Miles (Lieutenant Allan, Card Player), Johnny Mitchell (Policeman), Nestor Paiva (Tony Luce), Emory Parnell (Policeman Telling Eager to Move His Taxicab), Alexander Pollard (Farrell's Butler), Alonzo Price (Man No. One Watching Dog Run at Track), Stanley Price (Man with News of Rankin's Death), Janet Shaw (Alice, Secretary in Verne's Office), Elliott Sullivan (Ed Nolan), Charles Thomas (Bus Conductor), Gohr Van Vleck (Councilman French), Beryl Wallace (Mabel), Anthony Warde (Guard Outside Luce's Office Door), Pat West (Eddie, Hanger-on), Joe Whitehead (Mr. Ruffing).

Sullivan's Travels (1942) ["social problem" satire]

Credits: Directed by Preston Sturges; Produced by Paul Jones, Buddy G. DeSylva and Preston Sturges; Screenplay by Preston Sturges; Director of Photography: John F. Seitz (black and white / 1.37:1 ratio); Film Editor: Stuart Gilmore; Musical Score: Charles Bradshaw, Leo Shuken; Stock Music: Gerard Carbonara, John Leipold, Joseph J. Lilley, Albert Hay Malotte, Ernest Toch, Victor Young; Musical Direction: Sigmund Krumgold; Art Directors: Hans Drier, A. Earl Hedrick; Casting: Robert Mayo; Costume Designer: Edith Head; Makeup Artists: Wally Westmore, Hal Lierley; Hair Stylist: Merle Reeves; Hair Stylist Supervisor: Leonora Sabine; Unit Manager: Joseph C. Youngerman; Assistant Director: Anthony Mann; First Assistant Director: Hollingsworth Morse; Second Assistant Director: Barton Adams; First Props: Oscar Law; Second Props: Robert Goodstein; Set Dresser: Ray Moyer; Sound Recordists: Harry D. Mills, Walter Oberst, Grant Rymal; Stage Engineer: Wallace Nogle; Boom Operator: George Ziegler; Process Photography: Farciot Edouart; Stunt Doubles: Wesley Hopper, Allen Pomeroy, John Sinclair; Assistant Camera: Francis Burgess; Gaffer: Earl Crowell; Company Grip: Walter McCloud; Still Photographer: Talmadge Morrison; Second Camera Operator: Otto Pierce; Electrician: James Tait; Mike Grip: George Ziegler; Animators: Norman Ferguson, Dick Lundy; Casting Assistants: Bill Greenwald, Bert McKay, Alice Thomas; Wardrobe: Clayton Brackett (men); Hazel Hegarty (women); Costume Jeweler: Eugene Joseff; Assistant Cutter: Chandler House; Publicist: Teet Carle; Script Clerk:

Nesta Charles; Secretaries: Edwin Gillette, Marie Morris; Location Manager: Norman Lacey; Assistant Writer: Ernest Laemmle; Script Assistant: Isabelle Sullivan; Double (Veronica Lake): Cheryl Walker; Producer ("Playful Pluto" Sequence): Walt Disney; Director ("Playful Pluto" Sequence): Burt Gillet; Budget: $689,665; Paramount Pictures; Production Dates: May 12–July 22, 1941; New York Premiere January 28, 1942; Running Time: 90 minutes.

Cast: Joel McCrea (John L. Sullivan), Veronica Lake (The Girl), Robert Warwick (Mr. LeBrand), William Demarest (Mr. Jones), Franklin Pangborn (Mr. Casalsis), Porter Hall (Mr. Hadrian), Byron Foulger (Mr. Valdelle), Margaret Hayes (Secretary), Robert Greig (Sullivan's Butler), Eric Blore (Sullivan's Valet), Torben Meyer (The Doctor), Victor Potel (Cameraman), Richard Webb (Radio Man), Charles R. Moore (Colored Chef), Almira Sessions (Ursula), Esther Howard (Miz Zeffie), Frank Moran (Tough Chauffeur), Georges Renavent (Old Tramp), Harry Rosenthal (The Trombenick), Alan Bridge (The Mister), Jimmy Conlin (Trusty), Jan Buckingham (Mrs. Sullivan), Robert Winkler (Bud), Chick Collins (Capital), Jimmie Dundee (Labor), George Anderson (Sullivan's Ex-Manager), Myrtle Anderson, Elizabeth Ashley, Ruth Bias, Grace Boone, Ari Lee Branche, William Broadus, Anita Brown, Ruth Byers, Matilda Caldwell, Mark Carnahan, Laurence Criner, Frances Curry, Gladys Davis, James Davis, Joan Douglas, A. Downs, LeRoy Edwards, Fay Fifer, Elizabeth Gray, Inez Hatchett, Pearl Lancaster, Cora Lang, Artie Overstreet, War Perkins, Mary Reed, Irving Smith, Lillian Taylor, Henry ("Hot Shot" Thomas, Maggie Thomas, Notable Vines, Jack Winslow (Churchgoers), Roscoe Ates (Hollywood Diner Counterman), Ted Billings (Tramp in Soup Kitchen), Billy Bletcher (Entertainer in Hospital), Monte Blue (Policeman in Slums), Ed Brady (Hobo Hopping Train), Jess Lee Brooks (Church Preacher Showing Movie), Chester Conklin (Old Bum), Edgar Dearing (Motorcycle Cop), Robert Dudley (One-Legged Hobo), Kit Guard (Convict), Jester Hairston (Charlie, Church Projectionist), Chuck Hamilton, Bert Moorhouse, Cyril Ring (Reporters), Edward Hearn (Policeman at Beverly Hills Station), Arthur Hoyt (Preacher at Revival Mission), Sheldon Jett (Man in Bathhouse/Studio Executive), Payne B. Johnson (Boy), Bob Kortman, Lon Poff (Convicts Watching Movie in Church), Pert Launders, Emory Parnell (Rail Yard Bulls), J. Farrell MacDonald (Desk Sergeant), Pat McKee (Tramp at Revival Meeting), Esther Michelson (Woman on "Poor Street"), Ray Milland (Near Collison Man on Studio Street), Frank Mills (Drunk Eating in Theater), Howard M. Mitchell (Railroad Clerk), (Reporter), Paul Newlan (Truck Driver), Gus Reed (Mission Cook), Willard Robertson (Judge), Dewey Robinson (Charlie, Sheriff), Sheila Sheldon (Child on "Poor Street"), Preston Sturges (Studio Director), Madame Sui-Te-Wan (Church Harmonium Player), Julius Tannen (Public Defender), Harry Tyler (Railroad Information Clerk), Pat West (Las Vegas Diner Counterman), Bill Wolfe (Toothless Man at Revival Meeting).

They Made Me a Fugitive (1947) a.k.a. *I Became a Criminal* [crime gang]

Credits: Directed by Alberto Cavalcanti; Produced by Nat A. Bronstein, James A. Carter and Noel Langley; Screenplay by Noel Langley; Based on the Novel *A*

Convict Has Escaped by Jackson Budd; Director of Photography: Otto Heller (black and white / 1.37:1 ratio); Film Editor: Margery Saunders; Musical Score: Marius-Francois Gaillard; Musical Conductor: John Hollingsworth; Art Director: Andrew Mazzel; Makup Artist: Natalie Taylor; Hair Stylists: Jean Bear, Ida Mills; Assistant Makeup Artist: George Turner; Production Manager: Fraser Foulsham; Assistant Directors: Dicky Leeman, Guy Hamilton; Second Assistant Director: Pat Kelly; Head Carpenter: Peter Dukelow; Draftsman: Thomas Gosman; Sound Director: George Burgess; Sound Recordist: John Mitchell; Boom Operator: Moray MacFarlane; Dubbing Editor: Jack Slade; Stunts: Jock Easton; Camera Operators: Robert Day, Gus Drisse; Assistant Cameras: Gerry Fisher, Walter Lassally; Lighting Camera Operator (Second Unit): Bert Mason; Still Photographer: Curil Stanborough; Camera Operator (Second Unit): John Winbolt; Wardrobe Supervisor: Dorothy Sinclair; Wardrobe Mistress: Amy C. Binney; Cutter: Anne Barker; Editorial Supervisor: Reginald Beck; Continuity: Shirley Barnes; Assistant Continuity: Jean Dyball; Location Manager: Kenneth Horne; An A. R. Shipman Production; Alliance Film Studios, Limited–Warner Bros. Pictures; Produced at Hammersmith, London; Released June 24, 1947 (U.K.); Running Time: 78 minutes.

Cast: Sally Gray (Sally), Trevor Howard (Clem), Griffith Jones (Narcy), Rene Ray (Cora), Mary Merrall (Aggie), Charles Farrell (Curley), Michael Brennan (Jim), Jack McNaughton (Soapy), Cyril Smith (Bert), John Penrose (Shawney), Eve Ashley (Ellen), Phyllis Robins (Olga), Bill O'Connor (Bill), Maurice Denham (Mr. Fenshaw), Vida Hope (Mrs. Fenshaw), Ballard Berkeley (Rockliffe), Derek Birch (Police Constable Murray), Peter Bull (Fidgity Phil), Gordon Court (Sergeant), Lyn Evans (Lorry Driver), Enid Cruikshank (Club Hostess), Sebastian Cabot (Club Proprietor), Ida Patlanski (Soho Girl), Howard Douglas (Chief Warder), Charles Doe (Electrician), Diana Graves (May), Sam Kydd (Eddie), Beatrice Varley (Farmer's Wife).

Chain Gang (1950) [chain gang]

Credits: Directed by Lew Landers; Produced by Sam Katzman; Screenplay by Howard J. Green; Director of Photography: Ira H. Morgan (black and white / 1.37:1 ratio); Film Editor: Aaron Stell; Musical Score: George Duning, Hugo Frey, Louis Greunberg, Carol Rathaus, Hans J. Salter (stock music); Musical Direction: Mischa Bakaleinikoff; Art Director: Paul Palmontola; Set Decorator: Sidney Clifford; Makeup Artist: Ray Sebastian; Hair Stylist: Helen Hunt; Production Manager: Herbert B. Leonard; Assistant Director: R. M. Andrews; Sound: J. S. Westmoreland; Grip: Al Becker; Still Photographer: Don Christie; Gaffer: Howard Robertson; Camera Operator: William P. Whitley; Script Supervisor: Violet Newfield; Kay Pictures, Inc.–Columbia Pictures; Production Dates: May 17–24, 1950; Released November 1, 1950; Running Time: 70 minutes.

Cast: Douglas Kennedy (Cliff Roberts), Marjorie Lord (Rita McKelvey), Emory Parnell (Captain Duncan), William ("Bill") Phillips (Roy Snead), Thurston Hall (John McKelvey), Harry Cheshire (Henry ["Pop"] O'Donnell), Fred Aldrich (Convict), Stanley Blystone (Convict on Chain Gang), Paul E. Burns (Dr. Evans),

Benny Burt (Convict in Bunk), Jack Chefe (Convict), James Conaty (Pop's Influential Friend), George Eldredge (Guard Adams), William Fawcett (Zeke), Eddie Foster (Convict Operating Crane), John Hart (Chain Gang Member), Don C. Harvey (Guard Langley), Charles Horvath (Convict in Skirmish), Billy Lechner (Eddie Jones), Herbert Rawlinson (Senator Harden), George Robotham (Guard Reagan), John Rogers (Joe, Lunch Counterman), Larry Steers (Senate Committee Hearing Attendee), Bert Stevens (Newspaper Office Worker), Brick Sullivan (Guard), William Tannen (Harry Cleaver), Dorothy Vaughan (Mrs. Briggs), Rusty Westcoatt (Guard Yates), Frank Wilcox (Lloyd Killgallen).

Carbine Williams (1952) [work gang]

Credits: Directed by Richard Thorpe; Screenplay and Story by Art Cohn; Inspired by the Article "The Most Unforgettable Character I've Met," by Captain H. T. Peoples, in *Reader's Digest*, March 1951; Director of Photography: William C. Mellor (black and white / 1.37 ratio); Film Editor: Newell P. Kimlin; Musical Score: Conrad Salinger; Musical Orchestrations: Robert Franklyn, Johnny Green; Art Directors: Cedric Gibbons, Eddie Imazu; Set Decorators: Ralph S. Hurst, Edwin B. Willis; Costume Designer: Walter Plunkett; Makeup Designer: William Tuttle; Hair Stylist: Sydney Guilaroff; Assistant Director: Al Jennings; Recording Supervisor: Douglas Shearer; Sound: Ralph A. Pender; Special Effects: A. Arnold Gillespie, Warren Newcombe; Stunts: Charles Horvath, Stubby Kruger, Bert LeBaron, Ted Mapes, Duke York; Camera Operator: Neal Beckner; Assistant Camera: Bobby Moreno, William Riley; Still Photographer: Bill Thomas; Publicity Director: Howard Dietz; Technical Advisor: David Marshall Williams; Metro-Goldwyn-Mayer Pictures–Loew's Incorporated; Production Dates: Early December 1951–January 15, 1952; Fayetteville, North Carolina, Premiere: April 24, 1952; New York Premiere: May 7, 1952; Released May 16, 1952; Running Time: 92 minutes.

Cast: James Stewart (Marsh Williams), Jean Hagen (Maggie Williams), Wendell Corey (Captain H. T. Peoples), Carl Benton Reid (Claude Williams), Paul Stewart ("Dutch" Kruger), Otto Hulett (Mobley), Rhys Williams (Redwick Karson), Herbert Hayes (Lionel Daniels), James Arness (Leon Williams), Porter Hall (Sam Makley), Fay Roope (Ed, District Attorney), Ralph Dumke (Andrew White), Leif Erickson (Feder), Henry Corden (Bill Stockton), Frank Richards (Truex), Howard Petrie (Sheriff), Stuart Randall (Deputy Sheriff Tom Vennar), Dan Riss (Jesse Rimmer), Robert Hyatt (David Williams), Bob Alden (Messenger), Jimmy Ames (Trusty), Baynes Barron (Whipped Convict), Willis Bouchey (Joseph Mitchell), Marshall Bradford, Sam Flint, Nolan Leary, George Pembroke (Board Members), Margaret Brayton (Secretary), Roy Butler (Newton), Douglas Carter, James Cronan, Billy Dix, Roy Enge, Harry Hines, Charles Horvath, Robert Stevenson, Guy Wilkerson, Ward Wood (Prisoners), Harry Cheshire (Judge Kerr), Ken Christy (Bailiff), Heinie Conklin, Mark Herron, William J. O'Brien (Courtroom Spectators), Norma Jean Cramer (Mary Ruth Williams), Jordan Cronenweth (Will Williams), Wade Crosby, Paul Kruger, Bert LeBaron, James Logan, Lee Phelps, Duke York (Guards), Lillian Culver (Mrs. Laura Williams), John Doucette (Gavrey, Prisoner at Chain Gang Camp),

Watson Downs (Foreman), Michael Dugan (Frank Gregory), Tony Epper (Wesley Williams), Robert Foulk (Chain Gang Guard), Jon Gardner (Wesley Williams), Jonathan Hale (Judge Henry P. Lane), James Harrison (Trusty), Fred Kohler, Jr. (Lathe Worker), George Lloyd (Mess Hall Trusty), Marlene Lyden (Mary Eloise Williams), Harry Macklin (John Williams), John Maxwell (Dr. McDonald), John McKee (Worker), David McMahon (Prison Guard), Emile Meyer (Head Guard), Louis Nicoletti (Giacosi), Erik Nielsen (Gordon Williams), Fiona O'Shiel (Mrs. Rimmer), Marilee Phelps (Mrs. Gregory), Richard Reeves (Guard in Cage), Dick Rich (Trusty), James A. Robertson (Black Assistant), Gene Roth (Railroad Construction Boss), Ralph Smiley (The Ferrett), John Smith (Robert Williams), Leonard Strong (Robak), William Vedder (Minister), Emmett Vogan (Mrs. Swanson), Bennie Washington (Black Woman), Robert J. Wilke (Guard on Train).

Hellgate (1952) [work gang–innocent man]

Credits: Directed by Charles Marquis Warren; Screenplay by Charles Marquis Warren; Story by Charles Marquis Warren and John C. Champion; Director of Photography: Ernest Miller (black and white / 1.37 ratio); Film Editor: Elmo Williams; Musical Score and Direction: Paul Dunlap; Art Director: Frank Paul Sylos; Set Decorator: Ralph Sylos; Makeup Artist: Web Overlander; Production Supervisor: Andrew Magginetti; Assistant Director: Andrew V. McLaglen; Sound Engineer: John K. Kean; Sound Recording: Don Keith; Special Effects: Ray Mercer; Stunts: John L. Cason, Kermit Maynard; Grip Foreman: Noble Craig; Camera Operator: Archie R. Dalzell; Wardrobe: Wesley Jeffries; Assistant Editor: Robert L. Lippert, Jr.; Music Editor: Alan Jaggs; Script Supervisor: Marie Messenger; Locations: Bronson Canyon and Griffith Park, Los Angeles; Ray Corrigan Ranch, Simi Valley, California; Commander Films Corporation–Lippert Pictures; Production Dates: March 25–mid–April 1952; Released September 5, 1952; Running Time: 87 minutes.

Cast: Sterling Hayden (Gilman S. Hanley), Joan Leslie (Ellen Hanley), Ward Bond (Lieutenant Tod Voorhees), James Arness (George Redfield), Peter Coe (Jumper Hall), John Pickard (Gundy Boyd), Robert J. Wilkie (Sergeant Major Kearn), James Anderson (Verne Brechene), Richard Emery (Dan Mott), Richard Paxton (George Nye), William Hamel (Lieutenant Colonel Woods), Marshall Bradford (Dr. Pelham), Sheb Wooley (Neill Price), Rory Mallinson (Banta), Pat Coleman (Hunchy), Kermit Maynard (Barricade Guard), Nick Borgani (Guard), Timothy Carey (Wyand), John L. Cason (Prison Guard), Edmund Cobb (Frank), James Dobson, Mathew McCue (Prisoners), Frank Ellis (Man at Barricade), Ed Hinton (Ault), Jimmy Noel (Prisoner Tossing Rock), House Peters, Jr. (Witness), Stanley Price (Colonel Telsen), Mike Ragan (Army Corporal), Rodd Redwing (Pima), Mickey Simpson (Army Jailhouse Guard), Bert Stevens (Army Board Member), Jack Tornek (Guard/Horseman), James Harrison, Paul Marion, James Shaw (bits).

I Accuse! (1958) ["social problem"–innocent man]

Credits: Directed by Jose Ferrer; Produced by Sam Zimbalist; Screenplay by Gore Vidal; Based on the Book *Captain Dreyfus: The Story of a Mass Hysteria* by

Nicholas Halasz; Director of Photography: Freddie Young (black and white / 2.35:1 widescreen ratio); Film Editor: Frank Clarke; Musical Score: William Alwyn, Douglas Gamley; Musical Conductor: Muir Matheson; Art Director: Eliot Scott; Costume Designer: Elizabeth Haffenden; Makeup Artist: Charles Parker; Hair Dresser: Joan Johnstone; Production Manager: Dora Wright; Second Assistant Director: Otto Plaschkes; Recording Supervisor: A. W. Watkins; Sound Editors: Van Allen James, Kendrick Kinney, John Logan; Special Photographic Effects: Tom Howard; Locations: Metro-Goldwyn-Mayer British Studios, Boreham Wood, Elstree, Hertfordshire, England; Metro-Goldwyn-Mayer Pictures; Production Dates: April 3–Early June 1957; Released March 5, 1958 (U.S.).

Cast: Jose Ferrer (Captain Alfred Dreyfus), Anton Walbrook (Major Esterhazy), Viveca Lindfors (Lucie Dreyfus), Leo Genn (Major Picquart), Emlyn Williams (Emile Zola), David Farrar (Mathieu Dreyfus), Donald Wolfit (General Mercier), Herbert Lom (Major DuPaty de Clam), Harry Andrews (Major Henry), Felix Aylmer (Edgar Demange), Peter Illing (Georges Clemenceau), George Coulouris (Major Sandherr), Carl Jaffe (Colonel von Schwarzkoppen), Eric Portman (Bertillon), John Chandos (Drumont), Ernest Clark (Prosecutor, First Dreyfus Trial), Anthony Ireland (Judge, First Dreyfus Trial), John Phillips (Prosecutor, Esterhazy Trial), Lawrence Naismith (Judge, Esterhazy Trial), Michael Hordern (Prosecutor, Second Dreyfus Trial), Keith Pyott (Judge, Second Dreyfus Trial), Ronald Howard (Captain Avril), Charles Gray (Captain Brossard), Michael Anthony (Captain Leblanc), Arthur Howard (Captain Lauth), Michael Trubshaw (English Trubshaw), Violet Gould (Old Woman), Malcolm Keen (President of France).

The Defiant Ones (1958) ["social message"–chain gang]

Credits: Directed and Produced by Stanley Kramer; Screenplay by Nedrick Young and Harold Jacob Smith; Director of Photography: Sam Leavitt (black and white / 1.66:1 widescreen ratio); Film Editor: Frederic Knudtson; Musical Score: Ernest Gold; Musical Orchestrations: Jack Marshall; Production Designer: Rudolph Sternad; Art Director: Fernando Ferrere; Set Decorator: Joseph Kish; Makeup: Don Cash; Production Manager: Clem Beauchamp; Assistant Director: Paul Helmick; Property Master: Art Cole; Sound Effects: Walter Elliott; Sound Engineer: Jean L. Speak; Sound Editors: Wayne Fury, John Mick; Special Effects: Alex Weldon; Stunt Doubles: Ivan Dixon (Sidney Poitier), Robert F. Hoy (Tony Curtis); Stunts: Boyd ("Red") Morgan; Chief Gaffer: James Almond; Camera Operator: Albert Myers; Company Grip: Morris Rosen; Costume Supervisor: Joe King; Script Supervisor: John Franco; Presenter: Stanley Kramer; Dog Trainer: Cindy James; Curtleigh Productions-Stanley Kramer Productions–United Artists Pictures; Production Dates: Late February–Early April 1958; Released September 27, 1958; Running Time: 96 minutes.

Cast: Tony Curtis (John ["Joker"] Jackson), Sidney Poitier (Noah Cullen), Theodore Bikel , Charles McGraw (Captain Frank Gibbons), Lon Chaney, Jr. (Big Sam), King Donovan (Solly), Claude Akins (Mack), Lawrence Dobkin (Editor), Whit Bissell (Lou Gans), Carl ("Alfalfa") Switzer (Angus), Kevin

Couglin (Billy), Cara Williams (Billy's Mother), James Dime, Bill Lovett, Boyd ("Red") Morgan (Townsmen), Clem Fuller, Mickey Golden, Herman Hack (Search Party Members), Ned Glass (Doctor), Signe Hack (Townswoman), Harold Jacob Smith (Prison Truck Driver), Nedrick Young (Prison Guard in Truck).

Westinghouse Desilu Playhouse television series: "The Case for Dr. Mudd" (1958) [prison gang–innocent man]

Credits: Directed by Allen H. Miner; Produced by Jerry Stagg; Executive Producer: Bert Granet; Teleplay by Don Brinkley and Joseph Landon; Story by Don Brinkley; Director of Photography: Paul Ivano (black and white / 1.33:1 ratio); Film Editor: John M. Foley; Musical Score: Johnny Green; Art Directors: Ralph Berger, Frank T. Smith; Production Manager: Desi Arnaz; Desilu Productions–CBS Television Network; Broadcast October 20, 1958; Running Time: 60 minutes.

Cast: Lew Ayres (Dr. Samuel A. Mudd), Mary Anderson (Sarah Mudd), Donald Harron (John Wilkes Booth), Jack Weston (Root), Henry Brandon (Williams), Philip Coolidge (Stone), Charles Cooper (Lieutenant Lovett), Theodore Newton (Hennessey), Tom Pittman (Herold), Simon Scott (Holt), James Westerfield (General Ewing), Raymond Bailey, William Tannen, Dick Wilson (Bits), Desi Arnaz (Host).

Wanted: Dead or Alive television series: "Chain Gang" (1959) [chain gang]

Credits: Directed by Thomas Carr; Produced by John Robinson; Teleplay by Robert Leslie Bellem; Director of Photography: Harry J. Wild (black and white / 1.33:1 ratio); Film Editor: Lyle Boyer; Musical Score: Rudy Schrager; Art Director: Edward C. Jewell; Supervising Art Director: Bill Ross; Set Decorators: Chester Bayhi, Robert C. Bradfield; Production Manager: Norman S. Powell; Production Supervisor: Jack Sonntag; Assistant Director: Mike Salamunovich; Sound: Stephen Bass; Sound Effects: Albert E. Kennedy; Editorial Supervisor: Bernard W. Burton; Music Supervisor: Herschel Burke Gilbert; Four Star Productions–Malcolm Enterprises–CBS Television; Broadcast December 12, 1959; Running Time: 26 minutes.

Cast: Steve McQueen (Josh Randall), Dave Willock (Jethro Dane), Ted de Corsia (George Winters), Laurie Mitchell (Belle Colter), Chris Alcaide (Cree Colter), I. Stanford Jolley (Charlie Martin), James Burke (Sheriff Blore), William Schallert (Link Damon), Than Wyenn (Gib Rafford), Richard Reeves (Jenks), John Breen (Townsman), Jack Stoney (Prisoner).

Desire in the Dust (1960) [chain gang]

Credits: Directed by William F. Claxton; Screenplay by Charles Lang; Based on the Novel *Desire in the Dust* by Harry Whittington; Director of Photography: Lucien Ballard (black and white / 2.35 widescreen ratio); Film Editor: Richard W. Farrell; Musical Score: Paul Dunlap; Art Directors: Ernest Fegte, John B. Mansbridge; Assistant Editor: Oscar Denenberg; Production Secretary: Pat

Thomas; Locations: Clinton, Louisiana; Lippert Pictures–20th Century-Fox Pictures; Production Date: June 1960; Released October 11, 1960; Running Time: 102 minutes.

Cast: Raymond Burr (Colonel Ben Marquand), Martha Hyer (Melinda Marquand), Joan Bennett (Mrs. Marquand), Ken Scott (Lonnie Wilson), Brett Halsey (Dr. Ned Thomas), Edward Binns (Luke Connett), Margaret Field (Maude Wilson), Douglas Fowley (Zuba Wilson), Kelly Thordsen (Sheriff Wheaton), Rex Ingram (Burt Crane), Jack Ging (Peter Marquand), Ann Helm (Cass Wilson), Irene Ryan (Nora Finney), Paul Baxley (Thurman Case), Robert Earle (Virgil), Patricia Snow (Nellie), Elmore Morgan (Conductor), Audrey Moore (Frank), Joseph Sidney Felps (Roy), Joe Paul Steiner (Deputy).

The Fugitive television series (1963–1967) [framed man]

Credits: Series created by Roy Huggins; Directors include Lewis Allen, Abner Biberman, Richard Donner, William A, Graham, Jerry Hopper, Don Medford, Christian Nyby, Leo Penn, Joseph Pevney, Sydney Pollack, Mark Rydell and James Sheldon; Writers include John D. F. Black, Don Brinkley, Alan Caillou, John Kneubuhl, Philip Saltzman and Stanford Whitmore; Quinn Martin Productions–ABC Television; Broadcast 1963–1967; black and white & color / 1.33:1 ratio; Running Time (each of 120 episodes): 51 minutes.

Cast: David Janssen, Barry Morse; *guest stars* include Richard Anderson, R. G. Armstrong, Edward Binns, Antoinette Bower, Joseph Campanella, Richard Carlson, Ivan Dixon, Robert Duvall, Glenda Farrell, Murray Hamilton, Pat Hingle, Diana Hyland, John Larsh, Lois Nettleton, J. Pat O'Malley, Ed Nelson, Warren Oates, Susan Oliver, Paul Richards, Gilbert Roland, Janice Rule, Barbara Rush, Jacqueline Scott and William Shatner; Narrator: William Conrad.

Girl on a Chain Gang (1966) [chain gang]

Credits: Directed by Jerry Gross; Produced by Jerry Gross and Nicholas Demetroules; Screenplay by Jerry Gross; Story by Don Olson; Director of Photography: George Zimmermann (black and white); Film Editor: Israel Ortiz; Musical Score: Steve Karmen; Art Director: Nicholas Demetroules; Production Manager: Michael Blum; Sound: Lee Dichter, James Lynch; Camera Operator: Michael Konkos; Lighting Technician: Peter Nevard; Location Unit Manager: Henry Kaplan; Continuity: April Pollack; Production Coordinator: Jess Wolff; Jerry Gross Productions; Locations: Long Island, New York; Released October 21, 1966; Running Time: 96 minutes.

Cast: William Watson (Sheriff Sonny Lew Wymer), Julie Ange (Jean Rollins), Ron Charles (Deputy Luke), Arlene Farber (Nellie), Ron Segal (Ted Branch), Peter Nevard (Deputy Cal), Matt Reynolds (Les Davis), James Harvey (Claude Martin/Judge Farris Bean), Philip Vanyon (Doctor Rufe Hall), Henry Baker (Tom), Horace Bailey (Leroy), Sam Cutter (Cotton Ben Wymer), Wolf Landsman (Seth Waters), Earl Leake (Clyde Fuller), Richard Antony (State Trooper), Don Olson (Zeke Landers), Henry Kaplan (Justin Powers), Bernard Krauthamer (Jury Foreman).

Cool Hand Luke (1967) [chain gang]

Credits: Directed by Stuart Rosenberg; Produced by Gordon Carroll and Carter D. Haven, Jr.; Screenplay by Donn Pierce and Frank Pierson; Director of Photography: Conrad L. Hall (Technicolor / 2.35:1 widescreen ratio); Film Editor: Sam O'Steen; Musical Score: Lalo Schifrin; Art Director: Cary Odell; Set Decorator: Fred Price; Costume Designer: Howard Shoup; Makeup Supervisor: Gordon Bau; Supervising Hair Stylist: Jean Burt Reilly; Unit Manager: Arthur S. Newman, Jr.; Assistant Director: Hank Moonjean; Assistant Property Masters: John Barton, Don Miller; Set Dresser: Craig Binkley; Carpenter: Wes Webb; Sound: Larry Jost; Sound Re-recording Mixer: Dan Wallin; Stunts: M. James Arnett, Chuck Hicks; Camera Operator: Jordan Cronenweth; Assistant Cameras: Thomas Del Ruth, Robert C. Thomas; Assistant Chief Lighting Technician/Rigging Gaffer: Michael A. Jones; Chief Electrician: Harry Sundby; Musicians: Ben Benay, Barney Kessel, Tommy Morgan; Scoring Mixer: Dan Wallin; Title Designer: Wayne Fitzgerald; Locations: Lodi, Sacramento and Stockton, California; Jacksonville and Tavares, Florida; Budget: $3,000,000; Jalem Productions–Warner Bros. Pictures; Released November 1, 1967; Running Time: 126 minutes.

Cast: Paul Newman (Luke), George Kennedy (Dragline), J. D. Cannon (Society Red), Lou Antonio (Koko), Robert Drivas (Loudmouth Steve), Strother Martin (Captain), Jo Van Fleet (Arietta), Clifton James (Carr), Morgan Woodward (Boss Godfrey), Luke Askew (Boss Paul), Mac Cavell (Rabbitt), Robert Davalos (Blind Dick), Robert Donner (Boss Shorty), Warren Finnerty (Tattoo), Dennis Hopper (Babalugats), John McLiam (Boss Keen), Wayne Rogers (Gambler), Harry Dean Stanton (Tramp), Charles Tyner (Boss Higgins), Ralph Waite (Alibi), Anthony Zerbe (Dog Boy), Buck Kartalian (Dynamite), Joy Harmon (The Girl), Joe Don Baker (Fixer), James Gammon (Sleepy), Norman Goodwins (Stupid Blonde), Chuck Hicks (Chief), Rance Howard (Sheriff), James Jeter (Wickerman), Kim Kahana (Convict), Robert Luster (Jabo), Donn Pearce (Sailor), John Pearce (John), Cyril ("Chips") Robinson (Ben), Eddie Rosson (Luke's Nephew), Rush Williams (Patrolman), James Bradley (bit).

Nazarin (1968) [prison gang]

Credits: Directed by Luis Bunuel; Produced by Manuel Barbachano Ponce and Federico Amerigo; Screenplay by Luis Bunuel, Julio Alejandro and Emilio Carballido; Based on the Novel *Nazarin* by Benito Perez Galdos; Director of Photography: Gabriel Figueroa (black and white / 1.37 ratio); Film Editor: Carlos Savage; Musical Score: Rodolfo Halffter; Song, "Dios nunca muere": Macedonio Alcala; Art Director: Edward Fitzgerald; Costume Designer: Georgette Somohano; Makeup Artist: Armando Meyer; Hair Stylists: Bertha Chiu, Miguel Horcasitas; Production Manager: Enrique L. Morfin; Assistant Director: Ignacio Villareal; Sound Effects Editor: Abaaham Cruz; Sound Supervisor: James L. Fields; Incidental Sound Effects: Gonzalo Gavira; Boom Operator: Jose de Perez; Sound Re-recordist: Galdino R. Samperio; Gaffer: Daniel Lopez; Camera Operator: Ignacio Romero; Assistant Camera: Pablo Rios; Still Photographer: Manuel Alvarez Bravo; Production Advisor: Carlos Velo; Locations: Jonacatepec and Cuautla, Morelos, and Mexico City, Mexico; Producciones Barbachano Ponce–Altura Films International (Mexico); Released June 4, 1959 (Mexico); June 20, 1968 (United States); Running Time: 94 minutes.

Cast: Marga Lopez (Beatriz), Francisco Rabal (Padre Nazirio), Rita Macedo (Andara), Ignacio Lopez Tarso (El sacralego), Ofelia Guilmain (Chanfa), Luis Aceves Castaneda (El parracida), Noe Murayama (El pinto), Rosenda Monteros (El prieta), Jesus Fernandez (Ujo el enano), Ada Carrasco (Josefa), Antonio Bravo (Don Pablo, Architecto), Aurura Molina (La Camella), David Reynoso (Juan), Efrain Arauz (Vecino de Nazarin), Manuel Arvida (Companero de architecto), Socorro Avelar (Vecina de Josefa), Edmundo Barbero (don Angel-cura), Victorio Blanco (Viejo preso), Lupe Carriles (Prostituta), Arturo Castro ["Bigaton"] (Coronel), Jose Chavez (Capataz), Raul Dantes (Sargento), Felipe de Flores (Caminante con burro), Enedina Diaz de Leon (Anciana an casa de Josefa), Jose Luis Fernandez (Obrero), Lidia Franco (Sirvienta de don Angel), Salvador Godinez (Hombre vende caballo), Leonor Gomez (Mujer presa), Cecilia Leger (Mujer de la pena), Blanca Marroquin (Vecina de Nazarin), Roberto Meyer (Presidente municipal), Ines Murillo (Mujer entre multitud), Diana Ochoa (Vecina de Josefa), Pilar Pellicer (Lucia), Jose Pena (Sacerdote), Ignacio Peon (Sacerdote), Salvador Terroba (Amigo del pinto), Paz Villegas (Mama de Beatriz), Isabel Vazquez ["La Chicimeca"] (Vecina de Nazario), Amada Zumayo (Preso), (Ramon Sanchez (bit).

The Devil's 8 (1969) [chain gang]

Credits: Directed by Burt Topper; Produced by Burt Topper and Jack W. Cash; American International Pictures; Screenplay by Willard Huyck, John Milius and James Gordon White; Story by Larry Gordon; Director of Photography: Richard C. Glouner (Pathecolor / 1.85:1 widescreen ratio); Film Editor: Fred R. Feitshans, Jr.; Musical Score: Michael Lloyd, Jerry Styner; Art Director: Paul Sylos; Set Decorator: Harry Reif; Makeup Artist: Irving Berns; Production Manager: Jack Bohrer; Post-Production Coordinator: Buzz Feitshans; Assistant Directors: Lew Borzage, James Petsch; Properties: Randall C. Berkeley; Construction Supervisor: Ross Hahn; Sound Mixer: Al Overton; Special Effects: Roger George; Background Projection: William Hansard; Stunt Coordinator: Charles Bail; Stunts: Michael Haynes; Camera Operator: Vee Bodrero; Gaffer: Lloyd Garnell; Key Grip: Charles Hannawalt; Wardrobe: Richard Bruno; Music Director: Mike Curb; Music Arranger/Song Producer: Mike Curb; Musical Supervisor: Al Simms; Script Supervisor: Lynn A. Aber; Locations: The Lost Ranch, Big Bear Lake and Camp Pinecrest, San Bernardino, California; American International Pictures; Released June 18, 1969; Running Time: 98 minutes.

Cast: Christopher George (Ray Faulkner), Fabian (Sonny), Tom Nardini (Billy Joe), Leslie Parrish (Cissy), Ross Hagen (Frank Davis), Cliff Osmond (Bubba), Larry Bishop (Chandler), Robert DoQui (Henry Reed), Ron Rifkin (Stewart Martin), Joseph Turkel (Sam), Baynes Baron (Bureau Chief), Lada Edmund, Jr. (Inez), Marjorie Dayne (Hailie), Roy Thiel (Guard), R. L. ("Tex") Armstrong (Charley), Ralph Meeker (Burl).

Take the Money and Run (1969) [chain gang parody]

Credits: Directed by Woody Allen; Produced by Charles H. Joffe, Jack Rollins, Sidney Glazier, Jack Grossberg and Edgar J. Sherick; Screenplay by Woody Allen and Mickey Rose; Director of Photography: Lester Shorr (Technicolor & black and white / 1.85:1 widescreen ratio); Film Editor: Paul Jordan, Ron Kalish; Musical Score: Marvin Hamlisch; Casting: Marvin Paige; Art Director: Fred Harpman; Set Decorator: Marvin Match; Makeup Artist: Stanley R. Dufford; Unit Manager: Fred T. Gallo; Unit Production Manager: Jack Grossberg; Assistant Director: Louis A. Stroller; Second Assistant Director: Walter Hill; Second Second Assistant Director: Stanley Ackerman; Construction Supervisor: Theodore Moehnke; Set Propertyman: Ken Phelps; Chargeman Painter: Chardin W. Smith; Sound Mixer: Bud Alper; Sound Effects and Music Editors: Sanford Rackow, John Strauss; Re-recording Engineer: Richard Vorisek; Special Effects: A. D. Flowers; Stunts: Carol Daniels; Camera Operator: Til Gabini; Lighting Supervisor: Martin Gorowitz; Photographer, Second Unit: Fred Hoffman; Grip: Harry Stern; Gaffer: Jack H. Wilson; Camera Operator: William Mendenhall; Wardrobe Supervisor: Erick M. Hjemik; Set Wardrobe: Bob Wolfe; Supervising Editor: James T. Heckert; Editorial Consultant: Ralph Rosenblum; Music Supervisor: Felix Giglio; Music Recordist: Frank Kulaga; Musical Conductor-Orchestrator: Kermit Levinsky; Unit Publicist: Don Boutyette; Script Supervisor: Jeanetta Lewis; Production Assistant: Henry Polosky; Production Auditor: Bert Schneiderman; Production Secretary: Lynn Vogel; Location Manager: Fouad Said; Locations: San Francisco, California; Heywood-Hillary Productions–Cinerama Releasing Corporation; Budget: $1,500,000; Released August 18, 1969; Running Time: 85 minutes.

Cast: Woody Allen (Virgil Starkwell), Janet Margolin (Louise), Marcel Hillaire (Fritz, Director), Jacquelin Hyde (Miss Blair), Lonny Chapman (Jake, Convict), Jan Merlin (Al, Bank Robber), James Anderson (Chain Gang Warden), Howard Storm (Fred), Mark Gordon (Vince), Micil Murphy (Frank), Minnow Moskowitz (Joe Magneta), Nate Jacobson (The Judge), Grace Bauer (Farm House Lady), Ethel Mokolow (Mother Starkwell), Dan Fraser (Julius Epstein, the Psychiatrist), Henry Leff (Father Starkwell), Mike O'Dowd (Michael Sullivan), Louise Lasser (Kay Lewis), Stanley Ackerman (Stanley Krim, Photographer), Thomas Bellin (Member of Virgil's Gang), Michael L. Davis (Police Officer in Coffee Shop), Roy Engel (Prison Guard Captain), Lynn Foley (Parade Spectator), Mickey Rose (Chain Gang Man), Paul Schumacher (Patrolman Lynch), Mitchell Tunick (Young Virgil Starkwell), Dwight D. Eisenhower, Kaiser Wilhelm II, Richard Nixon (Themselves [archival footage]), Jackson Beck (Narrator).

Chain Gang Women (1971) [chain gang]

Credits: Directed by Lee Frost; Produced by Wes Bishop and Jeffrey Kruger; Screenplay by Lee Frost and Wes Bishop; Director of Photography: Lee Frost (color); Film Editors: Lee Frost, E. ("Red") Shryver; Musical Score: Porter Jordan; Production Manager: Donald Baker; Assistant Director: Michael T. Mikler; Key Grip: Merrick Martin; Assistant Cameras: James E. McLarty, Charles Minsky;

Still Photographer: Mike Paladin; Gaffer: Jim Stemme; Best Boy: Duke Wilmouth; Music Producer-Supervisor: Porter Jordan; Musical Conductor-Arranger: Billy Sprague; Production Secretary: Donna Anderson; Script Supervisor: Phyllis Di Rosa Frost; Production Assistant: Henry Fusco; Flamingo Productions, Ltd.–Crown International Distributing; Released September 22, 1971; Running Time: 85 minutes.

Cast: Michael Stearns (Weed), Robert Lott (Harris), Barbara Mills (Wife), Linda York (Ann), Ralph Campbell (Farmer), Wes Bishop (Coleman), William B. Martin (Willy), Bruce Kimball (Fat Sam), Phil Hoover (Gentry), Chuck Wells (Jones), Duke Wilmouth (Prisoner), E. ("Red") Shryver (Larson), Colin Male, Henry Fusco, Jim Stemme, Charles Minsky (Prisoners), James E. McLarty (Police Officer), John Bliss (Prison Guard), James Whitworth (Prisoner with Grayish Beard).

Sweet Sugar (1972) [chain gang]

Credits: Directed by Michael Levesque; Produced by Lawrence Woolner, Charles S. Swartz and Peter Cornberg; Screenplay by Don Spencer; Story by R. Z. Samuel; Director of Photography: Gabriel Torres (Metrocolor / 1.85:1 widescreen ratio); Film Editors: Ken Robinson, Barry Simon; Musical Score: Don Gere; Art Director: Carmen Rameriz; Production Manager: Alfonso Sanchez Tello; Assistant Directors: John Broderick, Cesar Armando Jimenez; Set Dresser: Jesus Duran; Propman: Miguel Padilla; Sound Mixer: Jesus Gonzalez Canzi; Special Effects: Laurencio Cordero; Head Electrician: Marcelino Iniestra; Key Grip: Antonio Ramirez ("Puma"); Wardrobe: Maria Esquivel; Assistant Editor: Allyson Moore; Main Title Design: Steve Orfanos; Script Supervisor: Patty Sue Townsend; Locations: Costa Rica; Dimension Pictures; Production Date: February 1972; Released June 9, 1972; Running Time: 90 minutes.

Cast: Phyllis Elizabeth Davis (Sugar), Ellaraino [a.k.a. Ella Edwards] (Simone), Timothy Brown (Mojo), Pamela Collins (Dolores), Cliff Osmond (Burgos), Angus Duncan (Dr. John), Jacqueline Giroux (Fara), Darl Severns (Carlos), Albert Cole (Max), James Houghton (Rick), James Whitworth (Mario), Elvira Oropeza, Ramon Coll, Nicholas Baker, Juan Antillon Freer, Antonio Casas Fugueroa, Frank Garcia, Diane Rojas, Ana Maria Rivera, Nicky Jacobstahl, Jose Luis Jimenez, Laurencio Cordero (bits).

Papillon (1973) [prison gang–innocent men]

Credits: Directed by Franklin J. Shaffner; Produced by Ted Richmond, Robert Dorfmann, Franklin J. Schaffner, Emanuel L. Wolf, Robert O. Kaplan and Robert Laffont; Screenplay by Dalton Trumbo, Lorenzo Semple, Jr., and William Goldman; Based on the Novel by Henri Cherierre; Director of Photography: Fred J. Koenekamp (color / 2.35:1 widescreen ratio); Film Editor: Robert Swink; Musical Score: Jerry Goldsmith; Casting: Jack Baur; Production Designer: Anthony Masters; Art Director: Jack Maxstead; Costume Designer: Anthony Powell; Makeup Creator: Charles H. Schram; Hair Stylist: Evet Hussey; Production Managers: Emmett Emerson, Francisco Ariza; Unit Production Manager: Robert Watts; First Assistant Directors: Jose Lopez Rodero, Kuki Lopez

Rodero; Second Assistant Directors: Joe Nayfack, Robert Parra; Property Master: Dennis J. Parrish; Assistant Property Master: Bill MacSems; Set Dresser: Hugh Scaife; Poster Artist-Designer: Tom Jung; Assistant Art Director: Alan Roderick-Jones; Sound Recordist: Derek Ball; Sound Editor: Gordon Daniel; Sound Re-recordist: Richard Portman; Special Effects: Alex Weldon; Special Photographic Effects: Albert Whitlock; Stunt Gaffer: Joe Canutt; Stunt Double (Steve McQueen): Loren Janes; Cliff Stunt Double (Steve McQueen): Dar Robinson; Stunts: Jophery C. Brown; Assistant Cameramen: Michael Benson, William McCreery, Stephen Yaconelli; Camera Operators: John Courtland, Owen Marsh; Key Grip: Reggie Jones; Camera Operator: Thomas Laughridge; Gaffer: Gene Stout; Electrical Equipment Supplier: Julio Garbi; Wardrobe Supervisors: Tony Pueo, Mickey Sherrard; Music Editor: Erma E. Levin; Musical Orechestrations: John Levin; Technical Advisor: Lucien Lamontagne; Script Supervisor: Marshall Schlom; Stand-in: Scott Alexander Tritt; Location Manager: Randy Spangler; Locations: Hawaii, Jamaica, Venezuela, France, Spain; Les Films Corona-Solar Productions–Allied Artists Pictures; Budget: $12,000,000; Production Dates: February 19–June 4, 1973; Released December 16, 1973; Running Time: 151 minutes.

Cast: Steve McQueen (Henri ["Papillon"] Cherierre), Dustin Hoffman (Louis Dega), Victor Jory (Indian Chief), Don Gordon (Julot), Anthony Zerbe (Toussaint), Robert Deman (Maturette), Woodrow Parfrey (Clusiot), Bill Mumy (Lariot), George Coulouris (Dr. Chatal), Ratna Assan (Zoraima), William Smithers (Warden Barrot), Val Avery (Pascal), Gregory Sierra (Antonio), Victor Tayback (Sergeant), Mills Watson (Guard), Ron Soble (Santini), Barbara Morrison (Mother Superior), Don Hanmer (Butterfly Trader), E. J. Andre (Old Con), Richard Angarola (Commandant), Jack Denbo (Classification Officer), Len Lesser (Guard), John Quade (Masked Breton), Fred Sadoff (Deputy Warden), Allen Jaffe (Turnkey), Liam Dunn (Old Trusty), Peter Brocco (Doctor), Richard Farnsworth (Manhunter), Billy M. Green (Old Man), Anne Byrne Hoffman (Mrs. Dega), Fred Lerner (Convict on Ship), Ellen Moss (Nun), Ken Muggleston (Border Official), Dalton Trumbo (Commandant), Harry Monty (bit).

Leadbelly (1976) [chain gang]

Credits: Directed by Gordon Parks; Produced by David Frost, Jack Grossberg and Marc Merson; Director of Photography: Bruce Surtees (Eastmancolor); Film Editors: Moe Howard, Thomas Penick; Musical Score and Direction: Fred Karlin: Production Designer: Robert F. Boyle; Set Decorator: John A. Kurl; Production Manager: Lindsley Parsons, Jr.; Assistant Director: Les Landau; Stunts: Denny Arnold, Jim Burk, Harold Jones; Camera Operator: Oscar Barber; First Assistant Camera: Timothy E. Wade; Second Assistant Camera: William D. Barber; Crane Operator: Mike Redding; Music Editor: June Edgerton; Musicians: Dick Rosmini, Sonny Terry, Brownie McGhee; Production Assistant: Mark Lyon; Locating Casting Director: Pamela Jaye Smith; Locations: Marlin, Texas; Brownstone Productions–David Paradine Productions–Zeeuwse Maatschappij N.V.–Paramount Pictures; Production Dates: Late September–Early December 1974; Released May 28, 1976; Running Time: 126 minutes.

Cast: Roger E. Mosley (Huddie Ledbetter), Paul Benjamin (Wes Lesbetter), Madge Sinclair (Miss Eula), Alan Manson (Captain Freeman), Albert Hall (Dicklicker), Art Evans (Blind Lemon Jefferson), James Broadhead (John Lomax), John Henry Faulk (Governor Pat Neff), Vivian Bonnell (Old Lady), Dana Manno (Margaret Judd), Lynn Hamilton (Sally Ledbetter), Rheta Greene (Lethe), Valerie Odell (Amy), Rozaa Jean (Sugar Tit), Melba Englander (Evaline), Peter Harrell (Ally George), Ernest L. Hudson (Archie), John McDonald (Pruitt), Leonard Wrentz, John Keith (Guards), William Wintersole (Sheriff Gibbons), Carole Lamond (Layra May), Pamela Singleton (Fat Bessie), George Williams (Shorty), Timothy Pickard (Gray Man), William Creamer (Conductor), Dearl Croft (Frank), John C. Johnson (Will), Bill Woodard (Alex), Robert C. Farrow (Blacksmith), B. T. Henderson (Boss No. One), Denny Arnold (Boss No. Two), James Taylor (Dog Boy), Drew Thomas (Sharecropper).

Mean Dog Blues (1978) [chain gang]

Credits: Directed by Mel Stuart; Produced by Bing Crosby, George Lefferts and Charles A. Pratt; Screenplay by George Lefferts; Director of Photography: Robert B. Hauser (color / 1.85:1 widescreen ratio); Film Editor: Houseley Stevenson, Jr.; Musical Score: Fred Karlin; Art Director: Jack Poplin; Costume Designers: Bill Milton, Christine Zamiara; Makeup Artist: Mike Moschella; Hair Stylist: Laura Lee Grubich; Unit Production Manager: Floyd Joyer; Executive in Charge of Production: John Pommer; First Assistant Director: Ken Swor; Second Assistant Director: Richard Luke Rothschild; Trainee Assistant Director: Ed Milkovich; Props: Michael Dunn; Construction Coordinator: Wally Graham; Sound Editor: James J. Klinger; Assistant Sound Editor: Teri E. Dorman: Production Sound Mixer: Dwight Mobley; Special Effects: Howard Jensen; Stunt Coordinator/Stunts: Bill Couch; Camera Operator: Jim Albert; Key Grip: Billy Beaird; Still Photographer: Durward Graybill; Steadicam Operator: Gilbert Haimson; Assistant Editor: Harold Wilner; Music Editor: Michael Tronick; Scoring Mixer: Dan Wallin; Transportation Captain: George Alden; Publicists: Jack Casey, Maury Foladare; Script Supervisor: Hazel W. Hall; Dog Trainers: Cindy James, Carl Spitz; Production Coordinator: Ted Langwell; Crab Dolly Operator: Ron Veto; Bing Crosby Productions-American International Pictures; March 1978; Running Time: 108 minutes.

Cast: Gregg Henry (Paul Ramsey), Kay Lenz (Linda Ramsey), Scatman Crothers (Mudcat), Tina Louise (Donna Lacey), Felton Perry (Jake Turner), Gregory Sierra (Jesus Gonzales), James Wainwright (Sergeant Hubbell Wacker), William Windom (Victor Lacey), George Kennedy (Captain Omar Kinsman), Marc Alaimo (Transfer Guard), Edith Atwater (Linda's Mother), Jimmy Boyd (Sonny), Edward Hall (Road Gang Guard), John Daniels (Yakima Jones), Christina Hart (Gloria Kinsman), Chris Hubbell (Elroy Smith), Stephen Johnson ("Mary" Emerson), Logan Ramsey (Edmund Oberlin), Geno Silva (Tonto), Lee Weaver (Cheatem), Ian Wolfe (Judge), David Lewis (Dr. Caleb Odum), Billy Beck (Deadman), Herb Armstrong (Bailiff), James Bacon (Court Clerk), Hunter von Leer (Guard at Conjugal Barracks), Kimberley Allan (Max), Andy Albin (Truck Driver), Georgie Paul (Masseuse), John Dennis (Deputy Sheriff), Bill Catching (Mr. Vogel).

39 Stripes (1979) [chain gang]

Credits: Directed and Produced by Ron Ormond; Screenplay by Ron Ormond and Tom Ormond; Directors of Photography: Ron Ormond, Tim Ormond (color); Film Editors: Ron Ormond, Tim Ormond; Hair Stylist: Mr. Vaughn; Production Manager: June Ormond; Constructors: Tommy Reese, O. C. Stewart, Amos Wipl; Dialogue Assistant: Joan Cruz; Sound: Tim Green, Steve Wallace; Sound Mixer: Gerald Somerville; Lighting Director: Stan Boring; Production Assistant: Ken Cherry; Production Secretary: Sharon Hawkins; Technical Advisors: Alfreda Martin, Ed Martin; Locations: Lynchburg, Virginia, and Tennessee; The Ormond Organization; Released June 17, 1979; Running Time: 61 minutes.

Cast: Tim Ormond (Ed Martin), Nancy Harper (Alfreda Enders), Craig Cortney (Dan), Duane Hahn (Tip), Steve Wallace (Mac), Sharon Burrus (Edna), Don Cruz (Big Willie), Tim Green (Sunday Preacher), Joseph Jones (Thief on the Cross), Andy King (Guard), Ed Moates (Camp Boss), Harold Mowyer (Guard), John Beller, Al Byers, Don Cabbage, Jack Cornelius, Vaughn Denton, Ron English, Brian O. Gallager, Les Harrison, Jonathan McPhail, Levi Pate, James T. Stine, Dick Tate, Jim Watson, Raleigh W. Wright (Supporting Roles).

Stir Crazy (1980) [framed men–prison satire]

Credits: Directed by Sidney Poitier; Produced by Hannah Weinstein; Executive Producer: Melville Tucker; Associate Producer: Francois De Menil; Screenplay by Bruce Jay Friedman; Director of Photography: Fred Schuler (Metrocolor / 1.85:1 widescreen ratio); Film Editor: Harry Keller; Musical Score: Tom Scott; Casting: Toni Howard, Lynn Stalmaster; Production Designer: Alfred Sweeney; Set Decorator: Arthur Jeph Parker; Set Designer: William Ladd Skinner; Costume Designer: Patricia Edwards; Makeup Artist: Richard Cobos; Hair Stylist: Lola Kemp; Unit Production Manager: Mickey McCardle; First Assistant Director: Daniel McCauley; Second Assistant Directors: Joseph Paul Moore, Don Wilkerson; Construction Coordinators: Harold Broner, Santos Raspa; Property Master: Donald B. Nunley; Welder/Fabricator: Gary Zink; Propmaker Foreman: Ron Frazier; Sound Mixer: Glenn E. Anderson; Sound Re-recording Mixers: Wayne Artman, Tom Beckert; Sound Effects: Tom Bushelman, Pat Somerset; Re-recording Mixer: Michael Jeron; Special Effects: Larry L. Fuentes; Stunt Coordinator: Mickey Gilbert; Stunts: John Ashby, Kerrie Cullen, Chuck Henson, Larry McKinney, Stoney Neufang, Jr., Scott Raftery, Gene Walker, Alex Green; Still Photographer: Sidney Ray Baldwin; First Assistant Camera: Dustin Blauvelt; Second Assistant Camera: Keith Lundy; Camera Operator: Joe R. Marquette, Jr.; Gaffer: Richard Martens; Grip: Robert Moore; First Assistant "B" Camera: Randall Robinson; "B" Camera Operator: Dennis Smith; Extras Casting: Jack N. Young; Wardrobe: (men) David Rawley; (women) Marie V. Brown; Assistant Editor: Thomas G. Jingles; Color Timer: Bruce Pearson; Music Editor: Cliff Kohlweck; Transportation Coordinator: James Langhorne; Unit Publicist: Herb Honis; Production Accountant: Herb Hourihan; Medic: David R. Lawson; Production Coordinator: Claire Mactague; Head Wrangler: Jimmy Medearis; Research Consultant: Patricia J. O'Donohue; Script Supervisor: Ray Quiroz; Choreographer: Scott Salmon; Stand-in: Robert Milicevic; First Aid: B. J. Smith;

Location Projectionist: Eliot Yaffe; Location Manager: Ronald L. Carr; Locations: Florence, Tucson, Arizona; Burbank, California; Overton, Nevada; New York City; Columbia Pictures Corporation; Production Dates: March 13–May 23, 1980; Released December 12, 1980; Running Time: 111 minutes.

Cast: Gene Wilder (Skip Donahue), Richard Pryor (Harry Monroe), Georg Stanford Brown (Rory Shultebrand), JoBeth Williams (Meredith), Miguel Angel Suarez (Jesus Ramirez), Craig T. Nelson (Deputy Ward Wilson), Barry Corbin (Warden Walter Beatty), Charles Weldon (Blade), Nicolas Coster (Warden Henry Sampson), Joel Brooks (Len Garber), Jonathan Banks (Jack Graham), Erland van Lidth (Grossberger), Karmin Murcelo (Teresa Ramirez), Franklyn Ajaye (Young Man in Hospital), Estelle Omens (Mrs. R. H. Broache), Peter Looney (Kicker No. One), Cedrick Hardman (Big Mean), Doug Johnson (Guard No. Two), Henry Kingi (Ramon), Joe Massengale (Caesar Geronimo), Herman Poppe (Alex), Luis Avalos (Chico), Esther Sutherland (Sissie), Pamela Poitier (Cook's Helper), James Oscar Lee (Kicker No. Two), Rod McCary (Minister), Claudia Cron (Joy), Bill Bailey (Announcer), Donna Kei Benz (Nancy), Grand L. Bush (Big Mean's Sidekick), Alvin Ing (Korean Doctor), Thomas Moore (Judge), Donna Hansen (Mrs. Sampson), Gwen Van Dam (Mrs. Beatty), Herb Armstrong (County Jail Guard), Herbert Hirschman (Man at Dinner Party), Don Circle (Bank Teller), Madison Arnold (Guard No. Three), Gene Earle (Sheriff), Mickey Jones (Guard No. Eight), Tracy Lee Rowe (Little Girl), Essex Smith (Blade's Friend), Kenneth Menard (Repairman), Billy Beck (Flycatching Prisoner), Lee Purcell (Susan), Tony Burton (Guy Who Punches Big Mean), Jim Henry (Rodeo Cowboy), Drasha Meyer (Lady in Restaurant), John Richard Peterson (Rodeo Spectator), Al Silvani (Inmate), Earl W. Smith (Jack Graham's Enforcer), Brien Varady (Young Inmate), Wendy Wells-Gunkel (Rodeo Guest).

Chain Gang (1984) [chain gang]

Credits: Directed by Worth Keeter; Produced by John Brock, Charles Heath and Earl Owensby; Screenplay by Todd Durham and Worth Keeter; Director of Photography: Irl Dixon (color / 2.35:1 widescreen ratio); Musical Score: Dee Barton; Art Director: Jeff Ginn; Head On-Set Dresser: Brit Babcock; Property Master: Richard Waldrop; Sound Re-recording Mixer: John Asman; Sound Effects Editor: Jerry Whittington; Stunts: David Boushey, John W. McEuen; Stunt Coordinator: Dick Langdon; Steadicam Operator: Dan Kneece; "B" 3-D Camera: Phil Smoot; Assistant Editor: Jerry Whittington; Transportation: Derek Whittington; E. O. Corporation–Regency Productions, June 1984; Running Time: 90 minutes.

Cast: Earl Owensby (Mac McPherson), Barry Bell (Defense Counsel), David Boushey Mark Alan Ferri (Convicts), Robert Bloodworth, Steve Boles, Carol Bransford, James Eric, Paul Holman, Gene Kusterer, Lash La Rue, Terry Loughlin (bits).

The Man Who Broke 1,000 Chains (1987) [adaptation of *I Am a Fugitive from a Georgia Chain Gang!*]

Credits: Directed by Daniel Mann; Produced by Michael Campus and Yoram Ben-Ami; Teleplay by Michael Campus; Based on the Book by Robert E. Burns and Vincent G. Burns; Director of Photography: Mikael Salomon (color / 1.33:1 ratio); Film Editors: Diana Friedberg, Walter Hannemann, Noel Rogers; Musical Score: Charles Bernstein; Casting: Cathy Henderson; Production Designer: Vincent M. Cresciman; Art Director: James Terry Welden; Costume Designer: Jack Beuhler; Makeup Department Head: Pamela S. Westmore; Production Manager: Robert Schneider; Executive in Charge of Production: Jan Wieringa; First Assistant Director: Robert J. Koster; Second Assistant Director: Bea Ellen Cameron; Set Dresser: Robert Heiser; Property Master: Dick Kyker; Sound Effects Editors: Doug Coleman, Randy Fife; Camera Operator: Paul C. Babin; Still Photographer: Ken Carter; Grips: Jimmy Leavens, Bob Myers; Additional Camera Operator: William Moffit; Transportation: Jim Petti; Transportation Coordinator: Jonathan A. Rosenfeld; Transportation Captain: Brian Steagall; Production Accountant: Lacia Kornylo; Location Manager: Kevin Halloran; Locations: Jefferson, Texas; Home Box Office; Broadcast October 31, 1987; Running Time: 105 minutes.

Cast: Val Kilmer (Robert Eliot Burns/Eliot Roberts), Charles Durning (Warden Hardy), Sonia Braga (Emily Del Pino Pacheco), Kyra Sedgwick (Lillian Salo), James Keach (Father Vincent Godfrey Burns), Elisha Cook, Jr. (Pappy Glue), Clancy Brown (Flagg), William Sanderson (Trump), Taj Mahal (Bones), Taylor Presnell (George Seales), Paul Benjamin (Big Sam), Bill Bolender (Raymond), Esther Benson (Mother Burns), Bert Conway (Father Burns), Charles Carrol (Hobo No. One), Ransom Andrews (Hobo No. Two), Stan Sturing (Burns' Atlanta Lawyer), John Mitchum (Atlanta Judge), Ray Morgan (Deebo), Bert Williams (Police Chief), Lawrence Parks (Merle McBain), Chris Mulkey (Burns' Chicago Lawyer), Billy Kane (Burley), Jerry Anderson (Speech Chairman), Rony Clanton (Cowboy), Warren Vanders (Stuckey), Tommy Bush (Chicago Judge), Bill Gratton (Georgia Parole Board Official), Michael Clark (Detective No. One), George Auld (Detective No. Two), Helen Hall (Bookstore Owner), Pat Minter (Trusty No. One), Joe McCaig (Trusty No. Two), Harlan Jordan (Backwoodsman), Julius Tennon (Nub), Desmond Dhooge (Dog Handler), Billy Bob Thornton (Conductor [scenes deleted]), John Franklin (scenes deleted).

An Innocent Man (1989) [prison gang–innocent man]

Credits: Directed by Peter Yates; Produced by Robert W. Cort and Bud Field; Executive Producer: Scott Kroopft; Associate Producer: Larry Brothers; Screenplay by Larry Brothers; Director of Photography: William A. Fraker (Technicolor / 1.85:1 widescreen ratio); Film Editors: Stephen A. Rotter, William S. Scharf, Joseph Gutowski; Musical Score: Howard Shore; Casting: Howard Feuer; Production Designer: Stuart Wurtzel; Art Director: Frank Richmond; Set Director: Chris Butler; Costume Designer: Rita Ryack; Makeup Artists: James Lee McCoy, (Mr. Selleck) Edward Lon Bentley; Hair Stylist: Carrol O'Connell; Unit Production Manager: Neil A. Machlis; First Assistant Director: Paul Deason; Second Assistant Directors: Paul G. Fonteyn, Kelly Wimberly; Second Second Assistant Director: Jeffrey Okabayashi; Construction Foreman: Robert Bonino; Standby Painters: Giovanni Castelenuovo, Jerry Gadette; Assistant Props: Randy Gunter; Leadman: Michael Schmidt; Set Designer: Sid Tingloff;

Property Master: Mark Wade; Paint Foremen: Ron Ashmore, Ward Welton; Labor Foremen: Curtis Geise, Anthony Tomeo; Swing Gang: Eugene J. Reed, Douglas M. Vaughn; Art Department Assistant: Samara Schaffer; Construction Consultant: Pat Tagliaferro; Foley Artists: Elisha Birnbaum, Brian Vancho; Foley Mixer: George A. Lara; ADR Editor: Jane McCulley; Assistant ADR Editor: Kristine Bulakowski; Sound Re-recording Mixer: Tom Fleischman; Sound Editors: Neil L. Kaufman; Bitty O'Sullivan Smith, Michael Kirchberger; Assistant Sound Editors: John Gilroy, David Grossack, Dan Korintas, Marissa Littlefield, Lynn Sable, Katherine Benedek; Supervising Sound Editor: Dan Sable; Boom Operator: Jules Strasser; Cable Operator: Charles J. Bond; Special Effects Coordinator: William H. Schirmer; Special Effects Assistant: Roland Tantin; Stunts: Kerrie Cullen, David Efron, Mike Johnson, Steven Lambert, Tom Lupo, George P. Wilbur, Jim Stephan; Stunt Coordinator: John Moio; Stunt Performer: Brian J. Williams; Stunt Double (Tom Selleck): Tom Lupo; Electrician: Chris Athy; Gaffer: Gerald H. Boatright; Grip: Steve Chase; Second Camera Assistant: Daniel Dayton; "A" Camera Operator: David E. Diano; Video Assist Operator: David Katz; Key Grip: Alexander La Verde; First Assistant Cameras: Marc Margulies, Robert Stradling; Second Assistant Camera: Nicholas S. McLean; Best Boy Grip: Ty Suehiro; Second Camera Operator: Joseph F. Valentine; Dolly Grip: Clay H. Wilson; Electrical Best Boy: Don Yamasaki; Lamp Operators: Paul Caven, Joel Stout, Michael ("Dutch") van Woert; Grips: John Powers, Edmond Wright; Camera Operator: Steve Randolph; Casting Assistant: David R. Brymer; Extras Casting: Ken Kitch, Franklin Warren; Casting (Atmosphere/Stand-ins): Sally Lear; Casting Associate: Dennis Osbourne; Costumer: Sandy Berke Jordan, David Mayreis, Key Costumer: Michael Dennison; Assistant Costume Designer: Daniel Orlandi; First Assistant Editor: Richard Friedlander; Assistant Editor: Holly Huckins; Apprentice Editors: Laura P. Krasnow, Alisa Lepselter, Stephen L. Meek; Color Timer: Bob Noland; Music Editor: Susana Peric; Assistant Music Editor: Suki Buchman; Orchestrator: Homer Denison; Music Scoring Mixer: Michael Farrow; Assistant Scoring Engineer: Vince Caro; Music Preparation: Brian Eddolls; Musician: John Moses; Drivers: Billy Baxter, Morris Bension, Gary Dally, D. Scott Guthrie, Ron Hinsley, Frank Mielcarek, Michael Ralph Price, Chuck Ramsey, Jerry Shore, Jr., Don Van Stry; Transportation Captains: Wayne Roberts, Mario Simon; Transportation Coordinator: Eddie Lee Voelker; Technical Advisors: Don Barfield, Joel Salce; Production Assistants: Scott Court, Daniel Earle, Marshall Peck, Carolyn Rothstein, Kris Shreffler; Assistant (Peter Yates): Patricia Freebery; Assistant (Robert Cort): Jordana Glick-Franzheim; Location Manager: Robbie Goldstein; Assistant Auditor: Alison Harstedt; Production Coordinator: Michele Imperato; Production Auditor: K. Lenna Katich; Assistant (Scott Kroopf): Penny Key; Assistants (Tom Selleck): Pua McGinness, David Muntz; Construction Coordinator: Pia Navales; Unit Publicist: Ellen Pasternack; Script Supervisor: Cynnie Troup; Stand-in: Joe Davis; Caterers: Carlos Garcia, Michael Schultz; Nurse: Anthony L. Pacquet; Staff Coordinator: Marl Scoon; Location Manager: Ken Lavet; Locations: Long Beach, Los Angeles, Pasadena, San Francisco and San Pedro, California; Carson City, Nevada; Norwood, Ohio; Interscope Communications–Silver Screen Partners IV–Touchstone Pictures–Buena Vista Pictures; Production Dates: February 4–March 10, 1989; Released October 6, 1989; Running Time: 113 minutes.

Cast: Tom Selleck (Jimmie Rainwood), F. Murray Abraham (Virgil Cane), Laila Robbins (Kate Rainwood), David Rasche (Mike Parnell), Richard Young (Danny Scalise), Badja Djola (John Fitzgerald), Todd Graff (Robby), M. C. Gainey (Malcolm), Peter Van Norden (Peter Feldman), Bruce A. Young (Jingles), James T. Morris (Junior), Terry Golden (Felix), Dennis Burkley (Butcher), Thomas B. Kackert (Dove), Vito T. Peterson (Handjob), Charlie Landry (Judge Kenneth Lavet), J. Kenneth Campbell (Lieutenant Freebery), Jim Ortlieb (Convict, Robby's Death), Ralph O. Benton (First Man on Tuna Boat), James Staszkiel (Second Man on Tuna Boat), Brian J. Williams (Third Man on Tuna Boat), Maggie Baird (Stacy), Alanniss Aldderro (Convict Toturer), Bob Maroff (Venucci), Derek Anunciation (Lester), Ben Slack (Woznick), J. J. Johnston (Joseph Donatelli), Brian Brophy (Nate Blitman), Ben Rawnsley (Cop at Jimmie's), Den Hill (Mike), Gary Matanky (Mechanic at Hangar), Jack R. Orend (Officer at Bust), Eric Lively (Donatelli's Dealer), David Rhodes Brown (First Convict), Larry Brothers (Basketball Con), Jeffrey Earl Young (First Guard), Michael J. Budge (Warden), David Melligan (Correctional Officer), Dave Florek (Court Clerk), Gary Velasco (Courthouse Guard No. One), Robert E. Nichols (Courthouse Guard No. Two), Dann Florek (Prosecuting Attorney), Dough MacHugh (Bailiff), Peter Adrian Owsley (Tortured Convict), Joseph Stillpass (Cafeteria Inmate), Joseph Carberry (bit).

Quantum Leap television series: "Unchained—November 2, 1956" (1991) [chain gang]

Credits: Series created by Donald P. Bellasario; Directed by Michael W. Watkins; Produced by Donald P. Bellasario, David Bellasario, Deborah Pratt, Michael Zinberg, Paul Brown, Jeff Gourson, Chris Rupenthal, Tommy Thompson, Jimmy Giritlian and Julie Bellisario; Teleplay by Paris Qualles; Director of Photography: Michael W. Watkins (color / 1.33:1 ratio); Film Editors: John Koslowsky, M. Edward Salier; Musical Score: Velton Ray Bunch, Mike Post (theme); Casting: Ellen Lubin Sanitsky; Production Designer: Cameron Birnie; Art Director: Ellen Dambros-Williams; Set Decorator: Robert L. Zilliox; Costume Designer: Jean-Pierre Dorleac; Unit Production Manager: Ronald R. Grow; First Assistant Director: Ryan Gordon; Second Assistant Director: Kate Yurka; Sound Editor: Greg Schorer; Sound Mixer: Barry Thomas; Special Visual Effects: Roger Dorney, Denny Kelly; Stunt Coordinator: Diamond Farnsworth; Stunt Double (J. C. Quinn): Brian J. Williams; Gaffer: Mark Abbott; Assistant Camera: Peter Gulla; Lighting Technicians: Ron Newburn, Joesph T. Terranova; Costume Supervisor: David Rawley; Colorist (Dailies): Greg Curry; Oboe Soloist: Tom Boyd; Music Editor: Bruce Frazier; Bellisarius Productions–Universal Television–NBC-TV Network; Broadcast November 27, 1991; Running Time: 46 minutes.

Cast: Scott Bakula (Dr. Sam Beckett), Dean Stockwell (Admiral Al Calavicci), Basil Wallace (Jazz Boone), J. C. Quinn (Boss Cooley), Claude Earl Jones (Captain Elias), Don Sparks (Jake Wiles), Robert V. Barron (Old Convict), Jed Mills (Monroe), Mark Kemble (Chance Cole), Deborah Pratt (Narrator).

The Fugitive (1993) [framed man]

Credits: Directed by Andrew Davis; Produced by Roy Huggins, Keith Barish, Arnold Kopelson, Stephen Brown, Nana Greenwald and Peter MacGregor-Scott; Screenplay by Jeb Stuart and David Twohy; Story by David Twohy; Director of Photography: Michael Chapman (color / 1.85:1 widescreen ratio); Film Editors: Don Brochu, David Finfer, Dean Goodhill, Dov Hoenig, Richard Nord, Dennis Virkler; Musical Score: James Newton Howard; Casting: Amanda Mackey Johnson, Cathy Sandrich; Production Designer: J. Dennis Washington; Art Director: Maher Ahmad; Set Decorator: Rick Gentz; Costume Designer: Aggie Guerard Rodgers; Makeup Artists: Pat Gerhardt, Rodger Jacobs, Linda Boykin-Williams; Hair Stylists: Mary ("Dugan") Buono, Dominic Mango; Makeup Supervisor: Peter Robb-King; Key Hair Stylist: Kathe Swanson; Additional Hair Stylist: Lun Ye Hodges; Additional Makeup Artist: James Lacey; Unit Production Managers: James A. Dennett, Robert Grand; First Assistant Director (Second Unit, North Carolina): Brian E. Frankish; Second Assistant Director (Second Unit, North Carolina): Dustin Bernard; Second Second Assistant Director: James A. Dennett II; First Assistant Director (Second Unit, Chicago): Kenneth A. Flisak; Second Assistant Director (Second Unit, Chicago): Gary B. Goldman; Second Unit Director (Chicago): Mike Gray; Second Assistant Director: David Kelley; Second Unit Director (North Carolina): Terry J. Leonard; First Assistant Director: Thomas J. Mack; Additional Second Assistant Director: Robert Schick; Second Unit Director: Joel Chernoff; DGA Trainees: Suzanne Geiger, Roger Senders; Property Master: Douglas E. Madison; Assistant Property Masters: Tighe Barry, David J. Chamerski, William Dambra; Construction Coordinator (Second Unit, North Carolina): Jack Cornish; Art Department Coordinator: Robby Green; Set Designers: Ann Harris, Nancy Mickleberry; Leadmen: Joel Prihoda, Robert Sica; Construction Coordinator: Richard Dean Rankin; Assistant Art Director: Tom Targownik; Sculptor: Tom Czarnopys; Gang Boss/Welder: Randy Kenan; Set Designer: David W. Krummel; Storyboard Illustrator (Train Sequence): Fred Lucky; Carpenter: Thomas C. Mentzer; Swing Gang: John Rozman; Propmaker: John J. Slove, Jr.; Set Dresser: Timothy W. Tiedje; Stand-by Painter: Richard Whitney; Dialogue Editors: Stu Bernstein, James Beshears, Gaston Biraben, Howell Gibbens, Kimberly Ellen Lowe, Gary Mundheim, Karen G. Wilson; Sound Effects Editors: Patrick M. Bietz, Lance Brown, Sam Gemette, Hector C. Gika, Glenn Hoskinson, Frank Kniest, Jay Nierenberg, Shawn Sykora, Donald L. Warner, Jr., Marshall Winn; ADR Editors: Barbara Boguski, Holly Huckins, Anthony Milch, Steve Schwalbe, Greg Stacy, Lee Lemont, Robert Ulrich; Assistant Sound Editors: Desmond Cannon, Rickley W. Dumm, Victor Iorillo, Ron Meredith, Michael Mirkovich, Valerie Schwartz; Processed Flashback Effects: John P. Fasal; ADR Assistants: Tim Groseclose, Laura P. Krasnow, Lori Martino, Bill Weinman; Re-recording Mixers: Michael Herbick, Donald O. Mitchell, Frank A. Montano; Boom Operator: Dale R. Janus; Assistant Sound Editors: Elizabeth Kenton, Dawn Michelle King, Lance Laurienzo, Ron Meredith; Foley Mixer: Mary Jo Lang; Supervising Sound Editors: John Leveque, Bruce Stambler; Foley Editors: James Likowski, Steve Richardson; ADR Mixer: Thomas J. O'Connell;

Boom Operator: Daniel Richter; Foley Artists: John Roesch, Alicia Stevenson; Supervising Foley Editor: Solange S. Schwalbe; Production Sound Mixer: Scott D. Smith; Supervising Dialogue Editor: Becky Sullivan; Cableman: Daryl Ziemke; Sound Technician: Andy Snavley; Sound Transfer: John Soukup; Special Effects Assistants: Michael Arbogast, Randy Cabral, Jim Jolly, Rodman Kiser, William Lee, Dick Wood; Special Effects Coordinators: Roy Arbogast, Tom Ryba; Special Effects Technician: John W. Weeks; Assistant Camera: Christopher Briles; Model Shop Supervisor: Douglas Calli; Producer (Introvision): Nick Davis; Cameramen: Chris Dawson, John P. Mesa; Visual Effects Supervisor: William Mesa; Model Makers: Timothy Niver, Scott Salsa; Art Director: Charles Wood; Visual Effects Second Assistant Camera: David Fogg; Digital Compositor (Digital FilmWorks): Peter W. Moyer; Art Department (Introvision): Matsune Suzuki; Model Builder: Gary Young; Stunts: Chris Branham, Troy Brown, Hal Burton, Thomas Dewier, Nick Dmitri, Jeannie Epper, Peter Epstein, Diamond Farnsworth, Teri Garland, Terry Jackson, Dean Jeffries, Rick Le Fevour, Stacy Logan, Mike H. McGaughy, Jeff Ramsey, Glenn Randall, Jr., John-Clay Scott, Gary J. Wayton, Paula Wayton, John Rottger; Stunt Coordinator: Terry Leonard; Stunt Double (Andreas Katsulas): Nick Dmitri; Stunt Double (Mr. Jones): Clifford Happy; Assistant Chief Lighting Technician: Alphonse Blumenthal; Second Assistant Camera: Chris Collins; Chief Lighting Technician: Eugene F. Crededio; Rigging Gaffer: John Formanack; Video Assist: Daniel H. Friedman; Camera Assistant: Jason M. Friedman; Second Assistant Camera: Linda Gacsko; Camera Operator (Second Unit, North Carolina): Brian C. Glover; First Assistant Cameras: Robert Heine, Steven Hiller; Aerial Cameraman: Frank M. Holgate; Director of Photography, Second Unit. Chicago and North Carolina): Gary Holt; Camera Operator (Second Unit, North Carolina): Michael Kohnhurst; Director of Photography (Second Unit, Chicago): George Kohut; Rigging Gaffer: Bob E. Krattiger; Key Grip: Morgan Michael Lewis; Best Boy: Mark E. Matthys; First Assistant Camera: Zoran Veselic; Second Assistant Camera: Tim Metivier; "A" Camera Operator: Frank Miller; Key Grip (Second Unit, North Carolina): Bob Rose; Best Boy (Second Unit, North Carolina): Erich O. Rose; "B" Camera Operators/Steadicam Operators: Stephen St. John, Robert Ulland; Dolly Grip: Joe Tomko, Jr.; Still Photographer: Stephen Vaughan; Grip: William Allen, Jr., First Assistant Camera, Second Unit: Joe Carroll, David Morenz; Electricians: Larry Cottrill, Tod Olivieri; Assistant Camera: Andrew Hoehn, Jr.; First Assistant Camera, Aerial Unit/Second Assistant Camera: David Moenkhaus; Film Loader: Hope A. Nielsen; Camera Technician (Wescam): David Norris; Rigging Key Grip: John S. Robertson; Gaffer (Second Unit, Chicago): Mark N. Woods; Casting (Chicago): Nan Charbonneau, Richard S. Kordos; Casting (North Carolina): Gloria Hancock; Casting Assistant (Chicago): Kirsten Nelson; Casting Assistant (North Carolina): Theresa Phillips; Casting Associate: Karen Miller; ADR Voice Casting: Sandy Holt; Extras Casting: Mark A. Ridge; Extras Casting Assistant: Joan Philo; Costumers: Jane Blank, Stella Cottini, Sybil Gray, Eileen McCahill, Gina Panno; Costume Supervisor: Linda Henrickson; Key Costumer: Jennifer Jobst; Wardrobe: Maryann Scinto; Assistant Film Editors: Joe Binford, Jr., Chris Boscardin, Richard Byard, James Durante, Roger Fenton, Rolf Fleischmann, Grant Gatzke, Joseph

Gutowski, John Morrisey, Patrick Paul Mullane, Mike Murphy, Mark Rathaus, Fred C. Vitale, David Young; Color Timer: Bob Putynkowski; Orchestrators: Chris Boardman, Bred Dechter, James Newton Howard; Score Co-Producer: Michael Mason; Assistant Music Editor: David Olson; Orchestra Conductor: Marty Paich; Musicians: (Saxophone Solos) Wayne Shorter; (Oboe Solos) Tom Boyd; (French Horn) James Thatcher; (Percussion) Steve Schaeffer; Scoring Mixers: Dan Wallin, Robert Shaper; Music Editor: Jim Weldman; Soundtrack Producers: M. V. Gerhard, Don Goldwasser; Transportation Captain: Michael P. Deal; Transportation Coordinator: Thaddeus E. Larkowski; Transportation Coordinator (Second Unit, North Carolina): Craig A. Pinkard; Production Driver: Roy A. Grace; Transportation Captain: John Rice, Sr.; Assistant to Mr. Ford: Leslie Adler; Staff Assistants: Dana Armonda, Kathleen ("Bo") Bobak, Mark Child, Michelle Clancy, Peter Hollocker, Martin L. Hudson, Michael Kase, Sarah Knight, Bill McLaren, D. Matt Patton; Script Supervisor: Drucilla A. Carlson; Technical Advisors: Tony Calabrese, Cory Franklin, M.D., Bruce L. Gerwertz, M.D., Dr. Norbert Gleicher, Marvin Lutes, James E. McLaughlin, Ed O'Donnell, Susan Phillips, John Rottger, Robb Smith, M.D., James M. Tantillo, Judge Toomin, Jack Uellendall, Sheldon Zenner; Assistants to Mr. Kopelson: Christy Gerhart, Maria Norman; Assistants to Mr. Davis: Laurie Hansen, Teresa Tucker-Davies; Assistant to Mr. MacGregor-Scott: Pamela Jaeckle; Executive Assistant: Frederic Mialaud; Computer Engineering and Graphics: John Monsour; Production Secretary: Diana Poppajohn; Assistant Production Secretaries: Rosemary Orlando, Bekki Vallin; Production Secretary (Second Unit, North Carolina): Stephanie Wertlake; Video and Computer Supervisor: Liz Radley; Computer Screen Graphics: Paul Conti; ADR Voice: Jeff Coopwood; Production Accountant: Ricki L. Stein; Assistant Accountants: Thomas Bianco, Laura Tiz; Post-Production Accountant: Bill Daly; Unit Publicist: Susan Steinlauf; Stand-in: Jeff Dlugolecki; Helicopter Pilots: (Chicago) Kevin LaRosa, Bruce Webb; (North Carolina) Cress Horne; Location Projectionist: Peter Juneau; Production Assistant: Jack Messitt; Title Designer: Nina Saxon; Script Supervisor, Second Unit: Patience Thoreson; Location Assistants: Wileen Dragovan, Robin E. Woldorf; Location Assistant (Second Unit, North Carolina): Lance Holland; Location Scout: Michael Anthony; Location Manager: Michael J. Malone; Location Manager (Second Unit, North Carolina): Rich Mockal; Locations: Chicago and Chester, Illinois; Blue Ridge Parkway, Bryson City, Dillsboro and Sylva, North Carolina; A Keith Barish–Arnold Kopelson Production; Warner Bros. Pictures; Budget: $40,000,000; Production began February 3, 1993; Released August 6, 1993; Running Time: 130 minutes.

Cast: Harrison Ford (Dr. Richard Kimble), Tommy Lee Jones (Samuel Gerard), Sela Ward (Helen Kimble), Julianne Moore (Dr. Anne Eastman), Joe Pantoliano (Cosmo Renfro), Andreas Katsulas (Sykes), Jeroen Krabbe (Dr. Charles Nichols), Daniel Roebuck (Biggs), L. Scott Caldwell (Poole), Tom Wood (Newman), Ron Dean (Detective Kelly), Joseph F. Kosala (Detective Rosetta), Miguel Nino (Chicago Cop No. One), John Drummond (Newscaster), Tony Forsco (Chicago Cop No. Two), Joseph F. Fisher (Otto Sloan), James Liautaud (Paul), David Darlow (Dr. Lenz), Tom Galouzis, M.D. (Surgeon), James F. McKinsey, M.D. (Surgeon), Mark D. Espinoza (Resident), John E. Ellis (Anesthesiologist), Gene

Barge, Thomas Charles Simmons (11th District Cops), Joseph Guzaldo (Prosecutor), Dick Cusack (Walther Gutherie), Nicholas Kusenko (Assistant Defense Attorney), Joan Kohn (Assistant Prosecuting Attorney), Joe D. Lauck (Forensic Technician), Joseph V. Guastaferro (Coroner), Andy Romano (Judge Bennett), Richard Riehle (Old Guard), Thom Vernon (Carlson), Ken Moreno (Partida), Eddie ("Bo") Smith, Jr. (Copeland), Frank Ray Perilli, Otis Wilson (Jail Officers), Pancho Demmings (Young Guard), Jim Wilkey (Bus Driver), Danny Goldring (Head Illinois State Trooper), Nick Searcy (Sheriff Rawlins), Kevin Crowley (State Trooper), Michael James (Head Welder), Michael Skewes (Highway Patrolman), Ila Cathleen Stallings (Duty Nurse), Linda Casaletto (Rural Hospital Nurse), Cody Glenn (Paramedic), Cythia Baker (Woman in Car), Johnny Lee Davenport (Marshal Henry), Mike Bacarella (Marshal Stevens), Bill Cusack (Training Technician), David Hodges (Marshal David), Lillie Richardson (Copeland's Girlfriend), Peter J. Caria IV (Billy), Tighe Barry (Windshield Washer), Monica Chabrowski (Polish Landlady), Lonnie Sima (Landlady's Son), Oksana Fendunyszyn (Myoelectric Receptionist), Orlando Garcia (Desmondo), Afram Bill Williams (Salesman), Bruce L. Gewertz, M.D. (Dr. Bruce), Jane Lynch (Dr. Kathy Wahlund), Joseph Rotkvich (Officer Joseph), Steven Lilovich (Officer Steve), Noelle Bou-Sliman (Myoelectric Technician), Roxanne Roberts (Trauma Doctor), Alex P. Hernandez (Trauma Doctor), Theron Touche Lykes (Orderly), Joel Robinson (Boy Patient), Greg Hollimon (Skating Orderly), Cheryl Lynn Bruce (O. R. Doctor), Marie Ware (Nurse Gladys), Bernard McGee (Man), Ann Whitney (Myoelectric Director), Lily Monkus, Willie Lucas (Desk Clerks), Turk Miller (Clearing Officer), Ana Maria Alvarez (La Cubana), Eugene F. Crededio (Visitation Guard), Maurice Person (Clive Driscoll), Terry Hard (Officer Hormel), Pam Zekman, David Pasquesi, Lester Holt, Jay Levine (Newscasters), Brent Shaphren, Stephen A. Landsman, B. J. Jones (Doctors at Bar), Dru Anne Carlson (Gerard's Secretary), Margaret Moore (Nichols' Assistant), Manny Lopez (Seminar Doctor), John M. Watson, Sr. (Bones Roosevelt), Kirsten Nelson (Betty), Juan Ramirez (Man on "El"), Neil Flynn (Transit Cop), Allen Hamilton (Host), Eric Fudala (Hotel Security Guard), Don Albert (Officer DuKakis), Suzy Brack (City Hall Employee), Roland Burris (Smiling Man), Darren W. Conrad (Deputy at Train Wreck), Ed Cray (Inmate), Reese Foster (Man Visiting Prisoner), Windy George (Doctor's Wife), Judy Carmen Gonzalez (Juror), Robert Dean Jacobs (Security Guard), Berniece Janssen (Spectator in the Courtroom), Gene Kelly (U.S. Marshal), Kevin Mukherji (Doctor), Richard Remppel (Man in Tuxedo in Restaurant), Todd Rice (Policeman), Sal Richards (Warrant Captain), Keith Schrader (Hotel Security Guard), John Clay-Scott (Mad Motorist at Tunnel), John Thurner (Parade Spectator).

The Shawkshank Redemption (1994) [prison gang–innocent man]

Credits: Directed and Screenplay by Frank Darabont; Produced by Niki Marvin; Executive Producers: Liz Glotzer, David V. Lester; Based on the novella *Rita Hayworth and the Shawshank Redemption* by Stephen King; Director of Photography: Roger Deakins (Technicolor / 1.85:1 widescreen ratio); Film Editor: Richard Francis-Bruce; Musical Score: Thomas Newman; Casting: Deborah

Aquila; Production Design: Terence Marsh; Art Director: Peter Lansdown Smith; Set Decorator: Michael Seirton; Costume Designer: Elizabeth McBride; Makeup Artists: Jeni Lee Dinkel, Monty Westmore; Key Makeup Artist: Kevin Haney; Hair Stylists: Roy Bryson, Pamela Priest; Key Hair Stylist: Phillip Ivey; Production Supervisors: Kokayi Ampah, Sue Bea Montgomery; Unit Production Manager: David V. Lester; First Assistant Director: John R. Woodward; Key Second Assistant Director: Thomas Schellenberg; Second Second Assistant Director: Michael Greenwood; Third Assistant Director: Jesse V. Johnson; Paint Foreman: Peter Allen; On-Set Dresser: Lee Lee Baird; Decorating Consultant: Bob Baker; Labor Gang Boss: John Barbera; Propmaker Foreman: Earl F. Betts; Labor Foreman: Barrett Fleetwood; Set Estimator: Susan Fraley; Painter: Blair Gibeau; Propman: Carey Harris, Jr.; Standby Painter: Todd Hatfield; Paint Gang Bosses: James Hawthorne, Robert Hawthorne; Propshop Foremen: Jim Henry, Isidoro Raponi; Set Dressers: Jack Hering, John M. Heuberger, Christopher Neely; Set Designer: Joseph A. Hodges; Lead Person: Alba Leone; Construction Coordinator: Sebastian Milito; Propmaker Gang Boss: Scott Mizgaites; Property Master: Tom Shaw, Jr.; Construction Foreman: Dixwell Stillman; Storyboard Consultant: Peter Von Sholly; Key Carpenter: Paul Wells; Art Department Assistant: Rhonda Yeater; Carpenters: Jim Heastings, Brent Peelor; ADR Supervisor: Petra Bach; Foley Artists: Kevin Bartnof, Ellen Heuer, John Roesch; Mixing Recordist: David Behle; Sound Editors: Bruce Bell, Jeff Clark, Zack Davis, Dale Johnston, Larry Lester, William R. Manger, Richard Oswald; ADR Recordist: Rick Canelli; Additional ADR Recordists: Mike Boudry, Michael Cerone; Cable Person: Kevin Boyd; Production Sound Mixer: Willie Burton; Foley Mixer: Marilyn Graf; Foley Recordist: Ron Grafton; Sound Re-recording Mixer: Michael Herbick; ADR Editor: Shelley Rae Hinton, Robert Ulrich; ADR Mixer: Thomas J. O'Connell; Additional ADR Mixers: Doc Kane, Paul J. Zydel; Mixing Recordist: Jack Keller; Boom Operator: Marvin E. Lewis; Temp Boom Operator: Jim Emswiller; Sound Re-recording Mixers: Robert J. Litt, Eliot Tyson; Assistant Sound Editors: Lori Martino, Janelle Showalter, Bill Weinman; Supervising Sound Editor: John Stacy; Technical Director of Sound: Donald C. Rogers; Recordist: John Soukup; Dolby Sound Consultant: Gary Wright; Special Effects: Bob Williams; Visual Effects: Melissa Taylor; Stunts: Daniel W. Barringer, Fred Culbertson, Mickey Guinn, Dick Hancock, Tom Morga, Ben Scott; Stunt Coordinator: Jerry Gatlin; Stunt Double (Tim Robbins) Tom Morga; Lighting Stand-ins: Tim L. Amstutz, James Burke, Max Gerber, David Gilby, Dexter Hammett, Bill Martin, Jon Stinehour; Second Rigging Grip: John Archibald; First Assistant Cameras: Robin Brown, Eric Swanek; Rigging Grips: Rex Buckingham, Jorgen Christensen, Charlie Quinlivan; Best Boy Grip: Keith Bunting; Grips: Brian ("Buzz") Buzzelli, Eugene C. DePasquale, Thomas Guidugli, James Harrington, Kenneth McCahan, Russ Milner, Pat Dames; Key Grip: Don Cerrone; Rigging Best Boy: Tony Corapi; Steadicam Operator: Gerrit Dangremond; Rigging Gaffer: Richie Ford; Electric Riggers: James Gribbins, Joseph Short; Dolly Grip: Bruce Hamme; Second Assistant Cameras: Andy Harris, Bobby Mancuso, William Nielsen, Jr.; Additional Second Assistant Camera: David Moenkhaus; Lamp Operators: William Kingsley, James ("Quincy") Koenig, Bill Moore, Ruben Turner; Best Boy Electric: James Knaster;

Film Loader: Hope Neilsen; Gaffer: Bill O'Leary; Video Assistant: Judy Scarboro; Video Assist Operator: Van Scarboro; Still Photographer: Michael Weinstein; Electrician: Kurt Dale Hartman; Rigging Electricians: Robert Bender, Jon D. Morrison, Brian Powers; Steadicam Assistant: Eric Swanek; ADR Voice Casting: Barbara Harris; Background Casting Intern: Adam Moyer; Casting (Ohio): Lynn Meyers; Background Casting: Ivy Weiss; Background Casting Assistant: Brent Scarpo; Casting Assistant: Julie Weiss; Wardrobe Assistant: Cookie Beard; Seamstress: Carol Buckler; Key Costumers: Kris Kearney, Mira Zavidowsky; Wardrobe Supervisor: Taneia Lednicky; Costumers: Donnie McFinely, Eva Prappas; Apprentice Editor: Jeff Canavan; First Assistant Editor: Patricia A. Galvin; Production Assistant: David Johnson; Second Assistant Editor: Robert C. Lustead; Color Timer: David Orr; Colorist (Mastering): Keith Shaw; Music Editor: Bill Bernstein; Music Preparation: Julian Bratolyubov; Assistant Music Editor: James C. Makiej; Music Contractor: Leslie Morris; Orchestrator: Thomas Pasatieri; Music Scoring Mixer: Dennis Sands; Concertmaster: Bruce Dukov; Musicians: (Oboe Soloist) Tom Boyd; (Harmonica) Tommy Morgan; Music Consultant: Arlene Fishbach; Transportation Captain: Fred Culbertson; Transportation Coordinator: David Marder; Drivers: Robert Conrad, William Culbertson, William P. Davis, Chick Elwell, Dick Furr, Harold Garnsey, Sally Givens, James Graham, Ray Greene, Mickey Guinn, Ronald Hogle, Neil Knoff, Roland Maurer, Douglas Miller, Gary Mishey, Glen Murphy, Ken Nevin, Jr., Tom Park, Chuck Ramsey, Judith Reed, Scott Ruetenik, David Smith, Donald Snyder, J. D. Thomas, David Turner, Chip Vincent; Picture Car Coordinator: Mario Simon; Accounting Assistant: Kelley Baker; Assistant (Frank Darabont): Robert C. Barnett; Craft Service: Brian Boggs; Gyrosphere Operator: Michael Kelem; Gyrosphere Assistants: Richard Brooks Burton, Ed Gutentag; Assistant (Tim Robbins): Tom Cotter; Assistant (Morgan Freeman): Alfonso Freeman; Script Supervisor: James Ellis; Assistant Production Accountant: Jane Estocin; Animal Trainer: Scott E. Hart; Additional Animal Wrangler: Therese Amadio; Production Office Coordinator: Beth Hickman; Office Assistant: Anne Hilbert; Set Production Assistant: Jesse E. Johnson; Unit Publicist: Ernie Malik; First Aid: Linda McKeon; Set Production Assistant: David McQuade; Accounting Assistant: Karin Mercurio; Craft Service: Mark Moelter, Don Speakman; Caterers: Carlos Garcia, Joe Schultz; Assistant Office Coordinator: Margaret J. Orlando; Script Coordinator: Sioux Richards; Location Manager: Kokayi Ampah; Location Assistants: Chris Cozzi, Scott Stahler; Production Accountant: Ramona Sanchez-Waggoner; Office Intern: Amie Tschappat; Accounting Assistant: Michael Vasquez, Assistant (Niki Marvin): Sophia Xixis; Helicopter Pilot/Aerial Coordinator: Robert ("Bobby Z") Zajonc: Press Attache (France): Michael Burstein; Production Assistant: Saxon Eldridge; Projectionist: Alan Jacques; ADR Voice: Tom Lent; Thanks: Dennis Baker, Warden of the Mansfield Correctional Institution; Manny Centeno, Director of the U.S. Virgin Islands Film Commission; Richard Hall, Assistant to the Warden of the Mansfield Correctional Institution; Eve Lapolla, Ohio Film Commission; Lee Tasseff, Mansfield Convention and Visitors Bureau, In Memory of Allen Greene; Locations: Mansfield Reformatory, Mansfield, Ohio; Butler, Ohio; Malabar Farm State Park, Lucas, Ohio; Upper Sandusky, Ohio; Ashland, Ohio; Bellville, Ohio; Yuma, Arizona; St. Croix, U.S. Virgin Islands; Budget: $25,000,000; Castle Rock Entertainment–Columbia Pictures; Released October 14, 1994; Running Time: 142 minutes.

Cast: Tim Robbins (Andy Dufresne), Morgan Freeman (Ellie Boyd ("Red") Redding), Bob Gunton (Warden Norton), William Sadler (Heywood), Clancy Brown (Captain Hadley), Gil Bellows (Tommy), Mark Rolston (Bogs Diamond), James Whitmore (Brooks Hatlen), Jeffrey DeMunn (1946 D.A.), Larry Brandenburg (Skeet), Neil Giuntoli (Jigger), Brian Libby (Floyd), David Proval (Snooze), Joseph Ragno (Ernie), Jude Ciccolella (Guard Mert), Paul McCrane (Guard Trout), Renee Blaine (Andy Dufresne's Wife), Scott Mann (Glenn Quentin), John Horton (1946 Judge), Gordon Greene (1947 Parole Hearings Man), Alfonso Freeman (Fresh Fish Con), V. J. Foster (Hungry Fish Con), John E. Summers (New Fish Guard), Frank Medrano (Fat Ass), Mack Miles (Tyrell), Alan R. Kessler (Laundry Bob), Morgan Lund (Laundry Truck Driver), Cornell Wallace (Laundry Leonard), Gary Lee Davis (Rooster), Neil Summers (Pete), Ned Bellamy (Guard Youngblood), Joseph Pecoraro (Projectionist), Harold E. Cope. Jr. (Hole Guard), Brian Delate (Guard Dekins), Don McManus (Guard Wiley), Donald Zinn (Moresby Batter), Dorothy Silver (1954 Landlady), Robert Haley (1954 Food-Way Manager), Dana Snyder (1954 Food-Way Woman), John D. Craig (1957 Parole Hearings Man), Ken Magee (Ned Grimes), Eugene C. DePasquale (Mail Caller), Bill Bolender (Elmo Blatch), Ron Newell (Elderly Hole Guard), John R. Woodward (Bullhorn Tower Guard), Chuck Brauchler (Man Missing Guard), Dion Anderson (Head Bull Haig), Claire Slemmer (Bank Teller), James Kisicki (Bank Manager), Rohn Thomas (Bugle Editor), Charlie Kearns (1966 D.A.), Rob Reider (Duty Guard), Brian Brophy (1967 Parole Hearings Man), Paul Kennedy (1967 Food-Way Manager), Neil Riddaway (Con), James Babson (Con), Dennis Baker (Old Man on Bus), Fred Culbertson (Police Officer), Richard Doone (Con), Rita Hayworth (Gilda Munson Farrell), David Hecht (Bank Teller), Alonzo F. Jones (Inmate), Gary Jones (Convict), Sergio Kato (Inmate II), Michael Lightsey (Con), Chris Page (Driver), Brad Spencer (1957 Parole Hearings Guard), Jodiviah Stepp (New Fish Con).

Life (1999) [prison work gang satire]

Credits: Directed by Ted Demme; Produced by James D. Brubaker, Karen Kahela Sherwood, Brian Grazer, Eddie Murphy, James Whitaker, Tina L. Fortenberry and Ray Murphy, Jr.; Screenplay by Robert Ramsey and Matthew Stone; Director of Photography: Geoffrey Simpson (color & black and white / 1.85:1 widescreen ratio); Film Editor: Jeffrey Wolf; Musical Score: Wyclef Jean; Casting: Margery Simkin; Art Director: Jeff Knipp; Set Decorator: John H. Anderson; Costume Designer: Lucy W. Corrigan; Special Makeup Effects: Rick Baker; Special Makeup Effects Key Artist (Eddie Murphy Old Age): David LeRoy Anderson; Makeup Artist (Mr. Lawrence): Kim D. Davis; Special Makeup Effects Artist: Bill Corso; Makeup Effects Technician: Richard Davison; Additional Makeup Artist: Rebecca DeHerrera; Assistant Makeup Artists: Debra Denson, Heather Koontz; Hair Stylists: Deena Adair, Louisa V. Anthony, Warren Lewis; Mold Maker: Richard Arguijo; Hair Stylists: (Mr. Murphy) Stacey Morris, (Mr.

Lawrence) Percy Burries; Key Hair Stylists: Sterfon Demmings, Julia L. Walker; Special Makeup Effects (Cinovation Studios): Clayton Martinez; Key Makeup Artists: Judy Murdock, Joseph Regina, Kazuhiro Tsuji; Hair Department Supervisor (Rick Baker/Cinovation): Sylvia Nava; Special Makeup Effects Artists: Mimi Palazon, Yoichi Art Sakamoto, Mark Shostrom; Makeup Artists: Ani Plotkin-Maloney, Bill Syner; Assistant Makeup Artist: JoAnn Stafford-Chaney; Makeup Production Supervisor: Bill Sturgeon; Makeup Artist (Mr. Murphy): Toy Van Lierop; Additional Makeup Artist: Phyllis Williams; Special Makeup Effects Artist: David Beneke; Unit Production Manager: James D. Brubaker; Production Supervisors: Arlene Kehela, Janet L. Wattles; First Assistant Director: Josh King; Second Assistant Director: Marcei A. Brown; Additional Second Assistant Directors: Marisa Farrey, Tommy Harper; Second Second Assistant Directors: Steve Booth, Evan Gilner; Second Unit Director: Don McCuaig; DGA Trainee: Elaine Wood; Set Designers: Maria L. Baker, Josh Lusby, Lori Rowbotham, Mary Saisellin; Set Dresser: Mark Boucher; Graphic Designer: Susan A. Burig; Art Department Coordinator: Francine Byrne; Paint Gang Boss: David B. Clark; Set Laborer: Joe Elvington; Standby Painter: Carmine Goglia; Construction Coordinator: Steve A. Hagberg; Assistant Property Masters: Corey Harris, Jr., Eugene McCarthy; Storyboard Artist: Alan Hoffman; Painter: Alan James; Construction Accountant: Marisol Jimenez; Head Paint Foreman: Steve Kerlagon; General Foreman: Randlett King Lawrence; Production Illustrator: Thomas W. Lay, Jr.; Props: Lauren Lustig; Propmaker: Kevin Wade McDonald; Carpenter: Larry Morgan; Art Department Production Assistant: Douglas Barrett Netter; Lead Man: Charles Nixon III; Construction Medic: Ahmed Saker; Paint Foreman: Chad Simpson; Character Designer: Aaron Sims; Weapons Specialist: Mike Sudrow; Assistant Property Master: Christopher Vail; Plasterer: Victor M. Shannon; Foley Mixer: James Ashwill; ADR Editors: Bobbi Banks; Sound Effects Editor: Odin Benitez; Dialogue Editors: Gaston Biraben, Norval D. Crutcher III, Avram D. Gold, Hari Ryatt; ADR Mixers: David Boulton, Alan Holly; ADR Recordists: Jeanette Browning, Rick Canelli; Foley Artists: John T. Cuzzi, Dan O'Connell; ADR Engineer: Will Edwards; Supervising Sound Editor: Michael Hilkene; Co-Supervising Sound Editor: Robert Fitzgerald; Foley Editors: Alexandra Gonzalez, Jason King, Victoria Rose Sampson, Christopher T. Welch, John T, Wilde; Sound Recordists: Frank Fleming, Brion Paccassi; Sound Effects Editors: David Grimaldi, Daniel Guth, Paul N. J. Ottosson; ADR Recordists: Bobby Johanson, Greg W. Lowe; Sound Effects Recordist: Michael Jonascu; Additional Sound Effects Recordist: Ken J. Johnson; ADR Mixers: Doc Kane, Greg Latimer, Thomas J. O'Connell; Sound Playback: Steve Klinghoffer; Sound Re-recording Mixers: Greg Landaker, Steve Maslow; Digital Mastering: Greg LaPlante; Foley Recordist: Linda Lew; Custom Looping: Mark Moseley; First Assistant Sound Editor: Douglas Parker; Apprentice Sound Editors: Eric Pinckert, Pernell L. Salinas; Foley Supervisor: Solange S. Schwalbe; Sound Engineer: Rick St. Hilaire; Second Assistant Sound Editors: F. Scott Taylor, Mark A Tracy; Boom Operator: Winfred Tennison; Production Sound Mixer: Russell Williams II; Cable Person: Ronald L. Wright; Sound Effects Editor: Daniel Evan Yale; Special Effects: Roy Augenstein, Hal Bigger, Robert E. Lamberth, Bruce Richter;

Sound Effects Foreman: Robert L. Olmstead; Special Effects Coordinator: Daniel Sudick; Foam Department Supervisor: Roland Blancaflor; Visual Effects: Randall Balsmeyer; Rear Projection Effects: Bill Hansard; Visual Effects Producer: Petra Holtorf; Inferno Artist (Opening Sequence): Toby Wilkins; Stunts: Mello Alexandria, Jophery C. Brown, Tony Brubaker, Eric Chambers, Lanier Edwards, Tony Gilbert, Irving E. Lewis, James C. Lewis, Gary Littlejohn, Jalil Jay Lynch, Rusty McClennon, Buck McDancer, Jeffrey McDancer, Bennie E. Moore, Jr., Gary Price, Stan Lee Price, Alphonse Walter, Big Daddy Wayne; Stunt Coordinator: Alan Oliney; Rigging Gaffers: Bob Allen, Jr., Richard Smock; Dolly Grip ("B" Camera): John Beran; Steadicam Operator/"B" Camera Operator: Harry K. Garvin; Wescam Camera Operator: Mark Hryma; First Assistant "A" Camera: Gregory Irwin; Key Grip: John Janusek; Assistant Chief Lighting Technician: Stephen Johnstone; Rigging Key Grip: Kenny King; Best Boy Rigger: Rick Maddux; Still Photographer: Bruce McBroom; Director of Photography (Second Unit): Don McCuaig; First Assistant Camera (Second Unit): Duane Mieliwocki; Video Assist Operator: Paul Murphey; Gaffer: Patrick Murray; Assistant Camera: Louis Niemeyer; Camera Operator: Bill O'Drobinack; Rigging: Travis Panarisi; Camera Loader: Jerry Patton; Dolly Grip: Michael C. Price; Assist Steadicam Operator/First Assistant "B" Camera: Joe Ritter; Best Boy Grip: John P. Shine; Second Assistant "A" Camera Operator: Joy R. Stone; Rigging Grip: Chuck Turner; Electrician: Carl A. Vidnic; Extras Casting: Jennifer Bender, Kevin Goldson, Carl Joy; Casting Associate: Carmen Cuba; Casting Assistants: Craig Harris, Susan Maas; Casting Administrator: Terry M. Landfers; Key Costumer: Dawn Y. Line; Costumer: Philip Maldonado; Key Set Costumer (Men): Joe McCloskey; Costume Illustrator: Michele Michel; Assistant Costume Designer: Maggie Morgan; Set Costumers: Johnny Pray, Nava R. Sadan; Costumer (Martin Lawrence): Kathleen Russo; Aging Assistant: Leticia Sandoval; Costume Supervisor: James W. Tyson; Apprentice Editor: John Bergstrasser; Post-Production Coordinator: Sharon Cannon; Negative Cutter: Marien Hill; Second Assistant Editors: Sophie Kil, Karen Kory; Additional Editor: Marty Levenstein; Apprentice Editor: Samara Levenstein; Color Timer: Mike Milliken; First Assistant Editors: Geoffrey O'Brien, Eric O. Schusterman; Music Contractor/Preparation: Emile Charlap; Music Consultant: Buck Damon; Score Recordist: Andy Grassi; Conductor/Orchestrator: Sonny Kompanek; Score Stage Administrator: Stephanie Murray; Supervising Music Editor: Allan K. Rosen; Music Supervisor: Amanda Scheer-Demme; Musician (French Horn): James Thatcher; Music Editors: Patty von Arx, Kevin Crehan; Music Recordist: Paul Wertheimer; Transportation Coordinator: Ed Arter; Transportation Dispatcher: Tina M. Arter-Duquette; Driver (Honeywagon): Roger Bojarski, Jr.; Drivers: Louis Dinson, Sean C. Ryan, Michael Vieira; Driver (Base Camp Generator): William P. Lafon; Driver (Cast): Fred Teague; Production Driver: Russ Tolliver; Transportation Captains: Mike Padovich, Daniel Quick, Ed Wirth; Title Designers: Bohnie Avanzino, George Cawood, Dina Mande, Nina Saxon; Wrangler: Jerry Bestpitch; Script Supervisor: Susan Bierbaum; Stand-ins: Fred Fein, (Mr. Lawrence) Darryl Brunson, (Mr. Murphy) Roger F. Reid; Accounting Assistant: Aillene Laure Bubis; Photo Double (Mr. Murphy): Virgil Carter; Second Assistant Accountant: Yolanda M. Thibodeaux; Executive Assistant to

Martin Lawrence: Peaches Davis; Dialect Coach: Jessica Drake; Production Coordinator: Jane Everett; Production Secretary: Julius M. Fletcher; Key Craft Service: Ronald E. Hairston, William Ramirez, Jr.; Post-Production Accountant: Ryan Hintz; Studio Teacher: Pat Jackson; Construction Accountant: Marisol Jimenez; First Assistant Accountant: Michael Morganthal; Second Assistant Accountants: Jennifer Koenig, Margo Romano; Payroll Accountant: Michael Wat; Set Medic: Tamara Maellaro; Textile Artist: Niamh Murphy; Production Auditor: Glen Richard; Archive Researcher: Deborah Ricketts; Production Assistants: Stephanie Neroes, Michael Rucker, George L. Tarrant, Jr., Brook Worley; Assistant Production Coordinator: Stacy Parker; Unit Publicist: Debbie Simmrin; Aerial Coordinator: Peter McKernan; Cast Associate: Karen Warendorp; Executive Assistant to James D. Brubaker: Regina A. Warendorp; Personal Assistant to Eddie Murphy: Randy Webster; Supervising Location Manager: Arlene Kehela; Location Manager: David Thornsberry; Assistant Location Managers: Brad Bell, Peter Martorano, Ken Struck; Locations: Los Angeles, Norwalk, Sacramento and Santa Clarita, California; Imagine Entertainment–Universal Pictures; Budget: $75,000,000; Released April 16, 1999; Running Time: 108 minutes.

Cast: Eddie Murphy (Rayford Gibson), Martin Lawrence (Claude Banks), Obba Babatunde (Willie Long), Nick Cassavetes (Sergeant Dillard), Anthony Anderson (Cookie), Barry Shabaka Henley (Pokerface), Brent Jennings (Hoppin' Bob), Bernie Mac (Jangle Leg), Miguel A. Nunez, Jr. (Biscuit), Michael ("Bear") Taliferro (Goldmouth), Guy Torry (Radio), Bokeem Woodbine (Can't Get Right), Ned Beatty (Dexter Wilkins), Lisa Nicole Carson (Sylvia), O'Neal Compton (Superintendent Abernathy), Noah Emmerich (Stan Blocker), Rick James (Spanky Johnson), Clarence Williams III (Winston Hancock), Heavy D (Jake), Bonz Malone (Leon), Ned Vaughn (Young Sheriff Pike), R. Lee Ermey (Older Sheriff Pike), Sanaa Lathan (Daisy), Allyson Coll (Young Mae Rose Abernathy), Poppy Montgomery (Older Mae Rose Abernathy), James D. Bruker (Judge E. M. Byrne), Walter K. Jordan (Slim), Brooks Almy (Billy's Mama), Hal Havins (Billy), Hildy Brooks (Nurse Doherty), Kenn Whitaker (Issac), Ernie Lee Banks (Bathroom Attendant), David Alexander (Doctor), Johnny Brown (Blind Reverend Clay), Armelia McQueen (Mrs. Clay), Nate Evans (Juke Bartender), Todd Everett (Deputy at Mansion), Don Harvey (Billy Bob), Venus De Milo Thomas (Juke Joint Waitress), Zaid Farid, Keith Burke (Shady Card Players), Kenneth White (Deputy), Leonard O. Turner (Superintendent Burke), Augie Blunt (Man in Prison), Quantae Love, Sean Lampkin (Trustys at Line), James Emory, Jr. (Goldmouth's Son), Bill Gratton (Fire Inspector), Reamy Hall (Mrs. Dillard), George Hartmann (Prison Guard), Zack Helvey (Captain Tom Burnette), Hall Vaughn Anderson III (Junkie), Kimble Jemison, Jordan Mahome (Gang Banger), William S. Taylor, Jay Arlen Jones (Bagmen), Oscar Jordan (Juke Joint Guitarist), Ronald Lee Moss (Bouncer), Betty Murphy (Mrs. Abernathy), Walter Powell, Jr. (Waiter), Christopher Prevost (Pilot), Dawn Robinson (Club Crooner), Leon Sanders (Barkeeper), Steve Boyles (Mule Cart Driver), Shayne Benton (Farm Boy), Sydney ("Big Dawg") Colston (Henchman No. Two), Thomas J. Larsen (Conference Teacher), Bridget Morrow (Cocktail Waitress), Leon Turner (Arm That Went Up), Muhammed Ali, Jimi Hendrix, Martin Luther King, Jr., Elvis Presley (Themselves [archival footage]).

Happy, Texas (1999) [chain gang parody]

Credits: Directed by Mark Illsley; Produced by Jason Clark, Mark Illsley, Rick Montgomery, Ed Stone, Norman Buckley and Glenn S, Gainor; Screenplay by Ed Stone, Mark Illsley and Phil Reeves; Director of Photography: Bruce Douglas Johnson (color / 1.85:1 widescreen ratio); Film Editor: Norman Buckley; Musical Score: Peter Harris; Casting: Joe Garcia; Production Designer: Maurin L. Scarlata; Art Director: Tobey Bays; Set Decorator: Phoebe O'Connor; Costume Designer: Julia Schklair; Makeup Artist: Karen Scherer; Key Makeup Artist (Additional Photography): Ania M. Harasimiak; Additional Makeup Artists: Carla M. Fabrizi, Susan Kaminga; Key Hair Stylist/Key Makeup Artist: Phillip Pico; Key Hair Stylist (Additional Photography): Solina Tobrizi; Assistant Hair Stylist/Assistant Makeup Artist (Additional Photography): Tania Goddard; Hair Stylist and Makeup Artist for Ms. Walker (Additional Photography): Kim Goodwin; Unit Production Manager: J. Patrick Clark; Production Supervisor: Debra L. Gainor; Post-Production Supervisor: Teresa Kelly; Production Supervisor (Additional Photography): Ron Schmidt; Post-Production Supervisor (Additional Photography): Kirk M. Morri; First Assistant Director: George Bamber; First Assistant Director (Additional Photography): Fernando Altshchl; First Assistant Directors (Second Unit): Shawn Hawley, Jose Clemente Hernandez; Second Assistant Director: Robin Jordan; Second Assistant Director (Additional Photography): Kelly Kiernan; Second Unit Director: Ricardo Mendez Matta; Second Second Assistant Director: Jody Spilkoman; Set Dressers: Wayne Acton, David Buckband, Anthony Kowloski, Ricky Zamudio; Lead Man (Additional Photography)/Set Dresser: Maxwell Jean Britton; Set Dressers (Additional Photography): Fred D'Amico, Peter Mathus; Property Assistant (Additional Photography)/Set Dresser: James L. Eddy; Set Decorating Shopper (Additional Photography): Camille Esposito; Property Master: Michele Spears; Assistant Property Master: Raf Lydon; Art Department Assistant: Susan Scarlata; On-Set Dresser: Ed Servaites; Scenic Artists: Suzanne Stotts, Robert Piser; On-Set Dresser (Additional Photography): Don Stroud; Painter: Nick Worsfold; Assistant Dialogue Editor: Pembrooke Andrews; Sound Re-recording Mixers: Wayne Artman, Robert L. Harman, Liz Sroka, Ken Teaney; Sound Consultant (MIDI): Kevin Bassinson; Sound Services Managers: Levon Broussalian, Wayne Gordon; Sound Effects Editor: Jeff K. Brunello; Sound Effects Assistant: Eric Corley; ADR Editor/Dialogue Editor: Paul Curtis; Additional ADR Supervisor: Andrew DeCristofaro; Sound Mixers (Second Unit): James Dehr, Clifford ("Kyp") Gin; Sound Effects Editors: Elisabeth Flaum, Michael Kamper, Jeffrey R. Whitcher; Sound Re-recording Assistant: Eric Justen; Sound Effects Editor/Sound Re-recording Assistant: Laura Kamper; ADR Recordist: Shawn Kennelly; Boom Operator: Dan Lipe; Boom Operator (Additional Photography): Kevin Maloney; Foley Recordists: Gred Louden, Greg Mauer, Susan Pusateri; Supervising Sound Editor: Michael Payne; Mix Assistant: Juan Peralta; Supervising Sound Effects Editor: Ann Scibelli; Dialogue Editors: Frederick H. Stahly, John C. Stuver; Assistant Dialogue Editor: Dan Scolnick; ADR Recording Assistant: Chris Staszak; ADR Mixer: Eric Thompson; Barber Boom Operator: Tom Van Otteren; Production Sound Mixer: Ed White; Stereo Sound

Appendix C

Consultant (Dolby): James Wright; Layback Mixer: Larry Hopkins; Pyrotechnician: Greg Landerer; Pyrotechnics Assistant: Lee McConnell; 2D Compositor (THDX): Michael Adkisson; 3D Animator (THDX): Inaka Imaz; In-Show Optical Process and Effects Compositor/Motion Control and Credit Sequence Optical Compositor (THDX): Christopher Dusendschon; Stunt Coordinator: Bobby C. King; Stunt Coordinator (Additional Photography): Manny Perry; Stunts: David Edward Garber, Gary Hugghins, April Littlejohn, Brian Burkhardt, Garner Clark; Stunt Double: Christopher J. Tuck; Utility Stunts (Additional Photography): Dick Ziker; Steadicam Operator (Additional Photography): Gavin Ames; Best Boy Grip (Additional Photography): Joe Backes; Grips: Clint Borden, Tom Feucht, Ted Kennedy, Ryan Meyer, Calvin Starnes, Robert Stillman; Electricians (Additional Photography): Kevin Cadwallader, Somsy Vejsiri, Jonathan Weiner; Electrician (Second Unit): Zoran Milosavljevic; Gaffer: Marcello L. Colacilli; Security Gaffer: Chacho Dominguez; Still Photographer: Dina S. Khouri; Additional Still Photographer: Richard Foreman, Jr.; Film Loaders: Isaac Friedman, David Tang; Electricians: Harry H. Gradzhyan, Greg McCurley, Vladimir Melnick, Euripides Nunez, Doug Rymes, Mike Schwabenland; Electrician (Additional Photography): Josh Liberman; Camera Loader (Additional Photography): Akos Gulyas; Crane Operator (Jib Arm): Shane Harness; Best Boy Electric: Orlando Hernandez; Director of Photography (Second Unit): Bengt Jonsson; Dolly Grip: Geoffrey D. Knoller; Company Grips (Additional Photography): Nick Liampetchakul, Jennifer Newell; Best Boy Grip/Electrician (Additional Photography): Richard Oliver; First Assistant Camera: Christopher C. Pearson; First Assistant Camera (Additional Photography): Michael Ortiz; Grip (Second Unit): Rell Putt; Dolly Grip (Additional Photography): Paul Reyes; Camera Intern: Ruben Russ; Key Grip: Kurt Wolfe; Key Grip (Additional Photography): David A. Santos; Second Assistant Camera: Allan Telias; Steadicam Operator: Rick Tiedeman; Set Lighting Technician: Shane Buttle; Assistant Camera: James R. Powell; Extras Casting: Dave Castro, Joseph Hicks; Casting Assistants: Michael G. Miller, J. P. Shields; Set Costumers: Denise Caplan, Jessica Hastings, Sherif Zaki; Set Costumer (Additional Photography): Denise Brandon; Assistant Costume Designer: Anthony Franco; Costume Supervisor: Mandi Line; Costumer (Additional Photography): Palmer Todd; Color Timers: Bob Frederickson, Mato; Post-Production Coordinators: Armand Garabidian, Douglas Salkin; Assistant Editor: Paul Millspaugh; Associate Editor: Jeff McEvoy; Post-Production Consultant: Harry B. Miller III; Score Producer: Peter Harris; Scoring Mixer: Scott Cochran; Music Coordinator: Audrey DeRoche; Composer: Additional Music/Score Producer: David Feinman; Music Editors: Ron Finn, Brian Kirk; Musician (Percussion): M. B. Gordy; Orchestra Contractor: Simon James; Music Supervisor: Alexandra Patsavas; Composer (Additional Music): James Stemple; Conductor: Alan Williams; Drivers: Mac ("Buck") Cook, Troy Gould, Duane Hale, Ray Stuart; Drivers (Additional Photography): Richard L. Burch, Nick Duron, Dave Earl, Dale Moser, Shaun Ryan, Eric Lazar, Joseph Taggert; Transportation Captain: Guy J. Graves; Transportation Captain (Additional Photography): Gene Ward; Transportation Coordinators: Billy Colbert, John De Troia; Transportation Coordinator (Additional Photography): Ted Moser; Cast Drivers (Additional

Photography): Beth Blanks, Deborah J. Chesebro, Valerie Bleth Sharp; ADR Voices: Newell Alexander, Steve Bulen, Mitch Carter, David Cowgill, Jackie Gonneau, Joyce Kurtz, Edie Merman, Gracie Moore; Office Production Assistant: Sarah Anthony; Graphic Artists (Tiles): Jose Avitia, Blake Busby; Chef: Pascal Besse; Assistant Chef: Frank Gunn; Craft Service: Christina Richard, Mary Beth Shewmake; Guards: Walter Bishop, Robert Mesa, James V. Navarro, James V. Navarro II; Dialogue Consultant: Michael Buster; Set Production Assistant: Randall Smoot; Set Production Assistant (Additional Photography): Amiee Clark, Steve Thomas; Safety Riggers: Garner Clark, Mike Cunliffe, Ken Forsgren; Assistant (Jason Clark): Warren Davis II; Production Assistant: Elizabeth Forsyth; Production Coordinator: Brendan Garst; Production Coordinator (Additional Photography): Ron Cosco Vechiarelli; Production Accountant: Michael Goldberg; Assistant Production Coordinator (Additional Photography): Jason Mundy; Production Accountant (Additional Photography): Robb Hastigan; Production Secretary (Additional Photography): Nawana Davis; Production Office Assistant (Additional Photography): Matthew Hirsch, Zoya Korper; Choreographer: Kelly DeVine; Script Supervisor: Samantha C. Kirkeby; Craft Service (Additional Photography): Melissa Larsen; Caterer (Additional Photography): Ramiro Lopez; Producer (Additional Photography): Mike Leahy; Production Legal: Ronald J. Levin, Paul Mayersohn; Technician: HotHead (Additional Photography): Gary Lucas; Studio Teachers: Roxa Crow, Joan Marks; Production Insurance: Kent Hamilton, Truman Van Dyke; Set Production Assistants: Robert Peralta, Lynn Struiksma, Robb Thomas; Payroll Services: John Switzer; Set Production Assistants (Additional Photography): Guy Pringle, Steve Thomas; Production Office Assistant (Additional Photography): Arron Turnbull; Key Set Production Assistant (Additional Photography): Robert Ohlandt; Office Production Assistant: Rick Saloomey; Production Office Assistant (Additional Photography): Raymond Prososky; First Assistant Accountant (Additional Photography): Claudia Soisson; Graphic Artist (Titles): Jennifer Rae Smith; Barber Boom Operator: Jayme Roy; Medic (Additional Photography): Ron Resch; Completion Bond: Matthew Warren, Kurt Woolner; Assistant to Producers (Additional Photography): Lauren Feige Keskinel; Location Scout: Guillermo Etcheberry; Location Managers: Joe Burk, Christopher Lee; Assistant Location Managers (Additional Photography): Ronin P. Nagle, Michael Paolillo; Locations: Lancaster and Piru, California; Marked Entertainment–Miramax Pictures; Budget: $1,700,000; Released October 1, 1999; Running Time: 98 minutes.

Cast: Steve Zahn (Wayne Wayne Wayne, Jr. ['a.k.a. "David]), Jeremy Northam (Harry Sawyer [a.k.a. "Steven," "Steve"]), William H. Macy (Sheriff Chappy Dent), Ally Walker (Josephine ["Joe"] McClintock, the Banker), Illeana Douglas (Doreen Schaefer), M. C. Gainey (Robert ["Bob"] Allen Maslow), Ron Perlman (Marshal Nalhober), Mo Gaffney (Mrs. Bromley), Paul Dooley (The Judge), Jillian Berard (Madison ["Maddie"]), Scarlet Pomers (Jency [Flaming Batons]), Scarlet Pomers (Another Happy Girl), Melissa Arnold (Another Happy Girl), Tiffany Takara (Another Happy Girl), Tim Bagley (David, Pageant Professional), Michael Hitchcock (Steven, Pageant Professional), Ed Stone (Alton), Rance Howard (Ely the Tractor Driver), Derek Montgomery (Bully Boy), Kiva Lawrence (Pageant Judge), Carley Fink (Little Light Girl), David Shackelford

(Varnel the Tire Collector), Kim Story (Guard), Tim Cowgill (Local Cowboy), Guy J. Graves (Tow Truck Driver), Mark Illsley (Guard on Horse with Shotgun), Krista Lewis (Bank Teller), Keo Woolford (Cabana Boy Kimo).

O Brother, Where Art Thou? (2001) [chain gang satire]

Credits: Directed by Joel and Ethan Coen; Produced by Tim Bevan, Eric Fellner, Ethan Coen, Joel Coen, John Cameron and Robert Graf; Screenplay by Ethan Coen and Joel Coen; Based on the Epic Poem *The Odyssey* by Homer; Director of Photography: Roger Deakins (color / 2.35:1 widescreen ratio); Film Editors: Ethan Coen, Joel Coen, Tricia Cooke; Musical Score: T. Bone Burnett; Casting: Ellen Chenoweth; Production Designer: Dennis Gassner; Art Director: Richard L. Johnson; Set Decorator: Nancy Haigh; Costume Designer: Mary Zophres; Makeup Supervisor: Jean Ann Black; Key Hair Stylists: Roy Bryson, Karen Huston, Amy Schmiederer; Head Hair Stylist: Paul LeBlanc; Hair Stylist (Mr. Clooney): Waldo Sanchez; Hair Stylist: Sheryl Blum; Makeup Artists: Linda Boykin-Williams, Laverne Caracuzzi; Unit Production Manager: John Cameron; Production Supervisor: Gilly Ruben; Post-Production Supervisor: David Diliberto; Executives in Charge of Production (Working Title Films): Jane Frazer, Michelle Wright; DGA Trainee: Peter Dress; First Assistant Director: Betsy Magruder; Second Assistant Director: Jonathan McGarry; Second Second Assistant Director: Donald Murphy; Dayplayer Additional Second Assistant Director: Steve Lonano; Construction Foreman: Dean Allison; Storyboard Artist: J. Todd Anderson; Assistant Set Decorator: Paige Augustine; Standby Greensmen: Pedro Barquin, Jeff Brown, Michael Hendrick; Greens Foremen: Robert Loring, Jr., Tom McEldowney; Construction Purchaser: Melody Bishop; Construction Foremen and Women: Jerry G. Henery, Tom McDaniel, Mark Sparks, Debbie Nolan, Steve Roll; Greens Laborer: Clayton Boyman; Construction Coordinator: E. W. Bradford, Jeff Passanante, Randall S. Coe; Plaster Foremen: Shane Buckallew, John Dugan; Paint Foremen: Robert E. Denne, Larry Laurent, Andrew M. Scudier; Paint Supervisor: Thomas E. Brown; Signwriter: Casey Kasemeier, William H. Neff, Dave Kelsey, Stephanie Macomber; Props: Carisa Rosenthal; Assistant Signwriter: Stephanie Kern; Property Master: Ritchie Kremer; Assistant Property Master: Ron Patterson; Labor Foreman: John Leone; Set Dressing Gangboss: Leslie ("Tinker") Linville; On-Set Dresser: James P. Meehan; Set Dressers: Thomas Minton, Nashon Petrushkin; Assistant Art Director: Marco Rubeo; Standby Painter: Henry Schaub; Set Painters: Craig T. Shordon, Dan Dorfer; Set Consultant: Jonathan Short; Art Department Administrator: Monica Streed; Leadman: Marl Weissenfluh; Set Dressers: Richard F. Anderson, Jack Blanchard; Carpenters: John Blanchard, Sara Fanelli, Leo Lauricella, Douglas P. Newell; Scenic Painter: Gail Briant; Camera Scenic Artist: Cyd Fenwick; Propmaker Foreman: Nail Gahm; Painter: John Herbert; Modelbuilder: Jane Kilkenny; Props Assistant: Props Assistant; Standby Greensman: Bryan McBrien; Sound Re-recording Mixers: Michael Barry, Sean Garnhart, George Orloff; Sound Re-recording Mixer/Supervising Sound Editor: Skip Lievsay; Sound Recordist: Jesse Ehredt; Sound Editor: Jerry Ross; Layback Sound Mixer: Larry Hopkins; Stage Engineer: Hanson Hsu; Apprentice Sound Editor: Bill

Orrico, Alex Zaleski; Sound Effects Editors: Glenfield Payne, Paul Urmson; Utility Sound Technicians: Knox White, Mark Zimbibki; Boom Operator: Steve Bowerman; Foley Editors: Kam Chan, Frank Kern, Jennifer Ralston; Foley Supervisor: Benjamin Cheah; Foley Artist: Marko A. Costanzo, Jay Peck; Dialogue Editors: Fred Rosenberg, Philip Stockton; Consultant (Dolby): Tom ("Coach") Ehle; Assistant Sound Editors: Chris Fielder, Mike Poppleton, Alan Zaleski; Sound Designer: Eugene Gearty; Production Sound Mixer: Peter F. Kurland; Foley Engineer: George A. Lara; ADR Mixer: Greg Steele; Sound Intern: Steve Zimbicki; Special Effects Coordinator: Peter Chesney; Special Effects Foremen: Kyle Ross Collinsworth, Gintar Repecka; Special Effects Administrator: Blaine Converse; Special Effects Set Lead: Robert L. Oldstead; Special Effects: Jon Thackery; Special Effects Technicians: Steve Austin, Gary D. Bierend, Tom Chesney, Joe Heffernan, Chris Nelson, Sandra Stewart; Visual Effects Executive Producer: Nancy Bernstein; Datacine Assistant: Jill Bogdanowicz; Digital Mastering Editor: Shawn Broes; Imaging Technician: Jeff Christopherson; Miniature Effects Supervisor: Alan K. M. Faucher; Senior Colorist: Julius Friede; Visual Effects Coordinator: Julie Goldberg; Film Recording Operator: Glen Gustafson; Film Compositing Supervisor: Claas Henke; Digital Imaging Supervisor: Jeffrey Kalmus; Creative Imaging Supervisor: Michael Kanfer; Compositor (Balsmeyer and Everett): Daniel Leung; Visual Effects Producer: Lucian Levi; Visual Effects Supervisor: Erik Nash; Computer Graphics Supervisor: David Prescott; Manager of Operations: Sarah Priestnall; Vice President, Digital Imaging (Pat Repola); Datacine Assistant: Brian Shows; System Administrator: Tess Spaulding; Imaging Technician: Mike Tosti; Visual Effects Editor: Deborah Wolff; Visual Effects Compositor: Ted Andre; Digital Matte Painters: Laurent Ben-Mimoun, Phillippo Constanzo; Digital Artists: David Bleich. John Michael Courte, Sean C, Cunningham, Melanie Okamura, Josh Seata, Keiji Yamaguchi; Runner: S. Kai Bovaird; 3D Technical Assistants: Wally Chin, Robert Coquia, Jr.; Scanning and Recording Operators: Chad E. Collier, James Egstad; Data Integration Artist: Jennifer Doud; Data Integration Supervisor: Tim ("Timco") Conway; Character Rigger: Barry Dempsey; Digital Compositors: Feliciano di Giorgio, Mark Larranaga, Donovan Scott; Shader Technical Director: John Gibson; Systems Administrator: Jeff Goldstrom; Visual Effects Business Affairs: Molly Hansen; Visual Effects: Jongwoo Heo; Visual Effects Animator: Garman Herigstad; Visual Effects Production Assistant: Flame Assistant: Stephen Jennings; 2D Technical Assistant: Fred Jimenez; Technical Coordinator: Brian Peyatt; Lead Modelmakers: Jeff Phillips, Brian Ripley; VFX Coordinator (Cinesite): LeiLa Ratti; Digital Character Animator: David Earl Smith; Model Maker Crew Chief: George Stevens; Data Integration Team: Messrob Torakian; Production Controller (Pre-Production): Kieran Woo; Compositor: Rachel Wyn Dunn; Stunt Coordinator: Jery Edwards; Stunts: Danny Downey, Nicholas J. Giangiulio, Donald John Hewitt, Jeff Jensen, Jennifer Lamb, David Peterson, Keith Siplinger, G. Peter King; Stunt Double (George Clooney): Brad Martin; Camera Loader (Josh Blakeslee); Rigging Gaffer: Craig A. Brink; First Assistant Steadicam: Erik L. Brown; Rigging Best Boy Electrician: David Diamond; Camera Operator: Clinton Dougherty; Second Company Grip: Kevin Fahey; Assistant Chief Lighting Technicians: Alan Frazier, Jeremy Knaster; Key

Rigging Grips: Charley Gilleran, Charlie Marroquin; Second Assistant Camera: Adam Gilmore; Still Photographer: Melinda Sue Gordon; Rigging Gaffer: Joseph Grimaldi; Dolly Grip: Bruce Hamme; Rigging Best Boy Electrician: James McElroy; Steadicam Operators: Mark O'Kane, Kyle Rudolph; Chief Lighting Technician: Jonathan E. Salzman; Second Company Grip: Michael L. Smith; First Assistant Steadicam: Chuck Whelan; Grip (Los Angeles): Robert Anderson; Akela Crane Operator: John Bonnin; Grip: Al Bruce; Lighting Department: Willie E. Dawkins; Additional Camera Loader: Will Dearborn; Rigging Grip: Michael James Fahey; Set Lightning: Alexandre Naufel; Camera Department Intern: Ben Nekhi; Set Lighting (Los Angeles): Dylan Rush; Rigging Electrician: Chris Weigand; Electrician (Los Angeles): Abbe Wool; Underwater Assistant Camera: Maryan Zurek; Title Animation (Balsmeyer and Everett): Gray Miller; Additional Casting: Kathleen Chopin; Extras Casting Assistants: Carrie Crossman, April Hardcastle; Local Casting: Sandra Dawes; Casting Assistants: Brennan Dufresne, Jennifer Euston; Voice Casting: Sondra James; Costume Supervisor: Cha Blevins; Tailor/Cutter: Celeste Cleveland; Set Costumers: Steve Constancio, Linda S. Cormany, Cookie Lopez; Assistant Costume Designer: Danielle Valenciano, Linda Gardar; Seamstress: Giselle Spence; Costumers: Guy Miracle, Jason M. Moore, Lori Jean Sacks, Susan Thomas, Tammy Williamson; Additional Costumer: Fran Murphy; First Assistant Editor: Ian Silverstein; Second Assistant Editor: Karyn Anonia; Additional Assistant Editor: George Thompson; Associate Film Editor: David Filiberto; Negative Cutter: Teresa Repola Mohammed; Final Colorist: Mike Bellamy; Color Timer: Mike Milliken; Digital Intermediate Producer: Carole Cowley; Music Legal Services: Jill Berliner, Michelle Dixon, Deborah McCullough; Music Producer: T. Bone Burnett; Composer (Additional Music): Carter Burwell; Music Editor: Sean Garnhart; Music Researcher: Alan Larman; Music Clearances: Deborah Mannis-Gardner; Music Coordinator: Lee Olson; Music Production Coordinator: Valerie Pack; Music Recordist: Mike Piersante; Executive Music Producer: Denise Stiff; Associate Music Producer: Gillian Welch; Musicologist: Sandy Wilber; Music Assistant: Daniel S. McCoy; Singing Voice (George Clooney): Dan Tyminski; Transportation Captain: Timothy P. Ryan; Transportation Co-Captains: James R. Brown, Ken Nevin; Transportation Coordinator: Don Tardino; Transportation Office Administrator: Paul Ripple; Transportation: John Lelko; Drivers: Willie T. Partin, James Nordberg, Patricia Sammons; Title Designer: Randall Balsmeyer; Craft Service: Nancy G. James; Craft Service Assistants: Kirk Barton, Robert Bodenheaimer, Derek Hurd; Construction Medic: Michael Berry; Assistant (Mr. Clooney): Amy Minda Cohen; Accounting Clerk: Gerry Lee Crews; Assistant Production Coordinator: Matt DiFranco; Assistant (Mr. Bevan and Mr. Fellner): Juliette Dow; Production Assistants: Jenny Eagan, Caroline Eselin, Christian Fauntleroy, Glenn P. Klekowski, Anand Mahendra, Emily Palmer, Taylor Phillips, Scott Pitman, Paul Schmitz, Christopher Vitale, Chris Wessman, Josh Yates, Blake McClure, Sean Riley; Producer: Titles and Effects: Kathy Kelehan; Yodeler: Pat Enright; Translator (*The Odyssey* Introductory Excerpt): Benedict Fitzgerald; Cooks: Neda Redula, (Tony's Food Service) Renaldo Garcia, Ivan Kerum, Hiro Lam; Train Coordinator: Stan Garner; Accounting Clerk: Lauren Gaston; Production Coor-

dinator: Karen Ruth Getchell; Animal Coordinator: Jennifer Henderson; Business Affairs: Rachel Holroyd, Angela Morrison; Production Accountant/Post-Production Accountant: Barbara Ann Stein; Assistant Accountant/Post-Production Accountant: Andrew Sears; Post-Production Provost: Neil A. Stelzer; Insurance Services (AON/Albert G. Ruben): Kevin O'Shea; President of Operations (Mike Zoss Productions): Alan J. Schoolcraft; Second Assistant Accountant: Nicholas Irwin; Script Supervisor: Thomas Johnston; Company Coordinator: Nina Khoshaba; Payroll Accountant: Denyse Rossi; Choreographers: Bill Landrum, Jacqui Landrum; Assistants (Mr. Bevan and Mr. Fellner): Dominic Sardo, Lara Thompson; Set Medic: Mitchell Ray; Medic: Charlie French; Animal Wrangler: Jeff Galpin; Head Animal Trainer: April Mackin; Animal Trainers: James Riggs Davis, James P. Warren; Financial Consultant: Julian Tomlin; Assistant Production Coordinator: Susan Vercelli; First Assistant Accountant: Jerri Whiteman; Assistant to Cast: George Bott, Batou Chandler, Jimi Woods; Stand-in (Mr. Clooney): Troy Hartman; Crafts Service Assistant: Andrew Rozario; Extras Coordinator: Kristian Sorensen; Location Scout: Kim Davis; Location Assistant: Barbara Saunders; Assistant Location Managers: Kim Jordan, Keith Potter, John Read; Location Manager: Michael Riley; Locations: Los Angeles and Santa Clarita, California; Canton, D'Lo, Edwards, Jackson, Leland, Oxford, Valley Park, Vicksburg and Yazoo City, Mississippi; Working Title–Mike Zoss Productions–StudioCanal–Touchstone Pictures–Buena Vista Pictures–Universal Pictures; Budget: $26,000,000; Released February 2, 2001; Running Time: 106 minutes.
Cast: George Clooney (Everett), John Turturro (Pete Hogwallop), Tim Blake Nelson (Delmar O'Donnell), John Goodman (Big Dan Teague), Holly Hunter (Penny), Chris Thomas King (Tommy Johnson), Charles Durning (Pappy O'Daniel), Del Pentacost (Del O'Daniel), Michael Badalucco (George Nelson), J. R. Horne (Pappy's Staff), Brian Reddy (Pappy's Staff), Wayne Duvall (Homer Stokes), Ed Gale (The Little Man), Ray McKinnon (Vernon T. Waldrip), Daniel von Bargen (Sheriff Cooley), Royce D. Applegate (Man with Bullhorn), Frank Collison (Wash Hogwallop), Quinn Gasaway (Boy Hogwallop), Lee Weaver (Blind Seer), Milford Fortenberry (Pomade Vendor), Stephen Root (Radio Station Man), John Locke (Mr. French), Gillian Welch (Soggy Bottom Customer), A. Ray Ratliff (Record Store Clerk), Mia Tate, Museta Vander, Christy Taylor (Sirens), April Hardcastle (Waitress), Michael W. Fennell (Interrogator), Georgia Rae Rainer, Marianna Breland, Lindsey Miller, Natalie Shedd (Wharvey Gals), John McConnell (Woolsworths Manager), Isaac Freeman, Wilson Waters, Jr., Robert Hamlett (Gravediggers), Robert Cox, Evelyn Cox, Suzanne Cox, Sidney Cox (Cox Family), Buck White, Sharon White, Cheryl White (The Whites), Ed Snoddenly, David Holt (Village Idiots), Dan Andrieu (KKK Member), Seth Bailey (Banquet Patron, Cigar Smoker), Billy W. Blackwell (Rally and Banquet Patron), Ron Block (Banjoist), Dan Braun, Ryder Davis, Nathan Kornelis (Klansmen), Jerry Douglas (Dobro Player), Christopher Francis, Mark Munson (KKK Member), Gloria Gonnillini (Lady at Political Rally), Geoffrey Gould (Head of Mob), Stuart Greenwell, Shayne Tingle (Rail Men), Emily D. Haley (Partygoer), Nathaniel Lee, Jr. (Ice Boy with Straw Hat), Lamar Lott (Rally Attendee), Andy Sims (Rallygoer), Dan Tyminski (Mandolinist on Stage), Leon Walls (Guitarist), John Wilkie (Klansman/choreographer).

Chapter Notes

Introduction

1. John E. O'Connor, ed., in *I Am a Fugitive from a Chain Gang* (Madison: University of Wisconsin Press, 1981), p. 9.

Chapter 1

1. Vincent Godfrey Burns, *Out of These Chains* (New York: New World Publishing, 1942), no page number.
2. Burns, *Out of These Chains*, p. 26.
3. Robert E. Burns, letter to Vincent G. Burns, 21 July 1929.
4. New York *Herald-Tribune*, 25 May 1929.
5. Burns, *Out of These Chains*, p. 44.
6. Burns, *Out of These Chains*, p. 46.
7. Burns, *Out of These Chains*, p. 49.
8. Michael J. Harbin, Attorney and Counselor at Law, discussion with Scott Allen Nollen, Mobile, Alabama, July 2013.
9. Burns, *Out of These Chains*, p. 69.

Chapter 2

All direct quotations from the Robert E. Burns memoir *I Am a Fugitive from a Georgia Chain Gang!* are taken from the original first edition, published by New York's Vanguard Press in 1932.

1. Burns, *Out of These Chains*, pp. 103–104.
2. Burns, *Out of These Chains*, p. 118.
3. Burns, *Out of These Chains*, pp. 129–130.
4. Burns, *Out of These Chains*, pp. 168–69.
5. Matthew Mancini, in Robert E. Burns [and Vincent G. Burns], *I Am a Fugitive from a Georgia Chain Gang!* (Athens: University of Georgia Press, 1997), ps. vi, ix.
6. Mancini, p. xix.

Chapter 3

All direct quotations from the Robert E. Burns memoir *I Am a Fugitive from a Georgia Chain Gang!* are taken from the original first edition, published by New York's Vanguard Press in 1932.

1. Roy Del Ruth, to Hal B. Wallis, Studio Memorandum (Los Angeles: University of Southern California, Warner Bros. Collection Production Files), undated.
2. Jack Warner, with Dean Jennings, *My First Hundred Years in Hollywood* (New York: Random House, 1964), p. 218.
3. Burns, *Out of These Chains*, p. 181.
4. Syndicated in various national newspapers, including those in New York, Chicago and Los Angeles.
5. "Al Jolson in *The Singing Fool*: A Warner Bros.–Vitaphone Picture" souvenir book (Burbank: Warner Bros. Pictures, 1928).
6. Michael B. Druxman, *Paul Muni: His Life and His Films* (New York: A. S. Barnes and Company, 1974), p. 47.
7. Druxman, p. 56.
8. Burns, *Out of These Chains*.
9. Del Ruth to Wallis.
10. Burns, *Out of These Chains*, p. 197.
11. O'Connor, p. 21.
12. Thomas Schatz, *The Genius of the System: Hollywood Filmmaking in the Studio Era* (New York: Pantheon Books, 1988), p. 145.
13. O'Connor, p. 23.
14. Burns, *Out of These Chains*, p. 197.
15. *Motion Picture Herald*, 6 August 1932, p. 40.
16. *Picture Play*, January 1933, p, 47.
17. *Motion Picture Herald*, 13 August 1932, p. 10.
18. Schatz, p. 142.
19. *Motion Picture Herald*, 20 August 1932, p. 35.

20. *Modern Screen*, October 1932, p. 48.
21. O'Connor, p. 25.
22. *Motion Picture Herald*, 22 October 1932, p. 31.

Chapter 4

1. Burns, *Out of These Chains*, pp. 212–213.
2. *Motion Picture*, November 1932, p. 68.
3. *Photoplay*, November 1932.
4. *Film Daily*, 27 October 1932, p. 2.
5. Burns, *Out of These Chains*, pp. 204–05.
6. Burns, *Out of These Chains*, pp. 205–06.
7. Burns, *Out of These Chains*, pp. 207–08.
8. Burns, *Out of These Chains*, pp. 208–09.
9. Burns, *Out of These Chains*, pp. 211–212.
10. *Film Daily*, 6 December 1932, p. 2.
11. Druxman, p. 118.
12. *Variety*, 15 November 1932, p. 19.
13. *Variety*, 15 November 1932, p. 26.
14. *Photoplay*, December 1932, p. 58.
15. *Picture Play*, December 1932, p. 69.
16. *Picture Play*, December 1932.
17. *Motion Picture*, January 1933, p. 74.
18. *Movie Classic*, January 1933, p. 8.
19. *Movie Classic*, February 1933, p. 6.
20. *Close Up*, March 1933, p. 39.
21. Burns, *Out of These Chains*, p. 213.
22. Schatz, p. 148.
23. O'Connor, p. 44.

Chapter 5

1. Burns, *Out of These Chains*, no page number.
2. Burns, *Out of These Chains*, pp. 4–5.
3. Burns, *Out of These Chains*, p. 217.
4. Burns, *Out of These Chains*, pp. 217–218.
5. Burns, *Out of These Chains*, p. 222.
6. Burns, *Out of These Chains*, pp. 226–230.
7. Burns, *Out of These Chains*, p. 233.
8. Burns, *Out of These Chains*, pp. 236–245.
9. Murphy Halloway, letter to Vincent G. Burns, November 1932.
10. Burns, *Out of These Chains*, p. 297.
11. Burns, *Out of These Chains*, pp. 298–300.
12. Jack L. Warner to Governor Arthur Harry Moore, November 1932.
13. Burns, *Out of These Chains*, pp. 383–384.
14. *Los Angeles Times*, December 1932.
15. *New York Herald-Tribune*, November 1932.
16. Burns, *Out of These Chains*, p. 433.
17. Kenneth T. Rowe, letter to Vincent G. Burns, 9 November 1940.

Chapter 6

1. Burns, *Out of These Chains*, p. 234.
2. Richard Watts, Jr., *New York Herald-Tribune*, November 1932.
3. *Telegraph*, Macon, Georgia, December 1932.
4. W. T. Anderson, letter to Vincent G. Burns, October 1936.
5. *New York Times*, 8 September 1937.
6. *New York Times*, 17 October 1937.
7. Burns, *Out of These Chains*, p. 444.
8. Burns, *Out of These Chains*, p. 448.
9. Burns, *Out of These Chains*, p. 444–455.
10. Burns, *Out of These Chains*, p. 457.
11. Burns, *Out of These Chains*, p. 464.
12. James Cagney, *Cagney by Cagney* (New York: Doubleday and Company, 1976), p. 76.

Bibliography

Discussions

Harbin, Michael J., Attorney and Counselor at Law, with Scott Allen Nollen, Mobile, Alabama, July 2013.

Letters

Anderson, W. T., to Vincent G. Burns. Macon, Georgia, October 1936.
Burns, Robert E., to Vincent G. Burns. Chicago, Illinois, 21 June 1929.
Halloway, Murphy, to Vincent G. Burns. Atlanta, Georgia, November 1932.
Rowe, Kenneth T., to Vincent G. Burns. University of Michigan, 9 November 1940.
Warner, Jack L., to Governor Arthur Harry Moore. Burbank, California, November 1932.

Official Government Documents

Burns, James, and family. 1910 United States Federal Census. Washington, D.C.: National Archives and Records Administration.
Burns, James H., and family. 1905 New York State Census. Albany: New York State Library.
Burns, James H., and family. 1915 New York State Census. Albany: New York State Library.
Burns, Robert E., and family. 1940 United States Federal Census. Washington, D.C.: National Archives and Records Administration.
Burns, Robert Elliott. Draft Registration Card, World War II, 17 March 1943. Washington, D.C.: National Archives and Records Administration.
Burns, Robert Elliott. U.S. Veterans' Gravesites, ca. 1775–2006. National Cemetery Administration.
Burns, Vincent. Social Security Death Index, 1935–2014. Social Security Number 572–40–0177.
Burns, Vincent G. Abstract of Military Service, World War I, 22 November 1919. New York State Archives.
Burns, Vincent G. Draft Registration Card, World War I, 18 May 1917. Washington, D.C.: National Archives and Records Administration.
Burns, Vincent Godfrey. Draft Registration Card, World War II, 25 April 1942. Washington, D.C.: National Archives and Records Administration.
Burns, Vincent Godfrey. Masons Membership Card, Pittsfield, Massachusetts, 1932.

Film Studio Documents and Publicity Materials

"Al Jolson in *The Singing Fool*: A Warner Bros.–Vitaphone Picture" souvenir book. Burbank: Warner Bros. Pictures, 1928.
Del Ruth, Roy, to Hal B. Wallis. Memorandum, undated. Los Angeles: University of Southern California, Warner Bros. Collection Production Files.
Wallis, Hal B., to Brown Holmes. Memorandum, 14 April 1932. Los Angeles: University of Southern California, Warner Bros. Collection Production Files.
Warner Bros. and Robert E. Burns. Contract for the film rights to *I Am a Fugitive from a Georgia Chain Gang!* 25 February 1932. Madison: Wisconsin Center for Film and Theater Research, Warner Bros. Contract and Copyright File.

Newspapers and Other Periodicals

The Berkshire Eagle. Pittsfield, Massachusetts. 7 September 1930.
Bovson, Mara. New York *Daily News*, 25 July 2015.
Los Angeles Times, December 1932.
Minchew, Kay Lanning. "How Hollywood Reformed the Georgia Prison System," *Georgia Journal*, Spring 1992.
New Age, January 1933.
New York Herald-Tribune, 25 May 1929; 27 November 1932.
New York Times, 2 January 1933; 8 September 1937; 17 October 1937.
Newark Evening News, 18 and 22 December 1932; 12 February 1935.
Newark Sunday Call, 11 December 1932.
The Reading Eagle, 22 December 1932.
The Telegraph. Macon, Georgia. December 1932.

Film Industry Trade Publications and Periodicals

Close Up. March 1933.
The Film Daily. 25 October 1932; 27 October 1932; 31 October 1932; 1 November 1932; 6 December 1932; 9 December 1932.
Modern Screen. November 1932.
Motion Picture. December 1932; January 1933.
Motion Picture Herald. 6 August 1932, p. 40; 13 August 1932; 20 August 1932; 17 September 2015; 8 October 1932; 22 October 1932; 12 November 1932; 26 November 1932; 10 December 1932; 17 December 1932.
Movie Classic. January-February 1933.
Photoplay. November-December 1932.
Picture Play. December 1932.
Variety. 15 November 1932.

Memoirs

Burns, Robert E. [and Vincent G. Burns]. *I Am a Fugitive from a Georgia Chain Gang!* New York: Vanguard Press, 1932.
Burns, Robert E. [and Vincent G. Burns]. *I Am a Fugitive from a Georgia Chain Gang!* Athens: University of Georgia Press, 1997.
Burns, Vincent Godfrey. *The Man Who Broke 1,000 Chains: The Story of Social Reformation of the Prisons of the South*. Washington: Acropolis Books, 1968.
Burns, Vincent Godfrey. *Out of These Chains: Sequel to "I Am a Fugitive from a Chain Gang."* Los Angeles: New World Books, 1942.

Cagney, James. *Cagney by Cagney*. New York: Doubleday and Company, 1976.
LeRoy, Mervyn, as told to Dick Kleiner. *Take One*. New York: Hawthorn Books, Inc., Publishers, 1974.
Warner, Jack, with Dean Jennings. *My First Hundred Years in Hollywood*. New York: Random House, 1964.

Books

Colvin, Mark. *Penitentiaries, Reformatories, and Chain Gangs: Social Theory and the History of Punishment in Nineteenth-Century America*. New York: Palgrave Macmillan, 2000.
Doherty, Thomas Patrick. *Pre-Code Hollywood: Sex, Immorality and Insurrection in American Cinema, 1930–1934*. New York: Columbia University Press, 1999.
Druxman, Michael B. *Paul Muni: His Life and His Films*. New York: A. S. Barnes and Company, 1974.
Meyer, William R. *Warner Brothers Directors*. New York: Arlington House, 1978.
Nollen, Scott Allen. *Glenda Farrell: Hollywood's Hardboiled Dame*. Baltimore: Midnight Marquee Press, 2014.
Nollen, Scott Allen. *Warners Wiseguys: All 112 Films that Robinson, Cagney and Bogart Made for the Studio*. Jefferson, North Carolina: McFarland, 2007.
O'Connor, John E., ed. *I Am a Fugitive from a Chain Gang*. Madison: University of Wisconsin Press, 1981.
Roddick, Nick. *A New Deal in Entertainment: Warner Brothers in the 1930s*. London: British Film Institute, 1983.
Schatz, Thomas. *The Genius of the System: Hollywood Filmmaking in the Studio Era*. New York: Pantheon Books, 1988.

Film Releases

I Am a Fugitive from a Chain Gang. Commentary by Richard B. Jewell. Warner Bros. Entertainment, Inc.-Turner Entertainment Company DVD, 2005.

Websites

AMC Filmsite. http://www.filmsite.org.
Library of Congress National Film Preservation Board. http://www.loc.gov/programs/national-film-preservation-board/film-registry.
New York Times. http://www.nytimes.com/movies.
Turner Classic Movies. *I Am a Fugitive from a Chain Gang* articles. http://www.tcm.com/tcmdb/title/782/I-Am-a-Fugitive-from-a-Chain-Gang/articles.html.

Index

Numbers in ***bold italics*** refer to pages with photographs.

Aaronson, Charles 58, 62
Abraham, F. Murray 136, 184
Abraham Lincoln (1918 play) 107
ACE Awards 136
Adamson, Ewart 107–108, 153
Addams, Jane 10
Adolphi, John G. 50
African American chain-gang convicts (in reality and on film) 12, 17, 28, 35–36, 52, 57
African American slavery 3
Alcaide, Chris 127, 172
All Quiet on the Western Front (1930 film) 47, 118
Alleborn, Al 50, 143
Allen, Harvey 141
Allen, Lewis 128, 173
Allen, Woody 129–130, ***131***, 176
Alliance Films 121
Amadeus (1984 film) 136
American Civil Liberties Union (ACLU) 90
American International Pictures 132
American Legion 90
Anderson, W.T. 95
Andrews, Robert Hardy 108, 153
Ange, Julie 129, 173
Angels with Dirty Faces (1938 film) 116–***117***, 161–162
"Apostolic Age" 97
Argosy Productions 129
Armendariz, Pedro 129
Arnall, Ellis 98
Arnaz, Desi 126, 172
Arness, James 124, 126, 169, 170
Asner, Edward 128
Astor, Mary 45
Atlanta, Georgia 8, 10–14, 16, 20, 23, 29, 34–36, 38–39, 64
Ayres, Lew 47, 107, 126, 172

Bacon, Lloyd 50, 100, 157
Badalucco, Michael 139–140, 201
Bakula, Scott 136–137, 184
Barrat, Robert ***100***, 111, 148, 150, 157, 159
Barrymore, John 45
Barrymore, Lionel 108, 155
Barthelmess, Richard 61, ***100***, 148
Battle, George Gordon 36, 90
Baxter, Warner 61, ***106***–107, 137, 153
Beal, John 109, 156
Beery, Wallace 19
Bell, James 58, 143
Bellasario, Donald P. 136, 184
Benjamin, Paul 136, 179
The Berkshire Eagle 17
Biberman, Abner 128, 173
The Big House (1930 film) 1, 19
Bikel, Theodore 126, 171
The Birth of a Nation (1915 film) 109
Black, John D.F. 128, 173
Black and Tan (1929 short film) 103
Black Fury (1935 film) 73, 104, 152
Black Legion (1937 film) 109–110, 156
Blackmail (1939 film) ***119***–120, 165
Blake, Norman 141
Blane, Sally 76–77, 153
Blanke, Henry 82, 111, 143, 158
Blessed Event (1932 film) 61
Blondell, Joan 47, 75
Bogart, Humphrey 75, 102, 104, 109–110, 112–114, 116, 118, 124, 157, 160, 162
Bonanza (TV series) 126
Bond, Ward 67, ***101***, 104, ***114***–115, 123–***124***, 126, 148, 150, 152, 161, 164, 170
Boone, Richard 126
Booth, John Wilkes 106–107, 126
Booth, Shirley 136
Boys Town (1938 film) 116

Index

Braga, Sonia 136, 182
Brando, Marlon 136
Brandon, Henry 110, 126, 157, 172
Branford Theatre (Newark, NJ) 67
Bright, John 110, 157
Brinkley, Don 126, 128, 172, 173
Broadhead, James 132, 179
Broadway Bill (1934 film) 76
Bronson Canyon, Los Angeles 123, 143
Brooklyn, New York 5–6
Brother Orchid (1940 film) 118
Brown, Clancy 136, 182
Brown, Rowland 57, 64, 146
Brown, Tom 57, 61, 63, 146, 147, 151
Browning, Tod 108, 155
Bruce Scenics company 57, 145
Bullets or Ballots (1936 film) 109
Bunuel, Luis 128–129, 174
Bupp, Sonny 109, 156
Burbank, California 46–47, 156, 181
Burke, James 127, 172, 189
Burnett, T-Bone 139, 198
Burns, Clara (wife) 17, 98
Burns, Dorothy (sister) 6, 17
Burns, Frances (daughter) 17, 98
Burns, James H. (father) 5–6
Burns, James, Jr. (brother) 6
Burns, Jennetta (sister) 6
Burns, Katherine (mother) 5–6, 12–14, 17, 35–36, 44, 87, 89–90, 98
Burns, Robert (Scottish poet) 5, 77
Burns, Robert Elliott 5–56, 68–72, 78–94, 98, 123, 136, 141; as advisor on the film 47–56, 68–72; birth 5; continued efforts to obtain a pardon 78–99; death and burial 3, 98; as "Dynamite Dick" 22; early life 5–6; first chain-gang escape 10, 28–29; on the film 63; personal appearances at film theaters 81–82; second chain-gang escape 14–17, 22, 37–38; World War I service 6–7; World War II draft registration **99**
Burns, Robert, Jr. (son) 98
Burns, the Rev. Vincent G. (brother) 2–3, 5, 6–8, 10–14, 17–18, 21–23, 28, 33, 35–36, 39, 41, 43–44, 48–52, 54, 66–67, 73–74, 78–93, **79**, 95–99, **97**, 136, 141, 143, 182; academic honors and achievements 98; appearance at Newark screening of the film 68; death 99; education 98; possibility of his playing his counterpart in the film 50; on WOR radio 87, 89; World War I-era service 67
Burr, Raymond **127**–128, 178

Cabin in the Cotton (1932 film) 61
Cagney, James 1, 47, 50, 69, 75, **102**, 114, 116–**117**, 148, 162
Caillou, Alan 128, 173
Calabasas, California 59
Caledonia State Prison Farm 123
Campbell County Chain Gang 9–11, 27–28
Campus, Michael 136, 181

Cannes Film Festival 128
Capone, Al 49, 91
Capra, Frank 76
Captain Blood (1935 film) 116
Captain Dreyfus: The Story of a Mass Hysteria (book) 124
The Captain Hates the Sea (1934 film) 76
Carbine Williams (1952 film) 123, 169–170
Carlson, Richard 128, 173
Carter, R.B. 90
Casablanca (1942 film) 116
"The Case for Dr. Mudd" (1958 TV show) 126, 172
Cassavetes, John 139
Cassavetes, Nick 139, 194
Catholic Legion of Decency 67
"Catholic vs. Protestant" depictions of pastors in the cinema 67
Cavalcanti, Alberto 121, 167
"The Chain Gang" (1917 short documentary) 57, 145
"Chain Gang" (1930 Disney cartoon) 57, 146
Chain Gang (1950 film) 121–**122**, 150
"Chain Gang" (1959 TV episode) 127, 172
Chain Gang (1984 film) 135, 181
chain-gang system 3–4; investigations and reforms 94–96
Chain Gang Women (1971 film) 129, 176
Champion, John C. 123–**124**, 170
Chaney, Lon, Jr. 126, 171
Chaney, Lon, Sr. 48, 108
Chaplin, Charles 119
"Charleston Chain Gang" (1902 short film) 4, 57, 145
Charters, Spencer 113, 143, 161
Chatsworth, California 59, 143
Chattanooga, Tennessee 16, 29–30, 38
Chatterton, Ruth 61
Chicago, Illinois 10–11, 13, 19, 21–22, 30, 43, 48, 67
Chicago Association of Commerce 30
Chicago Real Estate Board 30
China Clipper (1936 film) 109
Churchill, Berton 59, 143, 147, 148, 150
Cincinnati, Ohio 38
Cinerama Releasing Corporation **131**, 176
Civil War (1862–65) 3, 6
Claxton, William F. 128, 172
Clemens, William 116, 163
Cleveland, Ohio 48, 67
Cline, Edward 47
Clooney, George 139–**140**, 198–201
Close Up (scholarly journal) 73
Coen, Ethan 139–140, 198
Coen, Joel 139–140, 198
Columbia Pictures 1, 121–122, 146, 168, 181, 191
Come Back, Little Sheba (1952 film) 136
Commander Films Corporation 123–**124**, 170
Conan Doyle, Sir Arthur 93

Index

Conan Doyle, Denis 92–93
Confessions of a Nazi Spy (1939 film) 116–120, 163–164
Conrad, William 128, 173
Conte, Richard 136
Cook, Elisha, Jr. 136, 182
Cool Hand Luke (1967 film) 129–*130*, 174
Coolidge, Calvin 36
Cording, Harry 108, 152, 154, 161, 163
Corey, Wendell 123, 169
Corinthians 135
Counsellor-at-Law (stage play) 49, 68
The Crash (1932 film) 61
Crime School (1938 film) 102, 112–114, 160–161
The Criminal Code (1930 film) 1
Crosby, Bing 67, 132, 179
Crothers, Scatman 133, 179
Culver City, California 45
Curtis, Ken 127
Curtis, Tony *125*–126, 171
Curtiz, Michael 102, 104, 107, 116–*117*, 148, 152, 153, 156, 161

Daniels, Josephus 36
Darabont, Frank 137, 188, 190
The Dark Horse (1932 film) 61
Darro, Frankie 102, 148, 150
Darrow, Clarence 89–90
Davidson, William B. 108, 154
Davis, Bette 102, 104
Davis, Phyllis 132, 177
Dead End (1937 film) 112
"Dead End" Kids 102, 112–113
Death in the Deep South (novel) 112, 159
de Corsia, Ted 127, 173
Dee, Ruby 128
The Defiant Ones (1958 film) *125*–126, 171–172
Dell, Gabriel 113, 160, 162
Del Pino Pacheo, Emily 10, 30–32, 55, 86, 136
del Rio, Dolores 129
Del Ruth, Roy 43, 50, 141
De Mille, Cecil B. 107
Demme, Ted 137, 191
Dempsey, Jack 80
Dern, Bruce 128
Desire in the Dust (1960 film) *127*–128, 172–173
Deutsch, Armand 123
The Devil Doll (1936 film) 108, 155
The Devil's 8 (1968 film) 129, 132, 175
Devil's Island (1939 film) *115*–116, 132, 163
Dickinson, Angie 128
Dies, Martin 118
Dieterle, William 73, 111, 117, 158
Dillinger, John 91, 129
The Dirty Dozen (1967 film) 129
Disney, Walt 57, 146, 167
Dix, Richard 57, *60*–61, 63–64, 76, 146

Dixon, Ivan 128, 171, 173
Dobkin, Lawrence 126, 171
Dr. Ehrlich's Magic Bullet (1940 film) 117–118
Don Juan (1926 film) 45
Donnelly, Ruth 104, 151
Donner, Richard 128, 173
Donovan, King 126, 173
The Doorway to Hell (1930 film) 47
Dorsey, Hugh M. 94
Douglas, Illeana 139, 197
Downey, Morton 80
Dreyfus, Alfred 111–112, 124–125
Dumbrille, Douglass 77, 100, 143, 147, 148, 150
Duncan, Angus 132, 177
Durham, Todd 135, 181
Durning, Charles 136, 139, 182, 201
Duvall, Robert 128, 173
Dvorak, Ann 104, 109, 151

East Orange, New Jersey 44
Eastwood, Clint 127
Echols, John 8–9, 34
Edison, Charles 98
Edison Company 4, 57, 145
Edwards, James 128
Elizabeth, New Jersey 41
Ellington, Duke 103
Ellis, Edward 52, *75*–76, 92, 143, 150
Elvey, Maurice 76
Emmerson, Louis L. 10–11, 33
The Emperor Jones (1933 film) *103*–104, 129, 149
Enright, Pat 141, 200
Enright, Ray 75
Erickson, Carl 104, 152
Evans, Art 132, 179
Everton, Paul 112, 159, 161

Fabian 129, 175
Fairfield Four 141
Farrell, Glenda 4, 55, 58, 63, 71–73, 75, 86, 92, 104–*105*, *114*–115, 120–*121*, 128, 143, 150, 151, 161, 166, 173
Female Fugitive (1938 film) 112, 160
Ferrer, Jose 126, 170–171
Fetchit, Stepin 152
Fields, Joseph 107, 153
Figueroa, Gabriel 128–129, 174
Finkel, Abem 104, 110, 150, 152, 154, 156
First National Pictures 46–47, 143, 148, 150, 152, 154, 157, 159, 160, 162, 164
Five Star Final (1931 film) 50, 99
Flagg, Sidney George 87
Fleming, Eric 127
Florida chain gang "sweat-box" torture death 64
Flynn, Errol 75, 116
Ford, Francis 152
Ford, Harrison 137
Ford, John 57, 102, 104–107, *106*, 111, 123–124, 129, 151, 153

Index

Ford's Theatre (Washington, DC) 106
42nd Street (1934 film) 50, 61
Foster, Dianne 128
Foster, Preston 59, 63, 77, 109, 143, 151, 156
Fountaine, William 57, 146
Fox, Jimmy 80
Fox, William 47
Fox Films 1, 48, 102, 104, 107
Foy, Bryan 108–109, 116, 154, 160, 163
Francis, Noel 53–54, 143
Frank, Leo 112
Frankenstein (1931 film) 99, 108
Freeman, Morgan 137, 190–191
Fromm, John 36
Frost, David 132, 134, 178
The Fugitive (1947 film) 129
The Fugitive (1993 film) 137, 185–188
The Fugitive (TV series) 128, 173
Fulton County Chain Gang 9, 24, 27
Fury (1936 film) 76

Gargan, Edward 113, 154, 158, 161
Gargan, William 104–105, 152
Genn, Leo 126, 171
George, Christopher 129, 175
German-American Bund 118–119
Gibney, Sheridan 47–49, 51–56, 61–62, 74, 143
Girl on a Chain Gang (1966 film) 129, 173
Goldman, William 132–133, 177
Goldwyn, Samuel 44, 112
Goodman, John 139–140, 201
Gorcey, Leo 102, 113, 160, 162
Great Depression 1, 18, 20, 35, 39, 41, 53, 62
The Great Dictator (1940 film) 119
Green, Howard J. 7, 52, 55, 74, 121, 143, 168
Greene, Lorne 126
Greene, Ward 112, 159
Griffith, D.W. 109
Gross, Jerry 129, 173
Grot, Anton 111, 158
Groves, George 45
Guess Who's Coming to Dinner (1967 film) 126
Gunsmoke (TV series) 126–127
Gunton, Bob 137, 191
Gwenn, Edmund 108, 154

Hackensack, New Jersey 38–39
Hadley, Reed 112, 160
Hagen, Uta 136
Hague, Frank 87
Haines, William Wister 110
Halasz, Nicholas 24, 171
Hall, Huntz 113, 160, 162
Hallelujah (1929 film) 57–58, 145–146
Halop, Billy 112, 160, 162
Hamilton, Hale 1, 66, 75, 99, 143
Hampton, John M. 87
Handler, Charles 90
Handy, W.C. 53

Happy, Texas (1999 film) 139, 195–198
Hard to Handle (1933 film) 68
Hardman, Lamartine G. 11, 22–23, 32, 35, 39
Hardy, Harold 90, 136
Hardy, Oliver 77
Harris, Sibyl 113, 159, 161
Harron, Donald 126, 172
Hart, Brooke 49
Hartley, Esdras 110, 148, 150, 157
Hauptmann, Bruno 91–92
Havana Widows (1933 film) 75
Have Gun, Will Travel (TV series) 126
Hawks, Howard 49
Hayden, Sterling 123–*124*, 170
Hayes, Arthur Garfield 90
Haynes, Daniel L. 57
Hayward, Lillie 108, 153
Hayward, Susan 136
Hearts in Bondage (1936 film) 107
Heat Lightning (1934 film) 104
Heflin, Van 120–121, 165
Hellgate (1952 film) 123–*124*, 170
Hell's Highway (1932 film) 56–57, *60*–61, 63, 70, 104, 129, 146
Henry, Gregg 132, 179
Herald, Heinz 111, 158
Herczeg, Geza 111, 158
Heroes for Sale (1933 film) **100**–101, 120, 148
Heyburn, Weldon 113, 161
Hi, Nellie! (1934 film) 104–**105**, 150
Hickox, Sid 110, 151, 157
Hicks, Russell 109, 156
High Sierra (1941 film) 116
Hitler, Adolf 97, 117–119, 164
Hoffman, Dustin 132–**133**, 178
Hoffman, Harold G. 80, 84
The Hollywood Reporter (trade paper) 92
Holmes, Brown 47, 49, 51–52, 54–56, 61–62, 120, 143, 150, 165
Holmes, William 74
Home Box Office (HBO) 135–136, 182
Homer 139
Hoover, Herbert 43
Hopper, Jerry 128, 173
Hopton, Russell 109, 147, 156
Hovey, Ann **101**, 150
Howard, Leslie 104
Howard, Trevor 121, 168
Howard, William Schley 11–13, 36
Huggins, Roy 128, 173, 175
Hugo, Victor 2
Hull House 10
Hussey, Ruth **119**, 165
Hyer, Martha **127**–128, 173
Hymer, Warren 102

I Accuse! (1958 film) 124–126, 170–171
I Am a Fugitive from a Chain Gang (1932 film) 1–2, 4, *43*, 47, 50–51, 53, 57, 59, **62**, 64, 85, 89, 94, 96, 101–102, 104, 106–108, 111, 114–115, 119–121, 126, 128, 135–136, 139,

Index

141, 143–145, 147; commercial and critical success of the film 67–71; effect on chain-gang reform 94–95; influence on future films and television 100–141; National Board of Review "Best Film of the Year" Award 73; 1956 theatrical re-release 124; reception in the Southern states *70*–71, 92; record first-run engagement 64–66, *65*; success outside the United States 93
I Am a Fugitive frm a Georgia Chain Gang! (1932 serialization and book) 1–3, 18–42, 80, 88, 96, 99, 143, 181
I Became a Criminal see *They Made Me a Fugitive*
I'll Cry Tomorrow (1955 film) 136
The Informer (1935 film) 106
Inherit the Wind (1961 film) 126
An Innocent Man (1989 film) 136, 182–184
The Invisible Man (1933 film) 101, 112

Jackson, Thomas 99
Janssen, David 128, 137, 173
The Jazz Singer (1927 film) 45–46
Jefferson, Lemon Henry ("Blind Lemon") 132, 179
Jenkins, Allen 53, 75, 143, 148
Jerry Gross Productions 129, 173
Jesus 97
"Jesus Movement" 97
Johnny Eager (1942 film) 120–*121*, 165–166
Johns, Vere E. 101
Johnson, Andrew 107
Johnson, Nunnally 106–107, 153
Johnson, Tommy 141
Jolson, Al 45–46
Jones, Bobby 36
Jones, Tommy Lee 137, 187
Jordan, Bobby 113, 160, 162
Juarez (1937 film) 73, 111
Judge Priest (1934 film) 104, 151–152
Judgment at Nuremburg (1960 film) 126

Kandel, Aben 112, 159
Karloff, Boris 99, 107–108, *115*–116, 132, 154, 163
Karson, David 61
Keach, James 136, 182
Keeter, Worth 135, 181
Kelley, John L. 91
Kendall, Cy 113, 159, 161, 165, 166
Kennedy, Douglas 121–*122*, 168
Kennedy, George 129, 133, 174, 179
Kilian, Victor 115, 161, 165
Kilmer, Val 136, 182
King, Chris Thomas 140–141, 201
King, Joseph 108, 154
King, Stephen 137, 188
King Kong (1933 film) 111
Kinoy, Ernest 132, 134
The Kiss Before the Mirror (1933 film) 101
Klugman, Jack 128

Kramer, Stanley *125*–126, 171
Krauss, Alison 141
Krims, Milton 118, 163
Kroll, Harrison 61
Ku Klux Klan (KKK) 110, 118
Kuhn, Fritz 119
Kyo, Machiko 136

Ladies of the Big House (1931 film) 1
Laemmle, Carl, Jr. 101, 147
Laemmle, Carl, Sr. 44, 147
Lancaster, Burt 136
Landau, David 77, 104, 143, 151
Landers, Lew 121–*122*, 168
Landon, Joseph 126, 172
Lane, Merritt 91
Lang, Charles 128, 172
Lang, Fritz 76
Larch, John 128
Lasky, Jesse L. 44
The Last Angry Man (1959 film) 136
The Last Days of Pompeii (1935 film) 111
Latter, Cameron 11
Laughter in Hell (1933 film) 100–101, 147
Laurel, Stan 77
Lawes, Warden Lewis E. 61
Lawrence, Martin 137–139, *138*, 193–194
Leadbelly (1976 film) 132, *134*, 178–179
Ledbetter, Huddie William ("Lead Belly") 132, 134, 179
Le Hand, Missy 87
Lenz, Kay 133, 179
LeRoy, Mervyn 47, 50–51, 56, 59, 62–63, 73–74, 92, 99–100, 104, 112, 120–*121*, 143, 147, 150, 159, 165; on *I Am a Fugitive from a Chain Gang* 69
Liberty (magazine) 63, 73
Life (1999 film) 137–139, *138*, 191–194
The Life of Emile Zola (1937 film) 73, 111–112, 158–159
Lights of New York (1928 film) 46
Linaker, Kay 108
Lincoln, Abraham 106–107
Lindbergh kidnapping case 91–92
Lindfors, Viveca 126, 171
Lippert Pictures 123–*124*, 170, 173
Little Caesar (1931 film) 1, 47, 50, 55, 64, 124
Little Miss Broadway (1938 film) 76
The Littlest Rebel (1935 film) 107
Litvak, Anatole 118, 163
Lockhart, Gene 120, 165
Loeb, Lee 128
Lom, Herbert 126, 171
Lomax, John 132
Long, Walter 77, 144, 147, 161
Lord, Marjorie *122*, 168
Lord, Robert 110
Los Angeles, California 44–45, 56, 66–67, 123, 143, 170, 183, 194, 200, 201
Louise, Tina 133, 179
Louisville, Kentucky 16, 38

Loy, Myrna 20, 45, 76
Lubin, Arthur 114, 161
Lucas, John Meredyth 128
Lyons, Cliff 57

Mac, Bernie *138*, 194
MacLane, Barton 105, *114*–115, 152, 154, 157, 161
MacMahon, Aline *100*, 104, 148, 151
Macy, William H. 139, 197
Magnani, Anna 136
Magnum P.I. (TV series) 136
Mahal, Taj 136, 182
The Maltese Falcon (1931 film) 52
The Maltese Falcon (1941 film) 116
The Man from Hell's River (1922 film) 45
The Man Who Broke 1,000 Chains (book) 136
The Man Who Broke 1,000 Chains (1987 TV film) 135–136, 139, 181–182
Mancini, Matthew 41
Mann, Daniel 136, 181
Martin, Ben 86
Martin, Ed 135
Martin, Tim 135
Master of the Range (1928 film) 57, 145
The Match King (1932 film) 61, *65*
Mayo, Archie 102, 109–110, 148, 156
The Mayor of Hell (1933 film) *102*, 112, 114, 148
McBain, Merle 32, 182
McCrea, Joel 120, 139, 167
McGlynn, Frank, Sr. 107, 153
McGraw, Charles 126, 171
McKinney, Nina Mae 57, 146
McLaglen, Andrew V. 124, 170
McLaglen, Victor 124
McQueen, Steve 127–128, 132, *133*, 172, 178
McRell, James A. 68, 83–87
Mean Dog Blues (1978 film) 132, 179
Meeker, Ralph 129, 175
Meisner, Sanford 136
Meredith, Burgess 76
Metro-Goldwyn-Mayer Pictures (MGM) 1, 13, 57, 108, 116, *119–121*, 123, 129, 146, 155, 165, 169, 171
Middleton, Charles 77, 108, 144, 146, 154, 165
Milestone, Lewis 45, 47, 76
Milne, Peter 108, 153, 157
Miner, Allen H. 126, 172
Miramax Pictures 139, 197
Les Miserables (1862 novel) 2
Mississippi State Penitentiary 139
Monogram Pictures 112, 160
Montgomery, Robert 19
Moore, Arthur Harry 82–83, 87–91
Moore, Victor 80
Morley, Karen 104, 152
Morosco Theatre, Broadway 48
Morris, Chester 19
Morse, Barry 128, 173

Mosley, Roger E. 132, *134*, 179
Motion Picture (magazine) 63, 72
The Motion Picture Herald 58, 60, 62, 67, 101
The Mouthpiece (1932 film) 61
Movie Classic (magazine) 72
Mudd, Dr. Samuel M. 106–107, 126
Muni, Bella 49
Muni, Joseph 48
Muni, Nathan 48
Muni, Paul 1–2, 43, 49, 56, 59, 61–*62*, 67–73, *70*, *75*, 86, 92, 95, 104–*105*, 111, 117, 136, 141, 143, 150, 152, 159; on the film industry 48; on Mervyn LeRoy 50–51; on Robert Burns and making the film 71–72
Murphy, Dudley 103, 149
Murphy, Eddie 137–139, *138*, 191, 194
Museum of Modern Art 93

Naish, J. Carrol 105, 109, 152
Nazarin (1959 film) 128–129, 174–175
The Nazi Spy Conspiracy in America (book) 117
Nelson, George ("Baby Face") 139
Nelson, Tim Blake 139–*140*, 201
Nettleton, Lois 128, 173
New Age (periodical) 101
New York Herald-Tribune 11, 92, 94
New York Times 96
Newark, New Jersey 20, 38–39, 43, 67–68, 98
Newman, Paul 129–*130*, 174
Nigh, William 112, 160
Norris, Edward 112, 159
Northam, Jeremy 139, 197
Nyby, Christian 128, 173

O Brother, Where Art Thou? (2001 film) 139–141, *140*, 198–201
Oates, Warren 128, 173
O'Brien, Pat 67, 100, 110, 116, 124, 147, 157, 162
Odyssey (epic poem) 139
Oland, Warner 45
Oliver, Susan 128, 173
O'Malley, J. Pat 128, 173
On the Beach (1959 film) 126
O'Neill, Eugene 103, 149
O'Neill, Henry 108, 111, *121*, 152, 154, 159, 164, 166
Ormond, Ron 135, 180
The Ormond Organization 135, 180
Ornitz, Samuel 57, 64, 146
Out of These Chains (1942 book) 2, 5, 41, 78–99, *79*
Owensby, Earl 135, 181

Page, Gale 113, 160
Papillon (1973 film) 132, *133*, 177–178
Paramount Pictures 1, 50, 103, 107, 120, 132, 134, 167, 178
Parker, Norton S. 115, 161
Parks, Gordon 132, 134, 178

Parnell, Emory 123, 162, 166–168
Pasadena, California 59, 143, 183
Paul (apostle) 135
Pearlman, Ron 139
Penn, Leo 128, 173
Penny Arcade (stage play) 47
The Petrified Forest (1936 film) 104, 109–110
Pevney, Joseph 128
Phagan, Mary 112
Philadelphia, Pennsylvania 67, 80
Photoplay (magazine) 64, 71
Picture Play (magazine) 58, 71–72
The Plainsman (1936 film) 107
Poitier, Sidney **125**–126, 135, 171, 180
Polito, Sol 74, 143, 150, 162, 163
Pollack, Sydney 128
Potter, H.C. 120, 165
Powell, William 76
Prison Break (1938 film) **114**–115, 162
The Prisoner of Shark Island (1936 film) 105–107, **106**, 123–124, 137, 153
Production Code Administration of 1934 (PCA) 67, 112, 116
Proval, David 137, 191
Pryor, Richard 135, 139, 181
The Public Enemy (1931 film) 1, 47, 61, 102, 110, 124
Punsley, Bernard 113, 160

Qualen, John 105, 150, 152
Quantum Leap (TV series) 136–137, 184
Quinn Martin Productions 128, 173

Raft, George 116
Ragsdale, Isaac Newton 11
Raine, Norman Reilly 111, 158
Rains, Claude 112, 159
Ralston, Mark 137
Raphaelson, Samson 45
Rawhide (TV series) 127
Reid, Dorothy 115
Republic Pictures 107, 151–152
Reynolds, Craig 112, 160
Rin Tin Tin 45
Rita Hayworth and Shawshank Redemption (novella) 137, 188
Rivers, Eurith D. 96, 98
RKO Radio Pictures 44, 56–57, **60**–61, 75, 106, 109, 146, 156
The Road Back (1937 film) 118–119
Road Gang (1936 film) 108, 154–155
Robbins, Tim 137, 189–191
Robertson, Willard 77, 143, 151, 152, 167
Robeson, Paul 57, **103**–104, 149
Robinson, Edward G. 1, 47, 50, 61, **65**, 75, 80, 99, 109, 117, **119**–120, 164–165
Rogers, Will 104, 151
Rolph, James ("Sunny Jim") 49–50
Rome, Georgia 16, 38
Rooney, Mickey 128
Roosevelt, Franklin D. (FDR) 36, 87, 101, 118

Ropes, Bradford 61
The Rose Tattoo (1955 film) 136
Rosson, Robert 112
Route 66 (highway) 56
Rowe, Kenneth T. 93
Rowlands, Gena 139
Rule, Janice 128, 173
Russell, Richard B., Jr. 86, 91
Rydell, Mark 128, 173

St. Louis Blues (1929 short film) 103
"St. Louis Blues" (song) 53
Salo, Lillian 10, 19, 22, 31, 33–34, 136
Salomon, Mikael 136, 182
San Francisco, California 67, 176, 183
San Quentin (1937 film) 110–111, 113, 124, 157–158
Sandburg, Carl 10
Sanders, George 75
Sandy Springs Chain Gang Camp 24, 29
Saunders, Russ 111
Scarface (1932 film) 49, 61, 63
Schaffner, Franklin J. 132–133, 177
Schenck, Nicholas 13, 57, 153
Schildkraut, Joseph 111, 159
Schwartzkopf, Norman, Jr. 80
Schwartzkopf, Norman, Sr. 80
Scott, Ken 128, 173
Sedgwick, Kyra 136, 182
Seiler, Lewis 102, 112, 160
Selleck, Tom 136, 182–184
Semple, Lorenzo, Jr. 132–133, 177
Seven Faces (1929 film) 48
Shatner, William 128, 173
The Shawshank Redemption (1994 film) 137, 188–191
Sheldon, James 128, 173
Sherlock Holmes stories 93
Shuttleworth, John 22, 39
Sierra, Gregory 133, 178
Silver Dollar (1932 film) 61, **65**
Simandl, Harold 86
Simpson, Bill 88
Simpson, Mickey 124, 170
The Singing Fool (1928 film) 46
Sinner's Holiday (1930 film) 47
Sling Blade (1995 film) 136
Small, Edward 109, 155–156
Smith, Bessie 103
Smith, Leonard 108, 155
Southern Theatre Foundation 58
The Star Witness (1931 film) 61
Stevenson, Robert Louis 2
Stewart, James 123, 169
Stir Crazy (1980 film) 135, 180–181
Stockwell, Dean 137, 184
Stone, Milburn 127
The Story of Louis Pasteur (1936 film) 73, 111
The Strange Love of Molly Lovain (1932 film) 52
Stuart, Gloria 101, 147, 153

216   Index

Stuart, Mel 132, 179
Sullivan's Travels (1941 film) 120, 139–140, 166
The Sun Shines Bright (1953 film) 152–153
Sweet Sugar (1972 film) 132, 177

Take the Money and Run (1969 film) 129–130, *131*, 136
Talbot, Nita 128
Talmage, Eugene 98
Tasker, Robert 57, 64, 100, 146, 157
Tawes, J. Millard 99
Taylor, Robert 120, 165
The Teahouse of the August Moon (1956 film) 136
Telegraph (Macon, Georgia, newspaper) 95
Temple, Shirley 76, 107
They Made Me a Fugitive (1947 film) 121, 167–168
They Won't Forget (1937 film) 112, 159–160
The Thin Man (1934 film) 76
Third Reich 96–97, 116–119, 164
39 Stripes (1979 film) 133–134, 180
This One Wins (1930 stage play) 48
Thomas, Lowell 92
Thordsen, Kelly 128, 173
Thornton, Billy Bob 136, 182
Thorpe, Jim 111, 158
Thorpe, Richard 123, 169
Thorvaldson, Einar 61
Three on a Match (1932 film) 110
Toland, Gregg 128–129
Toledo, Ohio 47
Torrou, Leon 117, 163
Tracy, Spencer 61, 67, 76, 102, 116
Trans-Atlantic Tunnel (1935 film) 76
Troup County (La Grange) Chain Gang 12, 14, 19, 21, 34–36, 38, 86, 90, 92
Trowbridge, Charles 113, 161, 162, 164
True Detective Mysteries 21–22, 39–41, **40**, 80
Trumbo, Dalton 108, 132–133, 154, 177–178
Turner, Lana 112, 120, 159, 165
Turturro, John 139–***140***, 201
20th Century (Zanuck production company) 61
20th Century–Fox Pictures 61, ***127***–128
20,000 Cheers for the Chain Gang (1933 short film) 102, 149
20,000 Years in Sing Sing (1933 film) 61, 102
Two Against the World (1932 film) 52
Tyminski, Dan 141, 200–201

"Unchained—November 2, 1956" (1991 TV episode) 136–137, 184
United Artists ***103***, 149
Universal Pictures 44, 99–101, 114–115, 118–119, 147, 161, 184, 194
Up the River (1930 film) 1, 10

The Valiant (1929 film) 48
Vanguard Press 41

Variety 2, 44, 64, 69–70
Venable, Evelyn 112, 160
Veterans of Foreign Wars (VFW) 90
Vidal, Gore 124, 126, 170
Vidor, King 57, 76, 145
Vinson, Helen 54, 59, 63, 76, 143
Vitaphone sound system 45–46

Wagner, Bertha 20–21, 63, 66, 68–69, 82, 86
Wagon Master (1950 film) 111
Wagon Train (TV series) 126
Walbrook, Anton 126, 171
Walker, Ally 139, 197
The Walking Dead (1936 film) 108, 116, 153–154
Wallace, Basil 137, 184
Wallis, Hal B. 45, 50, 56, 118–119, 143, 148, 150, 152, 154–158, 160–161. 163
"Walls of San Quentin" (story) 114–115
Walsh, Raoul 111
Walthall, Henry B. 108, 151, 154
Wanted: Dead or Alive (TV series) 127–128, 172
Ward, Sela 137, 187
Warner, Abe 43–44, 46, 74
Warner, Ann 118
Warner, Harry 44–47, 74
Warner, Jack 43–46, 50, 74, 89, 109, 112, 117–119
Warner, Sam 44–46
Warner Bros. 1–4, 43–46, 51, 57–58, 62–63, 67–76, 80, 94–95, 99–102, 100, 101, 104–105, 107–112, 115–118, 117, 120–121, 124, 126, 129–130, 136, 137, 141, 143, 148–152, 154, 157, 159–160, 162–164, 168. 174, 187
Warner Ranch (Calabasas) 59
Warren, Charles Marquis 123–124, 170
Warwick, Robert 120, 143, 159, 163, 167
Waters, Ethel 57
Watts, Richard, Jr. 92, 94
Wattstax (1972 film) 132
We Who Are About to Die (1938 film) 109, 155–156
The Wedding Night (1935 film) 76
Week-End Marriage (1932 film) 52
Welch, Gillian 141, 200–201
Wellman, William 47, 101, 148–150
Western Electric Company 45
Westinghouse Desilu Playhouse (TV series) 126
Weston, Jack 126, 172
Wexley, John 118, 161, 163
Whale, James 101, 112, 118
Where the North Begins (1923 film) 45
White Heat (1949 film) 111
Whitman, Ernest 107, 137, 207
Whitmore, James 137, 191
Whittington, Harry 128, 172
The Widow from Chicago (1930 film) 47
Wiesenfreund, Dolores 111, 159
Wild Boys of the Road (1933 film) ***101***–102,

110, 120, 149–150
Wilder, Gene 135, 181
Wilkie, Robert 123
William, Warren 61, *65*
Williams, David Marshall 123
Williams, Emlyn 126, 171
Wilson, Frank R. *103*
Windom, William 133, 179
Winterset (1936 film) 76
Wolfit, Donald 126, 151, 154
Woods, Donald 108
Woods, Harry 73, 77, 144
World War I 6–7, 46, 53, 59, 67
World War II 41, 96–97
Wurtzel, Sol M. 104, 106

Yates, Peter 136
Young, Elizabeth *see* Blane, Sally
Young, Georgiana 76
Young, Loretta 76, *100*
Young, Polly Ann 76

Zahn, Steve 199
Zanuck, Darryl F. 2, 43–48, 51–54, 56, 58–59, 61, 64, 69, 74–75, 105–107, 110, 120
Zola, Emile 111, 126

www.ingramcontent.com/pod-product-compliance
Ingram Content Group UK Ltd.
Pitfield, Milton Keynes, MK11 3LW, UK
UKHW041954140426
5217IPUK00015B/793